TAKE A CHANCE!

TAKE A CHANCE!

101 Entrepreneurial Lessons for Making it Big

LARRY GAYNOR

Competition® | Focus® | Ideation® | Maximizer® | Strategic®

Advantage | Books

Published by Advantage Books, Charleston, South Carolina.
An imprint of Advantage Media.

ADVANTAGE is a registered trademark, and the Advantage colophon is a trademark of Advantage Media Group, Inc.

Printed in the United States of America.

10 9 8 7 6 5 4 3 2 1

ISBN: 979-8-88750-420-9 (Hardcover)
ISBN: 979-8-88750-421-6 (eBook)

Library of Congress Control Number: 2023923224

This publication is designed to provide accurate and authoritative information in regard to the subject matter covered. It is sold with the understanding that the publisher is not engaged in rendering legal, accounting, or other professional services. If legal advice or other expert assistance is required, the services of a competent professional person should be sought.

Advantage Books is an imprint of Advantage Media Group. Advantage Media helps busy entrepreneurs, CEOs, and leaders write and publish a book to grow their business and become the authority in their field. Advantage authors comprise an exclusive community of industry professionals, idea-makers, and thought leaders. For more information go to **advantagemedia.com**.

To my BUB, the Queen, and the love of my life.
You are always there when I need you most.

CONTENTS

AUTHOR'S NOTE

If there is one author that inspires me, it's Stephen King—I've read almost every one of his books. His novels open your imagination, and you are in constant wonder as to how he came up with the content. Being an entrepreneur is like being a Stephen King character: You live vicariously through curses, luck, and magic.

I wrote *TAKE A CHANCE!* for two reasons. One, I wanted to offer new entrepreneurs a real understanding of what it is like to start their own business and whether or not starting their own business is the right decision. Second, to provide established entrepreneurs with the valuable insight needed in finance and marketing, as well as management and leadership, to make optimal and strategic decisions. All too often entrepreneurs make costly mistakes because they did not know which decision to choose or which path to follow. My goal is to help you make the right choices—and if this book helps you to make just one right decision, then it will be worth reading (and worth my efforts writing—I am thrilled to share my insights).

Being an entrepreneur is a talent like singing, dancing, and acting. You have to have the genes—which often means being persistent and determined. Otherwise, you're just a person trying to start a business. Enjoy the journey.

LARRY GAYNOR

INTRODUCTION

There are over 5.4 million new business applications in the United States every year.[1] That means more than five million people will start their own business, and there are few things in life more exciting. But alas, almost half of new businesses will fail within five years. In this book, you will learn the inner workings of being an entrepreneur and 101 lessons that can help take your business to the next level and avoid failure. All that's required is to Take a Chance!

Here's why you need to read this book: As an entrepreneur, you are curious. You are impatient. Your mind is always racing. You are willing to take risks. Your friends and family might tell you that your idea for the new business is ludicrous, but you don't care because you have passion. It's not that you want to prove them wrong; you have a gut instinct that your idea will succeed. *Take a Chance!* is your guidebook to avoid costly pitfalls when starting your business. It will also prepare you for what to do in the second and third stages of growing your business.

I have been in the beauty business for more than fifty years. During those years, I have dealt with start-ups like Essie Cosmetics and

---

1   Stephanie Ferguson, "U.S. Chamber of Commerce," February 14, 2023, accessed July 1, 2023, https://www.uschamber.com/small-business/new-business-applications-a-state-by-state-view#:~:text=In%202021%20alone%2C%20a%20record,per%20capita%20in%20each%20state.

OPI that eventually went on to sell their companies for $150M and $950M, respectively. I have dealt with mega corporations including Amazon, L'Oréal, Unilever, Procter & Gamble, and ULTA Beauty, where I learned some of life's most difficult lessons.

My company, TNG Worldwide, is a Gallup®-trained organization, and if you have already taken the StrengthFinder's 2.0 test to learn your top-five strengths, then this book will be exceptionally helpful to you as an entrepreneur. If not, you will learn about StrengthFinder's 2.0 and why it is so important to focus on your strengths. You will also get a look inside the world of Gallup®.

TNG Worldwide is a small to medium-sized business started in 1985 as Nailco Manicurist Centers, a distributor of professional nail supplies to salons and manicurists. As the company evolved over the years and especially when TNG pivoted in 2020, it is now a manufacturer of beauty and personal care products. It's top-selling brands are ForPro Professional Collection and Ginger Lily Farms. I started the company with $50,000 and it now has a valuation of more than $100M. Annual sales exceed $50M but first-year sales were less than $500K. Less than 5 percent of all businesses exceed $1M in sales and less than 1 percent exceed $10M in sales. While TNG is small compared to an S&P company, TNG is the perfect size to give entrepreneurs the perspective they need to grow their business from nothing to more than $1M, and eventually to more than $10M.

Finally, I love to refer to myself as an "Amazonian" even though I have never worked for Amazon. TNG Worldwide is a top-200 Amazon beauty reseller, and if you are selling a product, chances are that you are thinking or already selling on Amazon. This book will provide insightful details about Amazon that can help you realize your ultimate sales potential.

Take a Chance! 101 Entrepreneurial Lessons for Making it Big is an owner's manual for new and established entrepreneurs. Think about putting together a gas grill or bicycle for the first time and how long it took. If you did it again, it would take less than half the time. This book is like that; my shared experiences will guide you to make the right decisions in less time and save you from making costly mistakes. Think of this book as your coach with my inside voice talking to your inside voice. It's magical being an entrepreneur. My inspirational inside tips and life lessons will help you win in the game of business because there is nothing worse than losing. Winners take all!

READER BONUS: I'm fully engaged in helping fellow entrepreneurs succeed in their business. As a special reader bonus and based on request, I am offering my readers a complementary thirty-minute Gallup® Strength-Based Discovery Session conducted by a certified Gallup® coach. To sign up, please email me at coach@tngworldwide.com. I will then connect you with one of my all-time favorite Gallup® coaches.

PART 1
THE EARLY DAYS

Why Starting Young Is a Huge Advantage for an Entrepreneur

LESSON #1

Learn as Much as Possible About
What You Love Doing So No One
Can Stop You from Doing It

The year of 1967 was a transformative one for me in more ways than I want to remember. I was only twelve years old when I went to work for my father's hardware store in Detroit, Cadillac Ace. ACE is a buying cooperative and allowed us to buy in almost every category you would expect to see in a hardware store. I'll never forget their slogan, "ACE is the place of the helpful hardware man."

Most of the customers were male, and the best customers owned apartment buildings and needed constant supplies to keep them operating. I learned how to cut pipe, make keys, cut glass, wire a transformer to a bell, cut window shades to size, unload ninety-pound bags of concrete and salt, custom mix paint colors, and assemble wheelbarrows and spreaders. I even bought a locksmith kit and learned how to make master locksets. I learned the inner workings of a toilet (ballcock, flush valve) and how to install a toilet. I learned the difference between latex and oil-based paint. I learned the difference between single- and double-strength glass. I learned more about grass seed than I wanted (Kentucky Blue was the favorite). I learned everything there was to running a hardware store.

I loved to upsell. My favorite upsell was selling something for $.29 or "three for a dollar." The customers always bought three. I also loved to recommend like items. For instance, if the customer was buying a light switch, I would sell them a light switch cover plate. If they were buying a garden hose, then they needed a high-quality nozzle.

LIFE LESSON TIP: Take the time to learn all aspects of your products and business. There is nothing worse than not knowing the answer to a question from a customer or employee.

LESSON #2

It's Not About How Many Times You Fall Down That Counts; It's About How Many Times You Get Back Up

Cadillac Ace was located on the west side of Detroit, at Davison and Linwood. Back in the day it was a thriving neighborhood, and my favorite spot was the Avalon Deli. I would go there in the morning and get coffee for the workers and homemade apple strudel for me. For lunch, their special was the cheeseburger deluxe with fries and coleslaw for $.99.

However, in 1967 times were changing and the neighborhood was too. It became more hardscrabble. Drug dealers scouted out street corners. Crime increased.

One morning, the store was held up. Until the gun is pointed at your face, you have no idea what will go through your body when it does. My adrenaline was so high that I was almost unconscious. The robber told me to open the register, take out the money, and give it to him. I opened the damn register thousands of times but at this moment nearly forgot how. The gun got closer to my face and somehow I opened the cash drawer, took out the money, and gave it to him. Luck was on my side and he ran out of the store without firing a single shot.

The register had a money clip that when a bill was removed sent a signal to the alarm company. Within minutes, the police showed up. The first question they asked was "What did the robber look like and what was he wearing?" Now mind you, I have a mathematical mind and can recall almost anything instantly. But I was in such a state of shock I could not answer their questions. Worse, after the police left, it was late morning, and the store wouldn't close until six that evening. I was left to wonder if this would happen again, and maybe next time I wouldn't be so lucky.

This was also the year the riots happened. Cadillac Ace was a concrete block building with nice plate windows. The chaos started only a few blocks from the store. Police sirens were everywhere. We locked the store door, but windows began to crash open as rocks were hurled through them. Somehow we were able to get plywood to cover the windows and secure the building. Law enforcement arrived on our block, and we escaped to our cars and got the hell out. The next day the neighborhood looked like a war zone. We hired a company to fill in the space where the windows had been with concrete blocks and fortify the front door. Shortly thereafter, security bars for windows and doors became one of our bestsellers.

After the riots many businesses shuttered. It became risky for our employees to walk to their cars at night.

A couple of years later, I was walking to the office in the back of the store where my father was working. We were being held up again, this time by two guys who had entered the store armed. They forced our employees and customers down on the floor, made me tie my father's hands behind his back, and brought me to the registers to clean them all out. Then they took off, but not before ordering me to the floor and firing two shots—thankfully in the ceiling.

This time when the police came, I remembered what the two guys looked like and what they wore. I was called down to the police station where they had four or five guys in a lineup. I instantly identified both of them, and they were eventually convicted and went to jail. We hired a full-time security guard after that—who charged extra for his services. But sometimes, peace of mind has no price.

LIFE LESSON TIP: When you can survive terror, you can survive almost anything. Remember, the difference between being a hero or not is the ability to hang in there for another minute when everyone else quits.

LESSON #3

Never Stop Learning What Customers Want

never fit into high school cliques. I never participated in sports because I had to work every weekend and summer. I did learn to type a hundred words a minute and became a teacher's assistant in many of my classes. Lunchtime was a great time to play poker and win some money. Otherwise, I was a pretty boring teenager who didn't drink, do drugs, or skip school. All I remember is working at Cadillac Ace, where the real action was.

The summer of 1971, I was sixteen years old. Did my father buy me a car? Of course not. I worked six days a week, Wednesday was my off-day. My father took Thursday off. We drove to work together daily except for our off-days, and on Thursday I took his station wagon. (He always had a station wagon because it held a four- by eight-foot piece of plywood.)

Next door was a laundromat. They sold Faygo pop out of a vending machine and the glass bottles were ice-cold. I loved pineapple-orange and fruit punch. Next to the Faygo machine was another vending machine dispensing laundry soap, softener, and bleach. As I was walking back to the store drinking my cold Faygo, a sense of magic washed over me. My thoughts instantly went back to the laundry vending machine and an entire new world opened up for me.

I found the Yellow Pages (remember them?) and looked up wholesale distributors for laundry detergent. I found among other listings, Fontana Brothers. I called them up and asked if they sold laundry detergent, bleach, and softener. And yes, they did. I drove to their warehouse in Detroit, loaded up the station wagon with Tide and Purex, Downy and Clorox bleach. I set up an endcap in the front of the store. Within two days, the endcap sold out. I went back to Fontana Brothers and loaded up again. The endcap didn't make it through the weekend. That's when they started to deliver pallets to us.

Now mind you my father was not involved with this as we rarely saw eye-to-eye on new products. But I saw this as a huge opportunity. Suddenly I was contacting SC Johnson, Boyle Midway, and a host of other consumer companies to buy direct. An entire aisle was devoted to cleaning products and air fresheners. Sales went through the roof. What was most fascinating was that we attracted a whole new customer type: women.

One day I went to Fontana Brothers and met with my salesperson to take a tour. I was like a kid in a candy store. They sold everything. Supermarkets back then were very expensive and you couldn't take the cart outside the door. I bought toilet paper (White Cloud was the favorite) and paper towels for a test. Like the laundry products, they sold out immediately.

Fontana's mainstay, however, was cigarettes and candy. Smoking was a big thing then, and everyone smoked Kool's and Newport's. I added single packs and cartons and suddenly customers were buying cigarettes with their hammers and nails. I then added chewing gum (Doublemint, Spearmint, and Juicy Fruit were the bestsellers) and candy. I was shocked at how customers loved Baby Ruth bars. So much so, I contacted the manufacturer and bought King Size bars direct. We sold fifty cases in less than two weeks. King Size candy bars were an overnight success, and I made a front endcap with them. Oh, and they were "three for a dollar"!

By this time, the non-hardware business was surging and getting close to 20 percent of the overall business. The best part was that it was all incremental sales. However, not all was magical as my father was not happy with the new mix.

LIFE LESSON TIP: Your original product idea might be good. However, a related product idea might even be better. There is a reason why Amazon shows related products when you buy something. Always keep your eyes open to related product ideas.

LESSON #4

Never Stop Pursuing Your Dream

Still in high school and working my ass off, my parents decided to buy a second home in Florida. My mother lived there from October through April, and my father commuted back and forth. Funny thing, I was the happiest when he was in Florida, and he was the happiest when he was in Michigan.

The Mod Squad premiered in 1968 and enjoyed a five-year run. Man, did I love that show. Peggy Lipton was so hot and Linc was so cool. Linc was so cool, in fact, that virtually every black male was sporting an Afro including our employees.

One day I asked the employees how they took care of their Afros. They all used a shine spray, and I quickly learned that there were three best-selling brands. Soft Sheen was number one, bright yellow bottle with red print. Sta-Sof-Fro was second and Posner was third. It was liquid gold in a bottle. I contacted the vendors, and they sent their salespeople to the store. They looked around and said to me, "You know, we never sold to a hardware store before." That I was quite certain of. Then I showed them the laundry detergent, toilet paper, and candy bars and told them you haven't seen these in hardware stores either. All agreed to an opening order.

Once again, I set up an endcap, and the products sold out quickly. After learning about all the additional products needed to maintain Afros along with relaxers and shaving powders that black men used as an alternative to shaving cream, I expanded the offerings. Within a few short weeks, an entire aisle was filled with personal care products. Hello P&G and Colgate! Have to have toothpaste and mouthwash too. Cadillac Ace became the first hardware store to sell health and beauty aids (HBAs) and within a year, we were the vendor's number-one selling location.

By now my father was going to: move to Florida full time OR kill me OR look the other way and pocket all the profits (that will be another chapter). He turned his head and smiled all the way to the bank. Until I added douches and makeup, that is. We had dinner monthly at a decent place, and he literally threatened to murder me if I kept makeup in the store. He was concerned with theft and that it would drive away the core customers. I told him to move to Florida full time. He told me to fuck off. Waiter, he'll take another Chivas on the rocks!

Now the store was doing more than 25 percent of sales non-hardware. How can you argue with success? Luckily, for both of us, I would be starting Michigan State University, and my working days at the store would be limited.

LIFE LESSON TIP: There will always be those that want to stop you, and your best friends and family could be the worst naysayers.

LESSON #5

Explore, Experiment, and Learn to Cut Your Losses Early

An entrepreneur's mind never stops working. This is no different from a musician like my favorites Jimmy Buffett (I will never forget September 1, 2023, when Jimmy Buffett set sail; it was one of the saddest days of my life) and Kenny Chesney. They never stop writing and singing songs. So, while I was doing high school full time during the week and working at Cadillac Ace on the weekends, my brain never stopped coming up with new ideas. Besides, I was an employee getting paid minimum wages at ACE, and entrepreneurs always dream about owning their own piece of the pie. Hence, the side gigs.

My first side gig was what I thought to be a very cool idea. Back then, aquariums were a big thing, and everyone had to have goldfish. Meijer added a live fish department, and hobby stores started selling tropical fish. But anyone ever owning an aquarium will tell you they are a pain in the ass. Alas, that was the start of *Coral Reef.* I made spiffy blue business cards and went door-to-door selling ten-, twenty-, and thirty-gallon aquariums fully serviced with weekly and biweekly maintenance programs. I enlisted a partner who was proficient with installations, and I took care of the fish and maintenance. We got many customers, but I quickly learned that I had no passion for this. Fish died; I would show up to clean the aquariums and no one would be home; and it was tough to generate income.

I loved to cut grass and had a Scott's silent mower, top of the line! Once again, I went door-to-door and found some willing customers. However, the first summer was a sizzler, and I quickly learned I had no passion for that either.

In my senior year of high school, I had the most brilliant idea! Dry cleaners were extremely popular, as everyone got dressed up for work. I noticed when I went to the dry cleaners, they did not have retail products. The idea came to me: *Closet Aid*. I bought self-standing hanger trees and the best-selling hangers from plastic to wood to tubular. The issue, however, was pricing. Dry cleaners were not retailers and did not want to deal with price tagging. I dealt with Monarch Labels at ACE and contacted them for my hangers. I came up with a very clever idea: color code the labels and sell hangers based on the color code of the label. It was brilliant. I bought fifty thousand labels, designed my prototype tree, and then took it to several dry cleaners. One of the biggest then was Janet Davis (they are still in business today), and they loved the idea. They were amazed at how many hangers they could sell. They added trees to their other locations.

One day I got a call from the owner. The owner told me customers complained because the labels were impossible to remove from the hangers. Little did I know that you could order removable adhesion labels for this reason. I ordered traditional labels with permanent adhesion. I bought fifty thousand labels! I contacted my rep, and he wouldn't exchange them. Moreover, all the hangers were labeled. It was a devastating lesson, and that was the end of Closet Aid.

LIFE LESSON TIP: Do one thing better than anyone else; side gigs can only get you in trouble.

LESSON #6

Expand Your Knowledge as Much as Possible

There are so many great things about being a teenager, and one of them is being able to experience wonderment for the first time. When you are an entrepreneur and get to experience your first trade show, there is nothing better. ACE Hardware held an annual trade show for its members. It was held in places like Las Vegas, New Orleans, NYC, Dallas, and other cool cities (never Detroit). I didn't care where it was located because it meant going on an airplane, staying at a hotel in my own room, eating out at restaurants, and going to an exhibition the likes of which I had never encountered before.

The convention center was enormous. We waited in line to get our show badge and show program, and then walked inside the hall. OMG! I had never seen anything like it in my life. There were hundreds of elaborate booths, each booth displaying its products in style. Not only did I see all the brands of products I bought from ACE, I also saw hundreds of new brands.

I was able to meet with the factory executives and talk shop. They were shocked as to how a seventeen-year-old kid knew so much about the industry and their product line. Each booth offered "show deals" and the prices were the best I've ever seen. Better yet, all the booths were allowed to ship directly to your store location. By the end of the two-day show, I visited every exhibitor, placed so many show orders I could not keep track, and added oodles of new products to our inventory. Little did I know then that trade shows would become a major part of my strategy when I started my own businesses.

Although I wanted to come back each year that was the only ACE trade show I attended. The following year I started MSU, and future endeavors would take me in different directions.

At this time, I subscribed to many business magazines including *Entrepreneur, Inc.*, *BusinessWeek*, and *Forbes*. These magazines are particularly suited for entrepreneurs because they delve into trends, new opportunities, and what other companies are doing well and not so well. More importantly, they offer insight and ideas that you can nurture.

LIFE LESSON TIP: Although trade shows are still around, they don't have the impact they once had because of the internet. Research trade shows for your particular industry. You will see on their websites a list of exhibitors with all their information. You can also click on the floor map and see which exhibitors are the most important based on the amount of space they take. In most instances, this information alone will give you the same insights as if you went to the show in person.

LESSON #7

Continuous Learning Is Critical for Continuous Success

B ack in 1973, Michigan State University had trimesters and cost about $3,000 a year with books, room, and board. With public college costs exceeding $100,000 for four years in 2023, the big question is "Is it worth it?"

My answer is YES! You are only eighteen once and going to college is a once-in-a-lifetime opportunity. Try to think of college as a trade show that lasts four years. Now let me tell you, what an entrepreneur experiences in college is far different from what typical students experience. More importantly, this was the only four-year period in my life that I didn't have to work on weekends and would be the only four years until I was over thirty-five years old.

The year 1973 was at the tail end of the hippie decade. If you must know, I did wear Nehru jackets, bead necklaces, and donned long and wild hair. I also wore tight bell-bottom blue jeans and, to this day, still love skinny jeans.

I stayed in dorms all four years figuring I had my entire life to live in an apartment or house. I loved the convenience of clean sheets weekly, hot meals three days a week except Sunday, the snack grill, study areas, and pinball machines. I'll never forget my first year at Wilson Hall. It set the tone for the next three years, and I can't begin to tell you how much I learned.

Did you know that a tiny little speck is enough to take you on the trip of a lifetime? Who needed Delta when you had acid! My RA introduced me to the sixth floor and told me acid was readily available. How's that for your first day on campus! The next day I learned all about streaking, and boy was that fun. There is nothing like running naked in a group on fresh-cut grass between dorm buildings.

Weekends were party time for sure, but I have to say the weekdays were pretty crazy too. The second weekend on campus I met up with a high school friend, and he asked me if I wanted to get high. As I told you earlier, I never drank or did drugs in high school. Let me tell you, MSU was not high school! I took a few hits, and before I knew it, I was passed out on his bed and wondering if I was ever going to be normal again. A couple of hours later, I came out of it, and he asked me if I was hungry. "You bet I am" I replied. I learned that night that I could eat an entire Domino's large pepperoni pizza with extra cheese by myself!

On weekends, the dorm regularly featured *Deep Throat* and *Behind the Green Door*. These movies were not like watching *Gilligan's Island*, *The Flintstones*, or *The Jetsons*.

The next month I learned everything about red wine that I needed to know for the next fifteen years. When I turned eighteen my roommate bought me a gallon of Gallo for my birthday. It was my first taste of red wine, and it wasn't bad. Until that is, we drank the whole gallon in an hour. I will spare you the details of what followed.

And my learning continued! Alcohol was legal for eighteen-year-olds at the time, and there was no better party than Friday afternoon's at the Alley Eye. $.25 Manhattan's, $.50 pitchers, and live music for dancing. I don't recall how many Manhattan's I consumed, but I always remember hitting the dorm at 6:45 p.m. because the cafeteria closed at 7:00 p.m. I danced so much the sweat was all over my body, but I was like everyone else and it was cool. After eating, I would pass out until 10:00 p.m. and start the party once again. Now tell me loyal reader, could you learn all this staying home?

I will always remember The Brewery known for its rock and roll acts. We saw Aerosmith and Peter Frampton for $3, and it was a hoot. I learned all about three-foot and six-foot water bongs, hash and hash oil, bean bag chairs, black lights and black light posters, and rock'n'roll. I had one of the baddest stereo systems and went to the record store weekly to buy at least two new albums. Frampton, Aerosmith, Zeppelin, you name it, I owned it. Guess who organized the first dorm parties? Yep, you guessed right! I was the DJ, and it was a blast.

Pinball was a big thing back then, and there were few games better than Jack in the Box and King Kool. I was a pinball addict and pinball wizard. I always won free games. Guess who organized MSU's first pinball tournament? Yep, you guessed right once again!

Here is where learning really came in handy. Double-deck pinochle. Never played it? WOW, it is one of the best games, but you best have a partner that knows how to play. It beats playing euchre hands down. I played at least four times a week, and the best part is you don't play for money. I also learned how to play chess and bridge, but not too many students got into that.

Another great advantage of living in dorms back then was that they were co-ed. Each building had six floors so there were plenty of boys and girls. One day I was eating dinner in the cafeteria and noticed this girl working. She was pretty cute, and there was something about her. I was going to introduce myself to her, but something happened and next thing I knew, she was gone. But I knew she lived in the dorm. A few weeks later, I found her, and this time did the proper introduction. We went on a date, and the rest is history. I ended up marrying her and having three kids, but I am saving what happened next for later in the book.

Academics. I had no idea back then that I would think about giving $3M to the Broad School of Business to help build The Pavilion building in 2017. So, you might ask, "Did attending MSU help to make me successful?" I have to say the answer is both yes and no. Everything I highlighted up to this point was yes because I used all those experiences in my businesses. Academics on the other hand did little for my creative business mind. For one, you had to take humanities. Who the hell is interested in humanities with the exception of history nerds? My interest in science was limited to NaCl and H2O. The only classes I enjoyed were business classes, especially marketing and cost accounting. I majored in accounting and graduated with a 3.1 overall and 3.5 in my core curriculum.

The problem with academics is that all the students are forced to learn the same material. How many students in my classes had my background in business? Very few. While the professor was teaching margins, discounts, percentages, and business plans, and students were wildly raising their hands to ask questions, I was yawning. The only class I was truly challenged in was cost accounting. The professor was the toughest in the business college. Very few students got a 4.0, and he loved to fail students. I met with Professor Mazzara after class one day and asked him, "How can I get a 4.0 in your class?" He looked at me, thought about the question, and then told me to study previous exams because they were in the library, take copious notes, and to focus on his teaching more than the textbook. I did exactly that. At the end of the semester, he congratulated me for my 4.0. And that my loyal reader was my academics at MSU.

> **LIFE LESSON TIP:** I firmly believe that going to college sets you on the learning path for the rest of your life. However, after those quick four years, it is up to you to continue the path. To this day, I am still learning. I spend thirty minutes daily on Duolingo learning Spanish, one hour learning chess, and read the *Wall Street Journal, Barron's* and *Detroit News* daily.

PART 2

NOW THAT YOU HAVE GRADUATED, WHAT'S NEXT?

1977–1994

LESSON #8

Once You Find the Passion for What You Want to Do, Never Stop

Oh man, did I love to play Monopoly. In fact, I loved to play many board games. My favorites included Life, Stratego!, Risk, Battleship, Clue, Connect Four, and who could ever forget Candy Land and Chutes & Ladders as a kid. Don't get me wrong, I loved video games too and back at MSU, I was a bit addicted to Pong, Space Invaders, Centipede, and my all-time fav, Ms. Pac-Man. When Nintendo introduced its first game deck with Super Mario Brothers, my life was consumed for hours upon hours each and every night. Did I mention Donkey Kong? I hate to admit this, but when Nintendo came out with *The Legend of Zelda* in 1998, I was a total addict. So addicted in fact, I bought the guidebooks at the bookstore and when I couldn't figure out the puzzle, I called their 800 number and paid to get the answer. Is that sick or what!

Slap me silly because here we are in 1977 and talking about the Chance card. You see, my number-one CliftonStrength® is Competition® (there will be an entire chapter devoted to Gallup®). I love to win and hate to lose. Monopoly is a game of luck and strategy. For one, I always play with $500 in Free Parking, how about you? I love to own the railroads and the Tennessee and Kentucky monopolies. However, it's always the Chance cards that get you because you never know if you are going to jail, paying $75 luxury tax, or inheriting $200! Life is all about Chance cards and the decisions you make when you come to a fork in the road. Which fork do you take? The choices we make in life are what separates winners and losers and make us optimists or pessimists. Fate is an amazing thing.

When I graduated from MSU the Chance cards were in front of me. There were two cards. One card said that I would work for a Big Eight accounting firm and the other card said that I would go into the family business. Which card did I pick?

I had to wear a suit to my interview with Peat Marwick. The interview was downtown at one of the fancy buildings that has a fancy restaurant inside. Back then, upscale restaurants were called "fancy" and people dressed up for both lunch and dinner. After seeing the firm (PM was the biggest firm in the industry at the time), we went to lunch. There were six of us. The five PM employees all ordered martinis, and the waiter came around and asked what I wanted. I never even heard of a martini, and besides, I didn't drink. I ordered a Tab soda. That was pretty much the end of the interview. Seriously, I'm not kidding.

My work attire at Cadillac Ace was always the same: Levi's that could stand up on their own from the dirt, work belt that had my tape measure and utility knife, work boots, and button-down shirt. And I always had a Monarch marking gun in my back pocket. Walking around the PM offices and seeing everyone in suits (even the few women at the time), it came to me that the term "stuffy" was appropriate. Don't get me wrong, accounting was my major, and I loved numbers more than anything. But I couldn't see myself working in this environment although the salary was great and the opportunity for partnership was amazing. Besides, all my college friends were interviewing at firms just like this. And what was more fun? Crunching numbers or unloading pallets of ninety-pound bags of concrete?

My first major life decision was easy, and I didn't even have to pick a Chance card. I decided to go into the family business.

LIFE LESSON TIP: Entrepreneurs are always exposed to Chance cards. Unlike in Monopoly where the player must do what the card states, you have the choice to make. It is these choices that define success or failure. Seek advice from mentors and colleagues but make the final choice based on your gut instinct.

LESSON #9

Never Be a Minority Shareholder in a Closed Corporation

The experts will tell you that father–son business relationships are terrible at best. They will beg you not to get involved unless you have to. I will tell you firsthand that they are right.

By now, you may have guessed that my father and I had a love–hate relationship. It's easy to know why. He was a businessman, and I was an entrepreneur. I made him a lot of money over the years, he got to go to Florida in the winter, and life was good. Now comes the family discussion about me coming into the business. My mother got involved in the conversation, and nothing good ever came about when that happened. It was always two against one. However, my father loved money and knew that I could make him a lot more of it.

We came to a mutual understanding that I would join the family business, and the goal was to open a second location in the suburbs. The neighborhood was getting scarier as drugs became more mainstream, and we had enough robberies and break-ins to last a lifetime. Now it was time to build the foundation. Just as you can't build a house without building a foundation first, in business too, you must establish a foundation. In business terms, it is called equity.

My father formed a sub-S corporation, Gaynor Enterprises. He gifted all three kids 5 percent equity in the company. He also gifted his mother 10 percent. The gift helped pay for all my grandmother's living expenses after my grandfather passed away. The gift for us kids helped to pay for college and other expenses. When my grandmother passed away, my father offered me her 10 percent but didn't gift it to me. I had to pay him for it over time. Now I had 15 percent equity in the business. What did that mean?

It meant that each year I would get 15 percent of the after-tax income from the business. Sounds good in theory, right? Cadillac Ace was a cash business. Our customers didn't have checking accounts or credit cards. Only the landlords we dealt with received credit. Let's say the business did $2M a year. Let's say the bottom line was $50,000. My father always made sure the bottom line was low so he didn't have to pay a lot of taxes. My father's distribution was $42,500 and mine was $7,500.

Now let's say that 5 percent of sales ended up in his pocket tax-free or $50,000. I never saw the cash. His total distribution was $92,500 compared to my $7,500. Here is one life lesson that you must never forget, and I repeat it for you: Never be a minority shareholder in a closed corporation. Don't worry my loyal reader, life has a saying "What goes around, comes around!" You will read that lovely chapter later in the book.

As the meeting continued, my father brought up the 5 percent that my brothers Steven and Bob owned. You notice that I have not written about them. Yes, they too had to work at Cadillac Ace, but both hated it. At the time, Steven was in college, and Bob was in high school. Both would need money after graduating from college for a new home. My father told me what he thought the value of stock was (non-negotiable), and I had to take the deal. I bought both Steven and Bob out and paid my father back over time. I now had 25 percent equity in Gaynor Enterprises. The foundation was built.

> **LIFE LESSON TIP:** Equity is the most important foundation for a successful business. Entrepreneurs are risk-takers and think differently than business-people or investors. As much as possible, invest more than 50 percent in your company when you start. It will be well worth it for reasons far more than financial.

LESSON #10

Get Inspired by Seeking Out the Best at What They Do and Learn Everything You Can to Improve on It

ere I was, twenty-three years old, married, and I had to trade in my shiny yellow Camaro I got my sophomore year at MSU for a stick shift Vega (which was the worst car I ever owned), because who would want to steal a Vega (I would be surprised to find out the answer). I continued my work schedule getting to the store by eight in the morning and coming home around seven each evening, daily except for Wednesday and Sunday (when the store was open 9:00 a.m. to 1:00 p.m.).

My wife was a teacher, and she worked during the week, sometimes in the evenings too for whatever reason. On those nights I would treat myself to McDonald's because in your twenties, what is better? My typical meal was a Quarter Pounder with Cheese, Filet-O-Fish, large fries, apple pie, and Diet Coke. Yum!

I continued to define and redefine the merchandise mix at Cadillac Ace, and now we had a full assortment of kitchen appliances, pots and pans, and utensils. Little did I know that I was creating a mini Lowe's (Lowe's and Home Depot opened their first Michigan stores in 1994). Business was good, and my father was planning to upgrade his condo in Boca Raton to a spanking new home. I loved it because he spent a lot of time in Florida with the contractors. While all along we were deciding where to open the second location.

One day we made a road trip to Cleveland. Let me give you a little background first. F&M opened its first store the year I was born in 1955. F&M was Fred & Margaret Cohen and their original location was a 7,000-square-foot store in Ferndale, Michigan. F&M Discount Drugs was the first store in the country that sold HBAs at deep discount prices. Their formula was simple, "Stack it high and watch it fly." I remember going to F&M for the first time, and I was awestruck. The line to get in was incredible, and once you got in the store, you saw stacks of assorted brand name products at deep discounts, at least 20 percent cheaper than anywhere else. They bought deals direct from manufacturers who had excess inventory and wanted to move it. For this reason, you never knew what products would be on sale. They were the first "treasure" store in which every visit was a surprise. This made you want to come back often so you never missed a great deal.

The store did more than $7M a year at its peak. Cadillac Ace did $2M so I was very impressed with their sales. The owners sold out in 1977 and that became the end of F&M, as everyone knew it. However, the concept caught the eye of others including Bernie Schulman.

Bernie opened his first store in Cleveland in 1969, and it was far bigger and more impressive. Not to be outdone, Drug Emporium opened its first store in 1977 in Columbus, Ohio, but unlike F&M and Bernie Shulman's, this store was a prototype for many more stores to come. Then in 1979, Marc's opened in Cleveland, and the war was on. Marc was an ex-employee of Bernie Schulman's and copied the format to a tee and then put his own spin on it. Long story short,

Marc's is the only deep discount HBA store operation still in business today and does over $1B in sales.

Bernie Shulman's store was what I expected, a larger format of F&M. However, when I walked into Marc's, it was like walking into my first trade show. It blew my mind. One thing about being an entrepreneur is that there is nothing like having your mind blown away. It is a better feeling than even having your home team win the Super Bowl or World Series.

Marc's was a huge store, and I never saw so much merchandise with such incredibly low prices. Further, the selection of goods was mind numbing. Besides HBA, food and beverage were huge. The Coke display was so enormous, you would have thought Coke leased the space and made sure it was constantly full. The store was packed, and women could not stick the goods in their shopping cart fast enough.

Even my father was impressed with the stores, and that is when the light bulb turned on for me. Forget the second hardware store. We had to open a discount HBA store! I knew that we could never compete with Marc's or Drug Emporium if they came to Michigan so I had to come up with a unique concept that would provide a competitive edge. Like magic, the idea came to me: open an upscale HBA store with personalized service, nice décor, and merchandise neither Marc's nor Drug Emporium sold but still at a discount. The name of the store was simple: GAYNORS: Health & Beauty Aids With A Flair.

LIFE LESSON TIP: The internet is great for research, but there is nothing better than seeing a product, concept, or new business in person. Whether you have to drive or fly, it is well worth the investment in time to experience inspiring ideas firsthand.

LESSON #11

Pioneers Always Get the Arrows; Steal
Other People's Ideas, and Make Them
Better, Just Like Steve Jobs Did

N ow that the concept was clear, I had to invent GAYNORS. My background at Cadillac Ace was in a poor neighborhood. Our customers were 95 percent black and 80 percent male. The merchandise sold was hardware, Black HBA, cigarettes, and candy. GAYNORS would be located in Farmington Hills, an upscale suburb. Customers would be largely white, mostly women and the merchandise would be HBA, food, and seasonal. The two stores could not have been more opposite.

Inventing GAYNORS involved a lot of research. One inherent trait of entrepreneurs is that they love to do research. If you asked me who my role model at the time was, I would have told you Steve Jobs and hinted at Bill Gates. What I loved most about Steve Jobs is that he didn't invent anything from scratch. His genius was that he took someone else's idea and made it better. That is what I had to do with GAYNORS to make it a success.

Another inherent trait of entrepreneurs is that we don't take no for an answer. We are maniacally committed to getting what we need to get to the next level. Remembering back to 1980, the PC had yet to be invented and, of course, there was no internet. Research involved subscribing to trade journals, going to the library, and more often than not, talking to the right people.

We found the perfect location in Farmington Hills. It was a brand-new strip center that was going to have T.J. Maxx and GAP as the anchors. It would also feature a B. Dalton bookstore, Dress Barn, a few boutiques, and a Coney Island restaurant. Better yet, right next door to the strip center was Tally Hall. Tally Hall was this amazing shopping district with its claim to fame being the first indoor food court in Michigan. It drew customers from all over, and it was within easy walking distance to the new strip mall. We met with the landlord and signed a five-year lease for 8,640 square feet. Now I had to figure out how to fill those feet up.

There are countless expressions when it comes to retail. One that I always loved was "know what your customers want before they know what they want." That would become the secret sauce at GAYNORS. However, the basic retail strategy of giving the customers what they want and always being in stock was important too. My research would be all about what our customers wanted and would want. I had six months to figure it all out before we would greet our first customer.

LIFE LESSON TIP: When it comes to launching your first product, research the market for competitive products extensively. Then decide what key variable you can add to your product to differentiate it from the others. Product differentiation is crucial to your success, and sometimes it is one key ingredient that makes all the difference.

LESSON #12

Don't Depend on Others to Do Your Research

The 1980s was one of the most prolific decades of the twentieth century when it came to retail and product innovation. It was a very lucky time to be in business. The 1990s was really good too. Sad to say, I don't see anything good about retail and product innovation in the near future and since the dot.com bust, it has been brutal.

The late 1970s and early 1980s was the birth of the professional hair care industry. Pioneers such as Jheri Redding and Paula Meehan Kent (they would invent Redken, the first three letters of each of their last names, and Redding would also invent Nexxus); Paul Mitchell and John Paul DeJoria (Paul Mitchell); Arnie Miller (Matrix); Jamey Mazzotta (KMS); and Horst Rechelbacher (Aveda) were just a handful of hairdressers who became entrepreneurs and launched their own brands. They created an entire new generation of beauty salons and hairdressers overnight. Trade shows, education, and excitement would prevail like never before for the next twenty years.

It was also the period in which women flourished in the workplace, and the WWII crowd was getting older. Cosmetics and skin care became huge categories, and most interesting is that the two most influential companies then are still the two most influential companies now: Estee Lauder and L'Oréal. Lauder focused on prestige brands, and I cannot emphasize the ongoing importance of this. Back then, cosmetics and skin care consisted of three categories: mass, masstige, and prestige. Mass beauty brands are sold at Target, Walmart, CVS, and Walgreens. Masstige brands are sold at Ulta, Kohls, and other mid-level department stores. Prestige brands are sold by high-end department stores and now, more often than not, their own stores. Maybelline is a mass brand. Calvin Klein is a masstige brand. Tom Ford is a prestige brand.

Retailers' understanding of the importance of these categories would determine if they survived and prospered or became extinct.

Lauder's claim to fame was in 1968 when it launched Clinique. The Estee Lauder brand was its most powerful and today still is, but Clinique ushered in an entire new customer base for Lauder, young and prosperous women. I will never forget their famous advertising campaign: 1-2-3. Cleanse; Exfoliate; Moisturize.

L'Oréal focused on all three categories but did especially well in mass and prestige. In 1964 L'Oréal bought Lancôme. It shortly became one of the best-selling prestige brands and remains so today. For the mass market, L'Oréal Paris became the top-selling brand, and they would eventually cement their leadership status by buying Maybelline.

Prestige department stores had exclusive distribution rights to sell both Lauder and L'Oréal products. Hudson's, Marshall Field's, Macy's, Bloomingdale's, Nordstrom, Dillard's, Lord & Taylor, Saks Fifth Avenue, Neiman Marcus, and others all bowed to the wishes of Lauder and L'Oréal so they could show off their exclusiveness. It was no wonder why cosmetic and fragrance companies always had the best space in department stores. Fast-forward forty years and nothing has changed, but, alas, ULTA Beauty has vastly diminished the power of department stores over the last decade.

I went to Hudson's and walked around their massive cosmetic department hinting that I needed products for my wife. I quickly learned their hot brands. I went to salons and was amazed to see so much retail displayed. I asked the receptionist which brands were the most popular. I quickly learned their top sellers.

I decided those were the brands that I would sell at GAYNORS. Now I had to figure out a way to get them since none of them would sell to a retailer, let alone a discount retailer. This is where the story gets really interesting.

Remember, drugs were infiltrating Detroit and not in a good way. Also, remember that while I was focused on the opening of GAYNORS, I was still working six days a week at Cadillac Ace. One day, an across-the-street neighbor approached me when I got out of my car in the morning. His name was Michael. I am naïve and should have known he was a drug addict. He came to me and asked for money. I told him I didn't have any money, and he started to beg. I said, "Come by the store. I'll get you a job, and you can make some money."

"No," he said, he needed the money now. I said "sorry" and walked across the street.

At 6:00 p.m., I left the store to go to the parking lot. My Vega was gone. I looked at Michael on his front porch, and he waved to me. Let me tell you, having your car stolen is not a good thing and having it stolen by a drug addict is even worse. My manager drove me home.

The next day, when my manager and I got out of his car Michael came up to me. I said to Michael, "I need my car back." He told me it was in the chop shop and too late. Then he said he needed more money. Bottom line is that I ended up giving Michael lots of money for protection and to get him off my back. It made Farmington Hills sound that much better. My reason for telling you this story is that drugs are nothing more than diverted merchandise, with the only difference being that they are illegal. And sorry to say, easier to get than professional hair care and prestige cosmetics and fragrances.

LIFE LESSON TIP: When it comes to research, others are not you. They don't have the same entrepreneurial mind to know what to look for. The more questions you ask, the more answers you receive.

LESSON #13

Never Give Up; There Is Always a Way to Succeed and to Move Forward

According to Google: Product diversion is when an unauthorized seller sells a product outside of authorized distribution channels. The product goes through various unauthorized channels in order to reach the shelves or listings on a website. This is a common practice with high-end and expensive beauty products.

Isn't it amazing, all these coincidences? There are millions of products, yet Google highlights "expensive beauty products." You are now going to learn the reason why: greed.

Greed is a human behavior that is the root cause of most wars and battles since humans were put on the planet. According to Merriam-Webster, the meaning of GREED is: "A selfish and excessive desire for more of something (such as money) than is needed."

The root existence of greed is money. I am working my ass off and not making very much of it. What if there was an easier way to make a lot of money? Boom, the reason for diversion.

Let me show you a simple formula that highlights the amount of money a hair care company like Paul Mitchell makes. Mitchell pays the factory $2 for an 8-ounce bottle of Awapuhi shampoo. Mitchell sells the bottle to an authorized beauty distributor for $6. Mitchell makes $4 a bottle. The distributor sells the bottle to the salon for $10. The distributor also makes $4 a bottle. The salon sells the bottle to their clients for $20 a bottle. The salon makes $10 a bottle. You are reading this correct. The salon actually makes more money than both Mitchell and the distributor combined.

Knowing this, certain individuals approach salon owners and tell them they want to buy wholesale quantities of certain brands and will pay cash. They start out small with a few dozen. The diverter pays the salon $15 a bottle in cash. Based on 100 bottles, the salon makes a quick $500. How many haircuts does that equal to? Next thing you know, the salon is diverting hundreds of bottles to the diverter and making a killing. The diverters line up as many salons as possible and now you know how salon products are found on retail drug store shelves.

Distributors know salons cannot be selling that much in retail, but hey, the money is good. The haircare manufacturers know that their brand is on fire and are partying as if it's the beginning of a new world. They never made so much money before. (It was years later that the same manufacturers would announce an anti-diversion program, which salons bought but it was pure smoke and mirrors.) Quality King is the undisputed leader in diverted salon goods as of this writing.

Luckily for me, I found the best salon product diverters, and they would be able to supply me with everything I needed when I opened. One category down, one to go.

Both Lauder and L'Oréal were public companies. They had to increase sales and profits for their shareholders. Many of their customers were also public companies with the same requirement to increase sales and profits for their shareholders. When a manufacturer saw that their numbers would be coming up short for a quarter, they would lean on their best customers to place large orders at the end of the quarter with a special discount provided. Back then and still to this day, prestige cosmetics and fragrances were never discounted. The whole damn department store could run a 20-percent-off sale, but cosmetics and fragrances were always excluded.

Department stores knew that they had to please their best manufacturers, and they obliged with big orders. However, the buyers knew they could not move the extra goods because they weren't allowed to promote them at a discount. They had to come up with another way. Hello diversion!

Unlike pro beauty products, diverted prestige goods were much more difficult to find. Luck came to me once again. A friend of a friend of a family member in NYC was a diverter of prestige goods. I got on the plane to NYC and had a meeting. Sure enough, the company had intimate contacts with the buyers at many of the prestige department stores in NYC. They could offer me virtually any brand I wanted, albeit fragrances were easier to source than cosmetics.

I was on cloud nine. The owners mentioned that I had to order well in advance because demand was so high and you never knew when the buyers could unload goods. Margins were very low but I didn't care, they would provide me the leverage I needed to get women into GAYNORS. And it worked.

LIFE LESSON TIP: The difference between winning and losing can be less than half a second or being able to hold on one minute longer. Winners never quit. Thomas Edison failed more than a thousand times before he eventually invented the light bulb. He never gave up.

LESSON #14

Plan, Plan, and Plan—And Then Plan on Changing the Plan

A plan-o-gram is simply a schematic drawing of what the store will look like when it sets to open. You can compare it to a blueprint for architects or an owner's manual for putting together a bike. Creating a plan-o-gram is essential for building out a store and one of the most difficult tasks of opening a new store.

The first part is the easy part: creating the store layout. I created six main aisles, an area in the back of the store for bulk items and the front of the store, which included the cash wrap and bulky paper items like diapers and toilet paper.

Aisle one included shopping carts, travel sizes (every deep discount store featured these, and it was amazing how many were sold), seasonal, and dental care. Aisle two was professional and retail hair care. Aisle three was pet, cleaning supplies, and household needs. Aisle four was candy, snacks, and featured items. Aisle five was vitamins, first aid, analgesics, and every other health category. Aisle six was cosmetics and fragrances. I built a special cosmetic counter for the diverted prestige cosmetics and fragrances.

The cash wrap was designed so that the customer would bring the cart to the cashier and the cashier would empty the cart. We did not allow the carts out of the store. When the customer had a large purchase, we took their shopping bags to their car.

Each aisle consisted of four-foot gondola sections. Each section had five shelves. So one gondola section had twenty feet for products. I had to determine product placement for every twenty-foot gondola section and there were more than a hundred.

Because of my experience at Cadillac Ace, I already had relationships with many manufacturers and met with them. They told me their best-selling products at competitive stores. But I had to establish meetings with lots more manufacturers that I never did business with. Not only did I need to select the initial product assortment, I also had to make opening orders. I opened direct accounts with over one hundred vendors including P&G, Lever Brothers (now Unilever), L'Oréal, Revlon, Maybelline, Hershey, M&M Mars, Colgate Palmolive, Beecham, Max Factor, Cover Girl, and Warner-Lambert just to name a few.

Once the product selection was completed, I then had to decide how much of each product to put on the shelf. One strategic decision I made early on is that GAYNORS would stock its SKUs on an ongoing basis and not sell deal-only goods. That meant buying goods at manufacturer list prices, and I countered that by buying heavy on deals. Finally, I was ready to complete the plan-o-gram, and I thought it was magnificent. Less than six months after opening I would learn that half the products would be discontinued and replaced with all new products.

LIFE LESSON TIP: Whether it's a plan-o-gram, new product, or service, be flexible in the developmental stages so you can react quickly to market conditions and make changes without much risk to yourself. For example, if you are launching a new lip plumper, always buy the smallest quantity and pay more per piece. This limits your risks and allows you to make changes quickly.

LESSON #15

If You Own a Business, You Need
Employees; the Better You Take
Care of Your Employees, the Better
Your Business Will Become

My father had a cousin who owned an employee-recruiting agency. We used his company to find employees for Cadillac Ace. Back then, newspapers were the only way to advertise for employees, and there were thousands of listings. Don Halper and his partner would run their own ads, do the initial interviews, and then pick out the best prospects for their clients.

Unlike Cadillac Ace that had only one shift per day, GAYNORS' hours were 10:00 a.m. to 9:00 p.m. daily and 10:00 a.m. to 5:00 p.m. Sunday. Retail hours in the suburbs sucked. Employees had to show up at seven in the morning to get the store ready, and the lights wouldn't be off until ten at night with last-minute customers coming in and taking their time to shop. I needed a lot of employees, both hourly and salaried.

I decided early on to focus on salaried employees, as they were exempt from overtime pay. Halper sent me over excellent candidates, and the hiring went smoothly. I hired two cosmetic artists for the makeup counter, four managers, an accounting clerk, cashiers, and stock clerks. I was the exclusive buyer except for mass cosmetics and fragrances for which I still needed a person. With less than two weeks to opening, I called Halper and asked him to dig deeper. He called me a day later and set up the interview.

Teresa was only eighteen years old, but I remembered what I was like when I was eighteen years old. Age didn't matter, results did. Teresa worked at the vitamin manufacturer that we were going to buy from in high school and knew everything about vitamins. I knew nothing except that it was going to be a big category. She also worked at Cecille's, another discount HBA store located a few miles away in Birmingham and bought cosmetics and fragrances. She had a falling out with the owner, learned about the job opening at GAYNORS, and was there in my office.

Truth be told, Teresa was one of the most stunning girls I had ever met. She had a "look" and could have come right out of *Vogue* or *Cosmopolitan*. Most intriguing, her makeup was perfect, and that is exactly what I was looking for in someone to deal with mass makeup and fragrances. The interview lasted five minutes, and she started the next week. Little did I know then that she would become my life partner.

Now let me tell you a little bit about employees. When I was at MSU, there wasn't a single class on dealing with employees. When you are an entrepreneur, the last thing you want to focus on is employees. All you want to do is focus on the big picture and results. Employees take a lot of time. You have to hire, fire, train, motivate, have empathy, give them time off and benefits, offer reviews, and that's just the top of the list. I loved dealing with manufacturers and customers. Employees not so much. However, I will say, turnover at GAYNORS was rare, and thinking back it was probably because I was so busy doing my thing, I let the employees do their thing. But it wouldn't always be so simple.

LIFE LESSON TIP: If you are a new entrepreneur and hiring your first few employees, read as many books on the subject as possible. Do your due diligence including background checks. Just as important, share your vision with the applicants and sense if they appreciate your vision. If they do, have them write on a piece of paper why they want to work for you. You want new hires to be nearly as passionate as you are for the success of the new business.

Thanks for letting me assist you.
If you need further assistance at any time,
please ask for Teresa.

(313) 855-0033

30905 Orchard Lake Road
Farmington Hills, MI 48018

LESSON #16

Always Differentiate Yourself from the Competition

As an entrepreneur, there is nothing more exciting than launch day. The store was set, employees were stocking the shelves, and I was preparing for the grand opening. My eighty-hour workweeks turned into ninety hours, but I didn't care.

Opening a new store is like planning a wedding. You have one shot. Just think of everything that goes into making a wedding and a wedding only lasts one day. When you open a store, you never think about it closing, you only think about opening another one. The second location only happens if the first one is successful. I had to make the grand opening not only successful but also memorable.

But first loyal reader let me tell you why I am spending so much time writing about GAYNORS. GAYNORS is how Nailco got started. Moreover, Nailco only got started in GAYNORS because of my obsession with customer satisfaction (I would later coin it "customer success"). Here is the genius idea that led to Nailco: I put clipboards with lined paper and pens at the end of each aisle. The paper had a heading "Customer Requests." I could only predict what our customers wanted, but if I was wrong, I wanted to know about it and, more importantly, know what they really wanted. I was shocked at how many items customers would write down each day and that is why just a few months after opening I completely revamped the store.

I spent weeks deciding how I was going to differentiate GAYNORS from other discount HBA retailers. We had four huge windows in the front of the store. I didn't need them because I put the sample size racks against the windows and the sunlight would do nothing good to the merchandise. Stealing ideas from NYC, I hired a designer that decorated the windows with seasonal themes. Not only did it give an inviting appearance to shoppers from outside the store, the displays blocked most of the natural light coming into the store.

I bought vests and jackets for all the employees with our logo. Our color theme was red and white. I wanted customers to know who GAYNORS employees were. I also made business cards for the makeup artists to pass out to customers thanking them for their business (and to refer a friend!).

Aisle six was where the real money was, and I wanted to make our makeup and fragrance department stand out. I installed elegant carpeting, attractive lighting, and beautiful built-in displays that allowed for product testing. The two licensed cosmeticians wore white lab coats with our logo.

The store would be spotless at all times. We did not have public restrooms but made sure the employee restrooms were always clean.

We had nice white plastic shopping bags and Monarch price tags with our logo. I wanted customers to feel shopping at GAYNORS was an experience and one they would share with their family and friends.

The store had to have fully stocked shelves. I opened an account with the biggest wholesale drug distributor, Frank W. Kerr, to fill in when we sold out of best-selling products. It sucked because it wasn't profitable, but it was worth it because it made the customers happy.

Everything was in place, and I just needed a grand opening event idea to draw women. Back in 1981, the most popular TV shows were soap operas such as *All My Children*, *General Hospital*, and *The Young and the Restless*. I hired a talent agency and they contracted the lead actors from *All My Children*. The cost was $10,000 for an hour (actually it was $25,000 with expenses and agency fees), but I knew it would be a smash hit.

To put the cost in perspective, my father borrowed $200,000 to open the store. This was a big investment for a grand opening. Now let's find out if it was worth it or not.

LIFE LESSON TIP: Mediocrity never wins first place. Your product or service has to stand out from the competition. Here are some ideas you can use: color, font, graphics, packaging, endorsements, certifications, ingredient(s), size, and price point. Like beauty manufacturers, decide if your product is mass, masstige, or prestige.

LESSON #17

Chaos Rules: Be Prepared to Deal with It When It Happens

Summertime. Eighty degrees and sunny. A beautiful Saturday morning. Radio ads were blasting GAYNORS grand opening. The store opened at ten. We were ready. And so were the customers.

The line extended forever with customers waiting to get in and it was only 9:30 a.m. We were ready for a rush but had no idea it was going to be this kind of rush. The limo appeared, and suddenly I was thinking to myself, are these customers or fans or are they both? The limo drove up to the front entrance, and you would have thought Elvis was reincarnated. The customers went crazy. The three soap stars emerged, and we shuffled them into the store. Inside the store, we set up a mock stage in the back, standing room only.

I forgot to tell you in the last chapter that I created a thirty-two-page flyer advertising the grand opening and the soap opera stars. I sent out twenty-five thousand of them. It was a great idea. To add to the excitement, we had the soap stars interviewed on local radio stations, and I recall one TV station showing up at the opening. This turned out to be a huge media event, and one thing you learned quickly: You have no control over the media.

We opened the doors at 10:00 a.m. You would have thought there wasn't a single other retail store in Farmington Hills with the number of customers that poured through the entrance. They grabbed shopping carts, shopping baskets, and some just ran to where the soap stars were. Virtually all the aisles were full by 10:15 a.m. The soap stars did their dialogue and answered questions for an hour. It was pandemonium. Afterward, we slipped them through the backdoor, and as a special surprise, we went to lunch with them. They were so nice and cooperative. I didn't want to leave the store with so many customers inside, but how often do you get to have lunch with soap stars?

We came back to chaos. Customers continued to come; the parking lot was packed. We sold out of more than a hundred bottles of Giorgio cologne. Clinique 1-2-3 was gone just like that. I learned that Maybelline makeup remover was a best-selling product when we had to restock it three times. The lines to checkout were long, but we had six registers and six baggers. I had three employees handle customer carryouts and restocking the carts and baskets.

When 9:00 p.m. came, we locked the door and were thrilled that the day was over. We were exhausted! It was the most exhilarating feeling ever, but at the same time, we knew the next day was only a short time away. We had to spend the next few hours restocking the shelves. That is when we found out that what we thought would be a thirty-day supply of many items turned into a one-day supply. Sunday would be another big day, and we had to be ready.

Opening day was the best sales day until the day GAYNORS was liquidated. It turned out that customers love a good store liquidation as much as a good store opening, and better yet, I didn't have to spend

$25,000 that day. However, I have a lot more to tell you before that delightful day.

> **LIFE LESSON TIP:** Chaos is normalcy for an entrepreneur. Successful entrepreneurs handle chaos like any other problem: They take the time to figure it out. Don't react to chaos instantly and, especially, don't raise your voice in front of employees or customers. When possible, address chaos the following morning. It is amazing how time is sometimes the best solution for solving a problem.

LESSON #18

Once You Learn What Your
Customers Want, Be Relentless
in Pursuing New Opportunities to
Keep Them Excited and Engaged

nlike Cadillac Ace, seasonal played a big part of business at
GAYNORS. When the store opened, back-to-school was
featured. I made sure we had plenty of candy for Halloween.
But for the holidays, I thought cosmetic and fragrance gift sets
would be all we needed. I couldn't have been more wrong. In fact, I
would learn quickly that our customers wanted the unexpected. That
meant they wanted to buy stuff at GAYNORS that they would not
find at other retailers.

Also, unlike Cadillac Ace, I was shocked to see so many babies
and kids in the store. Ace never had babies or kids. Sure, we sold
diapers (I had to follow Toys R Us and sell them at cost or below cost)
but what did I know about babies and kids? Perhaps a little bit as I
had my first baby boy in December 1981, hello Michael! I also knew
that there was nothing worse than the sound of a crying baby (some
things never change, right?).

My entrepreneurial mind went to work, and I did my research. Remember my first ACE Hardware trade show? I soon realized that there was a trade show for every industry. In fact, there was a trade show for trade shows! When I found out that there was an annual baby and kids show in Dallas, I hopped on a plane and checked it out.

OMG! It was just like the Ace show except it featured all baby and kids' items from furniture to strollers to soft goods and accessories. Unlike the Ace show in which I knew so many brands, I knew none of them here. I never knew that there could be so many pacifiers, baby bottles, baby foods, toys, stuffed animals, and you name it. Sorting through the booths, I always kept in the back of my mind that my customers wanted the unexpected. That's when I stopped at the Aprica Kassai booth. Founded in 1980, they made the best baby strollers in the world and were based in Japan. Their strollers sold for $200 and up. Back then, anything over $50 was a lot of money. GAYNORS was one of the first retailers to bring Aprica strollers in. They were an instant success.

The next booth of interest was Wee Sing. Don't ask me why, but there was something about the music cassettes that caught my attention. Wee Sing made music exclusively for babies and little kids. How does an entrepreneur sell baby music? I put in a sound system in the baby aisle (I'm coming to that) and from open to close, I played Wee Sing cassettes. We sold more than two hundred a week.

Golden Books and Random House featured kids' books. I bought an eight-foot fixture and filled it up with classics like *Dr. Seuss, Pat The Cat, The Little Engine That Could*, and hundreds of others. I was shocked to see how many books we sold.

I bought plenty of cool pacifiers, baby bottles, and opened an account with Gerber. They had just launched their natural baby food line, and I was all in. The magic really began when I stopped at the Russ Berrie booth. His story was amazing as he started with $500 and an idea. The booth featured stuffed animals and the most adorable hanging mobiles. Mobiles hung over the crib and attracted the baby's attention so the baby wouldn't cry. I had to have one for Michael. I had the rep come to our store, and we picked out an amazing selection. How does an entrepreneur sell mobiles? I installed hanging grids in the baby aisle and lined the entire aisle with mobiles. We sold hundreds.

To make room for the baby section, I got rid of all the bulk cleaning products at the back of the store and converted it to baby and kids land. The proliferation of moms and babies grew exponentially and of course, mom tossed a whole lot of other products into the shopping cart.

One last thing I have to mention. Babies cry, and kids whine. How does an entrepreneur solve both problems? The local bagel factory sold teething bagels, and I bought them by the gross (that's 144 if you are too young to know). Moms would instantly dart to the baby section and get their baby a teething bagel. It was amazing. Next to the bagels were a dispenser of Dum-Dum suckers. Both the bagels and suckers would need replenishment at least twice daily, and they were always complementary.

Now that the baby and kid stuff was taken care of, next came educational toys and games. I learned that the big toy show was in NYC, and when it opened, I was once again like a kid in a candy store. This show was different. It was in a skyscraper building and each floor featured manufacturer showrooms. Usually only open by appointment, they were all open during the show.

It's here that I found so many cool brands of educational toys that were niche enough you couldn't find them at Toys R Us. It is also where I found Selchow & Righter. In 1982, they licensed the game *Trivial*

Pursuit. It was among the first niche board games invented and would soon start an entire new category of board games. Their focus was on gift stores, not mass merchandisers like Toys R Us. I brought in the original version in early 1983 and we quickly sold out. In fall 1983, they were going to launch their next version, Trivial Pursuit Baby Boomer edition. I knew this would be big so I allowed our customers to preorder the game and this guaranteed that they would be the first to have it. Unbelievably, we took more than a thousand orders. It would be Selchow's & Righter's biggest order for a single store.

Remember Cabbage Patch Kids in 1982? If you were around then, you never saw anything like it. I missed that craze but was first in line when Coleco launched Furskins in 1983.

Last story about toys. I only tell you all these stories because they are all relevant to being an entrepreneur and how they molded me over the years. Little Tikes was a huge brand known for its durable toys. Their big business was their outdoor sets like their treehouse, slide, and fort. In 1983, I launched the first Little Tikes Truckload Sale. Customers would place their preorders in April at the best prices and then the truckload would arrive right before Memorial Day in the parking lot. Each year we sold a full truckload!

My next reinvention focus was the gift category. GAYNORS would be known for having the newest, coolest, and most innovative gifts that other retailers did not have. Once again, I did my research and learned that there were gift shows throughout the United States. This was indeed a big business. I headed to Chicago and McCormick Place. It was the largest convention show in the country, and it was filled with gift show booths. I was overwhelmed. But it was so much fun. The thing was, I didn't want GAYNORS to resemble a Hallmark store, and I wanted the gift selection to be transitional because our customers wanted something new every time they shopped the store.

Remember the Itty-Bitty Book Lite? Remember the Salton Shower Radio? These were the kinds of gifts I brought in, and they always sold out.

LIFE LESSON TIP: We always want to know what the latest restaurant is and to check it out. Why? Human behavior. Humans love new things. What do the most successful restaurants offer their guests? Daily specials. Why? Because those are chef recommendations. When it comes to your business, think like a restauranter: How can you make your product or service stand out to keep customers excited and engaged?

LESSON #19

Sometimes the Greatest Opportunities
Are Right in Front of You; All You Have
to Do Is Open Your Eyes to See Them

Business at GAYNORS could not have been better. We were doing $5 million a year, and I was making enough money to pay the mortgage on my $109,000 colonial home. It was such a relief moving from a 900-square-foot two-bedroom condo with two kids. Yep, my second kid was born in 1983, hello Daniel!

Before I get to Clipboard Magic, let's talk a moment about my parents. The original plan was for me to go to Cadillac Ace once or twice a month. That never happened. My parents built a new home in Boca, and my father bought a new Mercedes S500 convertible. My mother still went down there every October through May, and my father went more often than not. As you know, my relationship with my father was strained and very typical of father–son business relationships. The good news is that he did not show up at GAYNORS often. The bad news is that my mother decided to work the cosmetic counter on Saturdays for a few hours.

Suddenly my mother was an expert in business, running a store, and dealing with employees and customers. Mind you, she never spent a day at Cadillac Ace in her life. GAYNORS made her sort of a celebrity with her friends, and she couldn't wait to brag to her friends about her experiences working there. I dreaded each and every moment she was there, and Saturdays were our busiest day of the week. It turned out there was a solution to getting rid of my mother working at GAYNORS, and it had to do with the magic clipboard. In the meantime, I prayed for October to come every year.

I knew that hairdressers shopped the store because we sold a lot of Clairol and Wella hair color. However, I didn't know that manicurists did. Sure enough, manicurists came in looking for manicuring supplies. If we didn't have what they were looking for, they would write what they wanted on the clipboard: Polish remover gallon (we sold six-ounce Cutex); acetone (we sold that at the hardware store); Dragon Lady Nail Tips; Five Second Nail Glue; Zebra files; honey-tipped nail brushes, and other items. Little did I know that there was a manicuring craze going on in California at the time.

Hmm, I thought. I did it with baby and kids. I did it with gifts. Why not do it for manicuring? I opened my diverters' catalogs and saw that they had manicuring supplies. Why didn't I notice this before you might ask? Let me ask you: Did you know where the local maternity store was before you were pregnant or your wife was pregnant? Of course not! You only need a maternity store when one is pregnant. Why would I look at manicure supplies when I was focused on hairdressers? Anyway, they had most of the items I needed except for the honey-tipped brush. I created a three-foot endcap and filled it up with manicuring supplies.

I could not believe it. The endcap was devoured like a dog devours a steak. I reordered. Suddenly, more manicurists were coming to shop and wanted even more supplies. The magic clipboard was filled with more products. The three-foot endcap quickly became an inline eight-foot section in the cosmetic aisle. What was most amazing is that non-manicurists loved the products too as they were all new to them. Sales exploded.

All was good except for one thing. I still didn't have the honey-tipped nail brush in stock. I did my research. You guessed it, there were beauty trade shows! However, I didn't want to go to a trade show for a dozen brushes. Then I found out that there were trade magazines just for nails. After reading them, I finally found out that Creative Nail Design manufactured the honey-tipped brush. I gave them a call to order a dozen.

LIFE LESSON TIP: You're never going to spot an opportunity, trend, or fad sitting at home or in your office. If you are selling a product, visit as many stores as possible that sell your type of product. If you invented a home improvement product, where are you going to sell it? ACE, True Value, Lowe's, Home Depot, Menard's, Tractor Supply, or Amazon? Think about why there are all of these options for customers to shop and what differentiates each retailer from the other. That is the secret sauce successful entrepreneurs slurp up.

LESSON #20

Never Stop Pursuing Your Passion

L ife being an entrepreneur is filled with stories you cannot make up. This is one of them.

I called Creative Nail Design (CND) to order a dozen honey-tipped brushes. As you know, I had been dealing direct with the largest consumer companies in the world without a problem. What could be the big deal to buy from a small nail manufacturer?

The person on the phone said that I had to be a wholesale beauty distributor to buy from CND. She told me that their Michigan distributor was Pierce Brothers based in Lansing. She also told me I had to be a licensed manicurist or hairdresser to buy from them. I then asked her what a wholesale beauty distributor was. I knew all about manufacturers, retailers, and diverters. But wholesale beauty distributors? She told me that they sold exclusively to licensed beauty professionals.

[INSIGHT: If you are thinking about starting your own business, do not become a distributor. It is the lowest tier of business ownership because you are always at the mercy of the companies you distribute. I learned this the hard way and it took me thirty-four years to be liberated.]

So, what does an entrepreneur do? Research! I went to the Yellow Pages and looked up "wholesale beauty distributors." Sure enough, there was Pierce Brothers. I also found Beaute Craft in Troy, Maly's in Grand Rapids, Marlo's in Ferndale, Sally Beauty Supply, and a few others. Suddenly my mind was racing and thinking about this: I was already selling professional hair and manicuring products, but I had to buy them from diverters. If I could buy them direct, not only would I save money, I could get all the inventory I needed. Best of all, I could get brands I never knew existed and products like the honey-tipped brushes.

The decision was easy. I registered Nailco Manicurist Centers and started my next journey as a wholesale beauty distributor. All because of the magical honey-tipped brush.

LIFE LESSON TIP: Magnus Carlsen was born in 1990 and went on to become the best chess player of all time. He was a five-time world chess champion. And then he decided to take time off to pursue Texas Hold'em, and if he is as passionate about poker as chess, he will become one of poker's best players. His passion drove him to the top of chess. You too need to have the same passion for your product or service to get to the top.

LESSON #21

If You Decide to Start a Second
Business at the Same Time,
Prepare for the Consequences

Y ou have to admit that "Nailco" was a great name for the
company. Little did I know then that it would be the most
famous name in nail distribution and still lives today. You
see, TNG Worldwide stands for The Nailco Group. Back in
1985, how does an entrepreneur start a completely new company
from scratch with absolutely no experience or mentor? He works his
ass off and steals the best ideas.

First idea: Computerize Nailco from the start. Unlike
GAYNORS, Nailco would be shipping across the country and have
repeat customers. I had to have access to them easily and store their
information. The fourth IBM PC came out in 1984, the model AT,
and ran DOS 3.0 (Microsoft owned MS-DOS and licensed it to
IBM. It was Microsoft's big break). At the time, ComputerLand was
the biggest computer geek store (at one point they had more than
eight hundred stores and then would go broke in the 1990s). The
IBM AT was large and heavy, much like TVs back then. The monitor
was actually like a TV screen and was black and white (color came

out in 1983). I added an Okidata dot matrix printer (it took about twenty-five seconds to print a single page and the printer paper had to have strips on both sides to feed into the printer). But I needed software to run the computer. A local guy named Ted Ross was an independent contractor for ComputerLand and I hired him to write the software for Nailco.

Second idea: Create a catalog. Catalogs were a big business after WWII, and everyone got the Sears catalog among hundreds of others. Back then, catalogs were the equivalent of online shopping. I had no money to create a nice catalog so I went with the basics: sixteen pages, black and white, standard paper.

Third idea: Hire a manicurist. I could do every service at Cadillac Ace; I could buy from the biggest companies, but I did not know how to do a manicure. I did for a brief moment think about going to beauty school to become a manicurist so I would know how to do it, but that took too much time. I also knew hiring a manicurist would give Nailco authenticity. I hired Sandy Dusseau. Almost all my future hires would also be manicurists.

Fourth idea: Advertise. There were two trade rags at the time. *Mainly Manicuring* came out in 1980 and was a newspaper format. *NAILS* magazine came out in 1983. I subscribed to both of them and decided to advertise as well. The trade rags would become three in 1990, but that is another chapter.

Fifth idea: Create a separate space inside GAYNORS. There were certain products that could be sold only to manicurists such as the honey-tipped brush, so I installed a couple of showcases to put all those products inside. All other products were on the shelves accessible to everyone. Sandy ran the counter. It is also where we set up the UPS machine that would print labels and C.O.D. tags.

Sixth idea: Capitalize the company. All of the above ideas cost money. More important to me, Nailco was going to be my first business in which I was going to be the majority shareholder. You can imagine the conversation that ensued with my father. I told him that Gaynor Enterprises was his company (you recall I was a minority shareholder with 25 percent equity). I told him that Nailco would be my company, and I wanted the same equity proportion (I thought that was more than fair although it turned out to be to his advantage). I would own 75 percent of Nailco, and he would own 25 percent. We came to terms. We also came to terms on the cash infusion to get Nailco started and agreed to each put $25,000 into the company.

Seventh idea: Buy direct. The diverters served their purpose, but they couldn't keep up with our demand. There were also too many brands they could not buy that I needed. I read every page of both trade rags to learn the best-selling products, and I would contact the companies to buy direct.

Eighth idea: Hold a trade show. I saw in the trade rags that nail shows were the rage in California. Nailco would be the first nail distributor east of California in the country, so why not steal that idea! That's another chapter.

Ninth idea: Call CND and get the fucking honey-tipped brushes!

LIFE LESSON TIP: One of the greatest things about being an entrepreneur is that you never know where your ideas are going to take you. Sometimes when you start a business, there are going to be offshoot ideas that you never thought of that could turn out to be better than your original idea. You have to be flexible to capitalize on those ideas when they happen and be prepared to switch gears on a moment's notice, even if it means closing down your first business.

LESSON #22

Always Double Down When You Have
No Choice—Failure Is Not an Option

I called CND and told them I opened Nailco Manicurist Centers, a legitimate wholesale beauty distributor, and I wanted to order a dozen honey-tipped nail brushes. The person on the other line started to laugh. Then she went on to say, "Larry, we don't sell to 'any' wholesale distributor. We only sell to authorized CND distributors, and you have to be approved. Not only that, you have to carry the full line, not just one of our brushes." I replied, "OK, then I want to become a CND distributor." She told me she would relay my request to the team and someone would get back to me.

In the meantime, I started calling companies I wanted to do business with. Just a few of them included: IBD, No-Lift Nails, Delore, Forsythe, Essie, OPI, and Nail Secret. Virtually all of them told me that I would have to meet with their rep group and that they would notify their rep group to come to GAYNORS and set up a meeting. I asked, "What is a rep group?"

I compare rep groups to bookies; they get their juice for not doing much of anything. Real companies have their own salespeople. As it turned out, most companies in the professional beauty industry were not real. They were started by people that had no previous business experience, and they fell into the business because the nail category was so hot. It is like when a team is on a winning streak—no one pays attention to their mistakes. But as soon as the team starts losing, everyone highlights their mistakes. It's no wonder 95 percent of these companies are no longer in business or sold out long ago.

Rep groups got 10 percent of the sale. Some negotiated rates as high as 15 percent. They were extortionists. Nail companies signed up with rep groups because they had no money to hire their own sales force, and distributors were everywhere; they would need a huge sales force and they were a tiny company. I could write an entire book on rep groups, but I won't bore you. I will tell you this: The rep groups came to GAYNORS to meet with me.

They saw the store, they saw the eight-foot Nailco counter, and then they wondered why they wasted their time. One after another, they all said the same thing, "The companies we represent only sell to wholesale distributors, and you are running a retail operation." Further, they went on to say, "Our products can only be purchased by licensed manicurists. How would we know if you were selling them to your GAYNORS customers?" I showed them the catalog. I explained to them that we put all non-consumer products in the showcase and that we were going to sell a lot of goods through advertising in trade magazines, which catered exclusively to manicurists. They didn't buy it and told me they couldn't open me up. Now you know why I refer to them as the "fucking rep groups." They were going to make a quick 10 percent on every order without doing a thing. I would later find out that they were protecting their other customers, namely, the damn full-service distributors.

What does an entrepreneur do now? Hire a private investigator. I had the private investigator go to local beauty supply stores and buy several manicuring products. The investigator did not have a beauty license, and if the store asked for one, the investigator would make up an excuse as to why she didn't have it with her. She went to six stores. All six stores sold the goods to her without the license. The investigator took photos of the products and receipts. I made twenty-five copies of each.

I sent these by FedEx to twenty-five companies I wanted to do business with. Within a week, all of them responded that they would open Nailco up and the rep groups would be stopping by again. One company was so enthralled that the VP of Sales decided to come himself and visit with me. The company was IBD, and his name was Lorenzo Meija. He became a TNG cheerleader that would help open many more doors. In the meantime, I got a call back from CND.

LIFE LESSON TIP: One of the hardest things for an entrepreneur to learn is that business is not fair. There are gatekeepers that you would never expect. For example, if you want to do business with Target, you have to deal with an authorized Target rep group, not Target Corp. When you develop your business plan, make sure the product you are going to sell is available to you. Better yet, avoid being a retailer or distributor and manufacture it yourself.

LESSON #23

Sometimes Being the Underdog Has Its Advantages

For me, 1985 was turning out to be quite a year. My third son was born in February, hello Mark! Nailco was launched in July, and I turned thirty in October. Little did I know that my year would only get better when Paula Jacoby and Fred Shober visited me from CND.

[INSIGHT: It is no coincidence that all the nail companies were based in California. Just about everything American and invented was born in California. California was the thirty-first state admitted to the Union in 1850. That was the time of the Gold Rush in which more than 300,000 Americans came to California to partake in the rush from 1848 to 1855. Not only that, millions of immigrants would head west to find land to settle on and farm. California accounts for one-seventh of the U.S. population, and its GDP ranks in the top-five globally. Where else can you go to swim in the ocean, hike in the mountains, and ski all at the same time? Silicon Valley got its start in 1971 and Napa Valley became famous in 1976. As I mentioned earlier in the book, the 1970s and 1980s were boom times for new industries and product innovation. California also became the epicenter for the nail industry.]

CND was founded in 1979 by sheer luck. The father of the Nordstrom family was a dentist. One day a magical idea came to him that dental acrylic could be used on fingernails. He had three kids, two of whom were interested in his idea, Jan and Jim. CND was the first nail company to brand dental acrylic and sell it to manicurists. Their brand would become famous: Solar Nail. To apply Solar Nail to fingernails, you had to prep the nail, apply a coat of nail primer, dip a kolinsky brush into acrylic liquid followed by acrylic powder, and then deftly apply to the nail plate. The product would flow and the manicurist would sculpt it to fit the nail perfectly. The brand name of their brush was the honey-tip brush and no, it did not have honey on the tip of it!

I will never forget the meeting in my office. My office was so small I had to bring in two folding chairs for them. They wanted to know my strategic vision. They wanted to know my thoughts on education. They wanted to know my thoughts on how we were going to support their brand. They wanted to know about the catalog, trade advertising, and how I would protect their brand and not sell their goods to consumers. As the meeting progressed, I could see excitement in their eyes. I would later find out that Pierce Brothers had no interest in nails and was doing poorly with CND. They asked me if I could hit some sales numbers and I said absolutely. Next thing I knew, Nailco Manicurist Centers became an authorized CND distributor! The first thing I ordered was a dozen honey-tip brushes. When I told Paula and Fred the story, they sent me the dozen complementary via FedEx the next day. I now had the brush my customers wanted!

I would soon learn that becoming a CND distributor was a coveted thing. Neither Maly's or Beaute Craft had CND, and Marlo never had any premium brands. Overnight Nailco had status, and the other nail manufacturers soon found out. Suddenly, they started to call me to distribute their brand. It was pandemonium.

LIFE LESSON TIP: Always remember that when you start your business, you are one of five million others doing the same thing. Your business plan has to identify at least one unique lever that your company offers customers so others can buy in. There will be many instances in which that lever you need takes months or even a couple of years to get. Successful entrepreneurs never stop until they get that lever.

LESSON #24

Always Be Prepared to Accept the Unexpected

I f you thought 1985 was an exciting year for me, wait until you read what 1986 was all about. Up until now, I have not delved into my personal life. I mean, I could have told you as a kid I loved to play marbles and collect purees and boulders. Or that I loved and collected comic books. I was hooked on *Archie* (I could never decide if I was in love more with Betty or Veronica), but my favorite was Richie Rich. I was an avid coin collector as well and spent most of my earnings at Ernest Lush and subscribed to *Coinage*. I still have the coins, which were a terrible investment. And I was a hard candy addict and couldn't get enough watermelon Jolly Ranchers; I bought them by the box.

But looking at 1986, it's time to share some personal stuff because it is relevant. I have two younger brothers, Steven and Bob. Steven and Bob were never interested in the family business. Steven bought a podiatry practice with the money I gave him for his 5 percent and moved to Toledo. He eventually moved to Boca Raton, where he lives now. Bob moved right out of college to Boca Raton. He started his own business, Día Foot, and Steven ended up working for him.

Now you understand why my parents bought a place in Boca, and later on, they too moved there full time. I was the only Gaynor left in Michigan. And for shits and giggles, if you really want to know more about my background, Gaynor was a made-up name my father gave us. His father's last name was Ginsburg. He changed the name to Gaynor so it would be non-Jewish. Then again, my parents named me Larry, what kind of name was that!

My wife's name was Kathy, and I met her at MSU. One detail I didn't tell you is that she always wore a Jewish star necklace around her neck. Naturally, I thought she was Jewish. Kathy was one year younger than I, and we decided to get married after she graduated. I always told my high school friends that my plan was to go to college, get married, have three kids soon thereafter, and be free by the age of fifty. My plan worked to a tee. With the exception that I didn't know I would be married twice. When I proposed to Kathy, I learned that she wasn't Jewish. She liked dating Jewish guys, and that is why she wore the necklace. I dated girls that I was attracted to; they didn't have to be Jewish. However, I was stunned at this. Kathy agreed to become Jewish and converted, and let's just leave it at that. Kathy graduated from MSU and got her degree in teaching. She worked as a teacher until Michael was born.

By 1986, we had three kids and everything was great. Until it wasn't. I planned a really nice road trip to Toronto for the Memorial Day weekend. This was a treat because I never went on vacation. One day before we were ready to leave, Kathy told me that she was having an affair with her high school sweetheart and leaving me. I had no idea and was devastated. How could this have happened?

Let me tell you, I wouldn't blame you for going to the next chapter and skipping the rest of this blasted story. I am only including it because it is relevant to entrepreneurs and others who work long hours or travel frequently. It is the ultimate wake-up call.

Kathy was from North Muskegon. I am an old-fashioned type of guy and asked her father's permission to marry Kathy. He happily said yes. Charlie was an amazing father-in-law and the complete opposite of my father. He was also my first mentor. He owned a furniture store, and he would share many stories with me. He loved to play golf, and we played together when I could. He loved to play cribbage and taught me the game. He loved to cook, and I learned to make his corn meal pancakes. He loved his beer (only bought the cheapest) and his whiskey and daily happy hours with cheese and crackers. We had the best time together, and I tried to go to Muskegon for the weekend with the kids at least every two to three months. But weekends were tough for me as GAYNORS was the busiest then.

Kathy started to go to Muskegon with the kids by herself on weekends once a month. I was fine with that as I could work more hours and eat more fast food. Little did I know that when she was in Muskegon and after the kids went to bed, she hooked up with Dan. She told her parents that she was going out with high school girlfriends so they had no idea.

Now back to Memorial Day weekend. Kathy told me that we could still go to Toronto for the kids' sake and be civilized adults. I said no and broke down. She left with the kids, and I spent all weekend wondering what went wrong. But entrepreneurs are optimists, and I was optimistic that Kathy's fling with Dan would end and she would come back to me. I could not have been more wrong.

LIFE LESSON TIP: Only an entrepreneur can understand that our minds never stop working. We even dream about ideas and wake up remembering them. There are times that we are so wrapped up in our work that we forget those that are around us. Be cognizant of warning signs when they flash. However, more times than not, the warning signs never flash and shit happens. It's part of being an entrepreneur so learn to accept the unexpected.

LESSON #25

Patience Is a Virtue

Within a few months, business at Nailco was so good that we outgrew the space inside GAYNORS. Opportunity came when the store next door went out of business. Our lease would end in 1987. I had a good relationship with our landlord, and he agreed to give me the available space. The unit was 1,600 square feet and would be the first of more than eight expansions. Making the plan-o-gram this time was a piece of cake as most of the square footage would be devoted to UPS orders and warehousing. I did establish a really nice shopping environment for our customers and even had a manicure table for demonstrations. Additionally, I set up an intercom system between GAYNORS and Nailco so I could be reached at any time. But best of all, I got to put a sign on the door, "Open to Licensed Beauty Professionals Only."

In case you are wondering if my attention to GAYNORS was waning because of Nailco, the answer is yes. However, I still made sure GAYNORS had the latest cosmetics, fragrances, and hot gift ideas. I launched a line of beautiful Japanese lacquer-designed photo albums, contemporary picture frames, and partnered with Ann Marie who owned a perfume store so I could get more hot-selling fragrances.

Hudson's had hired a private investigator to find out where we were getting our high-end cosmetics from, so for this reason, we always removed the shipping tags from the boxes before we threw them into the dumpster. I couldn't believe how many boxes of Nips candy we sold and was even more shocked when we added Lite Delites hard candy and sold hundreds of bags every week.

GAYNORS business was steadily growing but not growing exponentially like Nailco's. I hired more nail techs, got more new brands, and came out with the second catalog, which was an upgrade; it was now two-color and featured thirty-six pages. Business was rocking, and I remember the first time we sent out more than a hundred orders in a single day. It was a day to celebrate, and we did.

There was another brand that was gaining momentum in California and already being sold at Beaute Craft and Maly's—OPI. George Schaeffer was both a shrewd businessman and an entrepreneur. He was the smartest guy in the nail business and knew how to take other people's ideas and make them better. Looking back, his true success as an entrepreneur compared to me was that his focus was on manufacturing and brand development, not being a lowly distributor.

George lived in California and saw what was going on in the nail industry. He was lucky too. In 1981, he bought Odontorium Products, a small dental supply company and renamed it OPI. Shortly thereafter, he collaborated with Suzi Weiss and his biochemist, Eric Montgomery, to develop his own acrylic system. Like Paul Mitchell and Arnie Miller, he too went door-to-door peddling his system. OPI would soon become CND's main competitor. Now mind you, CND was run by Jim and Jan, neither of whom were shrewd businesspeople or entrepreneurs. But we will get to more of that later. OPI became a must-have brand for me to carry. I called George.

George knew about Nailco, saw the first catalog, and was quite impressed. However, he told me he already had two Michigan distributors and that he was not interested in opening a third. I told him the two distributors knew nothing about the nail business and besides, we were shipping nationwide, not just in Michigan. George being George was intrigued because he loved growing his business, and Nailco would be a natural for him. But he had to protect his distributors. George flew in to meet with me.

George was one of those guys you loved at first sight. He was sort of a big guy who loved to eat and drink. He had a big face with big cheeks that you would love to squeeze (which I often did). He liked me right away, as we were both classic entrepreneurs. Unlike anyone else in the industry, George was a schemer. He came up with the most brilliant idea: "Larreeee [as he would call me], here's what I am going to do. You will buy from my Arizona distributor for a few months, and we will see what kind of business you can do. You will pay distributor pricing, and I will work it out with him. I also want to see what kind of reaction I get from Beaute Craft and Maly's." I was thrilled. OPI would make the cover of my next catalog!

We did a lot of OPI business. So much, in fact, that the Arizona distributor could not keep up. George made sure shipments to his Arizona distributor would take priority. After three months, George gave me a call. "Larreeee, I can't believe how much business you have done. But what really gets me is that neither Beaute Craft or Maly's contacted me about you selling OPI. Fuck them; you are now an authorized OPI distributor!" I was elated. Nailco would be among the very few distributors in the United States to have both CND and OPI. It was a day to celebrate, and I did.

Once word on the street hit that I had OPI, all the wannabes called me to take on their lines. No-Lift Nails, Alpha 9, Tammy Taylor, Linen

Batiste, and many others started filling up even more catalog pages. The catalog was now forty-eight pages. Business boomed, and we cracked $600,000 in sales that year. My goal was to beat Cadillac Ace's sales, and I would soon find out that didn't take too much time to do.

LIFE LESSON TIP: Entrepreneurs are impatient at heart. We want results now! We want it done now! Tomorrow is always too late. But this life lesson tip is a good one: Learn to be patient. Patience is a virtue only when you allow time to take its course and not intervene. There is an old proverb: "If it was meant to happen, it will happen."

LESSON #26

You Don't Know Until You Know

Manicure trade shows were a big thing in California so I decided to hold my first trade show in Michigan. It would be small and gauge demand for future trade shows. I have included this chapter so my loyal readers could read firsthand how even the smartest entrepreneurs fuck up every now and then.

Note: Some readers may gloss over when I use the "fuck" word, and some readers might wonder why I use the "fuck" word. "Fuck" is just another word. I remember when I was a kid watching TV. (You want more personal perspective, here you go. Back then, there were only three channels and I was the remote control. The internet connection was a premium set of rabbit ears and TV was black and white.) TV shows couldn't even use the words "hell" or "shit" let alone "fuck." After WWII and up until the Vietnam War, life was pretty good in America. Then came the Vietnam War and the hippie generation was born. Their slogan was "Make love, not war." It was a beautiful thing. Fast-forward to today, and we are in the midst of the greatest conflict and upheaval in our history—perhaps even more so than the first Civil War. Americans are less happy (at this time of writing), life expectancy is going down for the first time ever, and we are more divided than ever. So, what the fuck?

The first Nailco show was held at the Sheraton Oaks in Novi. Now mind you, I have been to quite a few retail trade shows so I pretty much knew the routine. There would be booths, education, and the hotel would take care of the catering. I decided to feature fifteen brands, and Sandy would take care of the classes. We sold an impressive three hundred tickets without much advertising.

The show opened at ten in the morning, and we were ready. The manicurists came running onto the show floor, eager to buy everything at show prices. I made up nice price cards for each item with the regular price and show price. All the products were arranged perfectly on tables, and I had order forms for the customers to fill out.

Suddenly, all hell broke loose. The customers were screaming at me. They expected the show to be cash-and-carry. I asked them what that was. They told me that at beauty shows, all the products were available for sale, and the customers paid for them and took them home. I said to them that I have been to many shows for hardware, baby stuff, toys, and gifts and I had never even heard of this concept. They wanted my head.

What does an entrepreneur do? He runs to his station wagon, drives a hundred miles per hour to his store, fills up the station wagon with as much product as he can and drives back to the hotel at 110 miles per hour. I got to the entrance of the hotel and started to carry the products to the show floor. One of the manicurists saw me doing this. The manicurist told a friend who told a friend. Suddenly three hundred manicurists were outside the hotel and literally taking the products they wanted to buy out of my hands. I was witnessing a zombie movie, but it was real. Sandy came outside and wrangled the crowd back inside. Eventually we got all the products unloaded from my car, and everyone was happy. When I drove back to the store after the show, there was nothing in the back of the station wagon—everything sold out.

I would make sure my next show would be much different. You will read about that in 1988, but I have so much to share with you before then.

LIFE LESSON TIP: You already know that you should never "assume": it makes an ass out of you and me. What I love about math is that 2 + 2 is always 4. What I hate about science is that 2 + 2 can be debated. Entrepreneurs love to assume, and that is when the costliest mistakes happen. As much as possible, fact check and never assume.

LESSON #27

Don't Waste Time Picking the Best Mentors

L ittle did I know when 1987 started that it would be my craziest year in business ever. Let's start with the really big move. The lease was up on both GAYNORS and Nailco, and decisions had to be made. I already outgrew the space for Nailco. My father and I looked for a new location in the Farmington Hills area thinking twenty-four hundred to three thousand square feet would be ideal. We took a few tours, but I didn't see anything I liked. Then one day I was looking at the classifieds in the newspaper and saw that a new 32,000-square-foot industrial building in Livonia was available. I didn't know much about Livonia, but I knew it was a thriving city in Wayne County. I went to visit it.

The building was divided into five 6,400-square-foot units. It was right off the I-96 freeway, which was a great location. I met with Zef, the landlord, and explained the situation to him: "Nailco is a fast-growing business and needs more space." I told him that 6,400 square feet would be four times the space I currently had. I wasn't sure if I needed that much room but, on the other hand, if the business continued to accelerate I told him I might need that and more. Zef gave me a sweetheart deal being that I would be his first tenant as well as first-right-of-refusal on the 6,400 square feet next door. Little did I know then that I would be taking up the entire building.

I told the news to my father. He was not a happy camper. He told me I was taking a big risk (no shit!) and that I should take a smaller space. We agreed to disagree. Now that I had the space, how was I going to lay it out? I became an expert at doing plan-o-grams, but designing a warehouse was all new to me. That's when I met my next mentor, Jack Miller, CEO of Quill Corporation.

This brings me to another flashback that I have to share with you because, once again, it is relevant to my entrepreneurial career path. Some people would call me a nerd. Why? I was fascinated with organization. Everything I owned had to be organized a certain way, and if anyone touched or moved anything, I would know it instantly. What better store for organizational nerds than an office supply store? Back then, they were such a thing and they were everywhere. Silver's was the ultimate office supply store where I lived and opened at the first suburban mall in Michigan, Tel-Twelve. Silver's featured every office accessory you could think of, including all the fancy brands. They also sold office equipment such as desks and chairs. I was into nifty four-way pens, mechanical pencils, colored markers, and colorful binders. I spent hours there.

Quill was started in 1956, and like every industry, key employees left Quill to start Viking in 1960. These guys were entrepreneurs ahead of their time. They saw the demand for office supplies and recognized that every state had lots of independent office supply stores. Their idea was to become the first department/warehouse store for office supplies. Quill's breakthrough came in 1963 when it introduced its first catalog. The catalog would grow to more than a thousand pages. I knew firsthand because you could see my drool marks on many of the pages. Eventually Silver's and all the other independent office supply stores closed (that was such a sad day for me) and catalog companies ruled the industry (until Staples bought Quill out in 1998 for $685M and we know the rest of the story after that). Truthfully, I feel bad for all the young entrepreneurs that will never get to experience shopping at an office supply store.

Anyway, I gave Jack a call, told him my story, and he agreed to meet me at his warehouse in Chicago. I hopped on a plane and met with him in his conference room. First thing I noticed was a giant bowl of M&M's. I asked him about them. He told me everyone loved them, and he always kept the bowl filled. As soon as I got back to Nailco, I made sure that we too had a bowl of M&M's (we still have them). We talked catalogs, we talked warehouses, we talked growing pains, and then he took me on a tour. WOW! The warehouse was enormous. For the first time I saw automated conveyors, packing lanes, picking totes, automated box makers, and so much more. Afterward, Jack said I could call him anytime. He was a great mentor.

So, what does an entrepreneur do? Go to the Yellow Pages and find a warehouse design firm. That's exactly what I did, and the company would not only build the first automated conveyor for me, it would be back several times expanding it. We were ready for the big times, and I was aiming to be just like Jack. But first, I needed a lot of money (next chapter).

One particular day, while all of this was going on, someone came into Nailco and asked for me. I came to see him and he handed me an envelope and said, "You've been served." I had no idea what he meant. I opened the envelope and saw the lawsuit. Kathy filed for divorce, and it was officially over. Suddenly, I needed to get away.

Teresa was at GAYNORS and gave me a call on the intercom. She had a couple of questions and asked how I was because I didn't sound so good. I told her what just happened, and she had total empathy for me. Unexpectedly I said to her, "I'm really in the mood to get drunk tonight, would you like to join me?" (Now mind you, I didn't drink in my twenties and not much in my thirties but am doing my best now to make up for it, HA!) I really have no idea why I said what I said to her, but when she told me "Yes!" I could not believe it.

Teresa left the store early, went home to change, and came over to my house. We went to the Sheraton Oaks because I knew they had a good bar, and we ordered Long Island iced teas at her recommendation. I will not elaborate as to what happened next but let's just say we would stay together forever from that day on. Who goes from being married one day to being with a new person the very next day for the rest of his life? I do! And I have been loving every minute of it since.

It was time to play Monopoly, and I had two Chance cards in front of me: One card had, "Congratulations, you decided to keep GAYNORS!" The other card had, "Congratulations, you decided to keep Nailco!" I knew that I couldn't keep both. I also knew warehouse clubs were starting to open (Ulta didn't open until 1990 if you were wondering), and the future of discount HBA would be fleeting at best. I knew that nails were just starting and it was a very exciting time. The answer was easy, but the conversation that took place with my parents and attorney was not.

We were all sitting at the kitchen table after dinner. A decision had to be made. Little did they know I already made it so no matter what they said, it would not have made a difference. My mother was selfish and wanted to keep GAYNORS. Our attorney, who was a relative of the family, was neutral. My father wanted to keep GAYNORS to placate my mother, and he wanted me to keep Nailco because he thought he would make more money long term. After a lot of bickering back and forth, I prevailed. However, it would turn out to be a brutal ending for GAYNORS, and our relationship turned even worse. GAYNORS liquidated shortly thereafter and Nailco now had my 100 percent undivided attention. What a year.

LIFE LESSON TIP: Mentors are invaluable. The trick is to know which mentors are best for you. Here are some tips: They have no vested interest in your business. They are not related to you. They do not charge for their time. They are excited to see you succeed. They are responsive when you need them. In most instances, one meeting with a mentor is all it takes to get the information you need to move forward. After meeting with Jack, I never called him again. But his advice was invaluable.

LESSON #28

When It Comes to Professional
Services, Pay for and Hire the Best

What a boring lesson, right? I mean, what's more boring than dealing with bankers, lawyers, and accountants? However, if you are reading this book as a new or established entrepreneur, this is one of the most important chapters. If you fuck this up, you can pretty much kiss away any chance for long-term success.

Let's start with the bank. The bank is the only thing I kept the same as my father. The reason was that Detroit Bank & Trust was the oldest bank in Michigan dating back to 1849, and it was also the most powerful bank (the name changed to Comerica in the early 1980s). When you borrow money from a bank, you need to establish a relationship with a lending officer. There is a famous expression that goes something like this, "It is best to use a bank when you don't need it." Moreover, if you have a growing business, there is no better way of getting money than from a bank. The only thing you have to deal with is interest payments. All other ways of getting money involve partnerships (YIKES!), equity sale (more YIKES!), or borrowing from friends and family (the absolute worst-case scenario).

In thirty-eight years with Comerica, I have had two loan officers. You could say that I am a loyal guy. In fact, I am the *most loyal* type of guy, and while there are pros and cons of being too loyal over the long haul, being loyal is the best. The ideal loan officer not only understands your business, they also want to see it succeed. Why? The more business you do, the more money you will need, and the more money they will make.

Borrowing money is one of the scariest things an entrepreneur can do. Not only do you have to pay it back, you have to pay interest too. In 1988, mortgage rates were around 10.5 percent and the prime rate was about the same. The prime rate is the rate the best corporations pay. Companies such as Nailco pay up to three to four points higher. That meant paying around 14 percent interest each and every month. To put things in perspective, Nailco's gross margin was in the low forties. Interest payments alone would reduce it to the low thirties. Luckily, for me, I was drawing a meager salary and put all the profits back into the business as I continue to do to this day.

My loan officer was impressed with my business, the catalog, the growth, and the potential. She gave me a $100,000 line of credit. I would learn that for my next increase, my home would be used as collateral. Thank God, I was always current on my payments. Comerica would be there each and every time I needed them for financing my new buildings, acquisitions, borrowing money to pay taxes, and other costly matters. Going into debt is not fun, and I will never forget the day I was finally debt-free.

My cousin, Mickey Zipser, was both my attorney and my father's, but he was limited in what he could do for me and I always felt there was a conflict of interest in him representing both of us. Don't ask me why, but I invented the Nail Taboret, a storage device for manicurists. It was really cool, and I decided to patent it. I needed a patent attorney. What does an entrepreneur do? Yep, back to the Yellow Pages. However, this time I decided that I would select a law firm for all of Nailco's work. You would be amazed at how often you need an attorney. I decided that if I was going to be sued or I was going to sue someone, I would want the best law firm in Michigan.

Dykema Gossett started in 1926 in Detroit (they would later change their name to Dykema), and they were the biggest law firm. Their intellectual office was located in Bloomfield Hills, and I went to visit them for my patent. I learned all about patents and trademarks. I also learned all about litigation, which was handled in their downtown Detroit office. Their rates were high, but they had clout. I wanted the peace of mind that if and when I filed a lawsuit, the defendant would see it was handled by Dykema and that Nailco was not a low-life company. I also wanted to know that when I was the defendant, the plaintiff would know that I wasn't going to roll over and die. My meeting with Robert Kelly was exceptional, and I hired Dykema on the spot. They are still my law firm today, and I hate to say it but I have spent more than $1M in legal fees since that first meeting.

As I said to you before, and I cannot reiterate this life lesson enough: Never become a minority shareholder in a closed corporation. My uncle was our accountant, and I knew I was being screwed. Mickey also did accounting, and I gave him the business. Eventually one of his employees left his firm, and I hired him to be my CFO. As Nailco grew, the bank demanded audited financial statements. Once again, I decided to go with the best firm in Michigan and that was Plante Moran. Plante started the firm in 1924 (can you believe, just two years before Dykema!), and Moran joined in 1950. Today they are the sixteenth biggest audit, tax, and management firm. Comerica loved the fact that we partnered with Plante as it gave them peace of mind. And that my fellow readers is what any entrepreneur wants when he goes to sleep at night: peace of mind.

LIFE LESSON TIP: Never wait until you need a banker, lawyer, or accountant. When you first start out, it's OK to use family and friend referrals. But as your business grows, hire the best firms and establish an excellent relationship with them. You'll be using these firms more than you think.

LESSON #29

When It Comes to Technology, Always Embrace Changes That Come with It

After GAYNORS closed, I only brought one employee with me to Nailco, and you guessed right, Teresa! She had the office next to mine. We shared buying responsibilities, and she took over HR.

I was always enthralled with magic. In high school, I went to magic shops to buy and learn tricks. I became a master card trick magician. I loved watching David Copperfield and other magicians on TV. So perhaps it was no surprise that when Nailco held its first trade show, I called it MAGIC and gave it a theme each year. The theme in 1988 was Main Street U.S.A.

Unlike the first trade show I did, this one would be far different. I took the entire exhibit space at the Hyatt Regency in Dearborn, and the show floor had more than a hundred booths. I also took space for classrooms and nail competitions. I advertised in *NAILS* and our catalogs. We sold more than three thousand tickets. The Solar Nail class alone attracted more than a hundred nail artists. I held competitions for acrylics, nail art, nail tips, and gave away more than five thousand dollars in cash prizes. More than three hundred competed. It was wild.

The show was held on a Sunday and Monday. To keep the nail artists at the Hyatt for both days, I created a special event for Sunday night. The event featured complementary food, a fashion show, "Nailco" dancers, and the winners of the competitions. More than six hundred attendees came and it was sold out.

[Sidenote: The acrylic nail boom changed the nail industry forever. Manicurists were now called nail artists, as they had to take a brush and sculpt acrylic flawlessly on the nail plate. Eventually the industry title for manicurists changed to nail techs. However, CND always referred to them as nail artists.]

Education would become the secret sauce that would separate Nailco from the competition. I started N.C.C.E. (Nailco College for Continuing Education) and held classes at local hotels and did weekend retreats twice a year. I chartered a plane from Detroit to Atlantic City and called it "Semin-air." The seminar was done on the plane going to Atlantic City and then we all had fun on the strip. I also launched the Nailco Educational Video Club: videos of how-to for all different categories.

Nailco launched Peau de Peche, the first formaldehyde-free nail enamel and the first nail enamel to retail for $5. It was an instant success.

I updated the Nailco Gold Card program and launched The Gold Card Frequent Buyer Program. Members earned free trips to Vegas and Disney along with gift certificates to Tiffany's and Bloomingdale's.

To compete with *NAILS* magazine, I launched *Nail World*. At first, it was a bimonthly newsletter that was sent to Nailco customers. Like the first catalog that was sixteen pages, this too would be sixteen pages. Customers loved it, and I always included educational articles.

The Nailco catalog expanded to sixty pages, and I started selling full-page ads to our vendors. The Nailco logo got its first of many updates. We ended the year with thirteen employees and did over a million dollars in sales.

Technology was a big part of Nailco's success, and I was an early adopter in every phase. The first commercial fax machine was available and it was huge, about four-feet square. It was amazing. Instead of calling in orders to vendors, we could now fax orders, saving hundreds of hours on the phone each year. I made our vendors get a fax machine or I took 10 percent off the invoice. They all got fax machines.

LIFE LESSON TIP: Outsource, outsource, and outsource. But even when you outsource, you have to have someone in charge of technology who keeps your company current. My design team and I love Macs, but all other computers are PCs; running both requires different expertise. Network computers, phones, fax, and cloud must work together seamlessly to limit downtime and anxiety.

LESSON #30

Be Careful What You Wish for, It Might Come True

B uddy and Harriet Rose started Forsythe in 1979. They were among the first to manufacture professional nail polish in hundreds of colors at $1 a bottle. Up until that time, manicurists used retail brands such as Revlon. Forsythe was very innovative and created a special shape for their bottle. They hired outside sales reps to call on salons. Two of the reps were Essie Weingarten and Janet Greenberg. They both learned all about Forsythe, and decided to start their own nail polish companies. One would turn out to be a winner and the other a loser.

Essie started in 1981, and she created a square-shaped bottle. There was no logo on the bottle or cap, just a label on the bottom. Essie's claim to fame was her talent in naming the colors. She sold her polish for $1 a bottle and hired outside reps.

Manicurists wanted to buy Essie from Nailco, not Essie's local rep and wait for delivery. So I called Essie to buy direct. She told me she only worked with reps and not distributors. I decided to contact her local rep, and we met. The plan was to give her half the commission on Nailco's sales and that we would more than quadruple her business. She wasn't interested.

What does an entrepreneur do? In this case, two things.

Janet also launched her own company in 1981 and used a standard round bottle without a logo on the bottle or cap. She too came up with her own names for the colors but certainly not as creative as Essie. She sold her polish for $1 a bottle and hired outside reps. Essie and Janet became instant competitors. I called Janet and flew out to NYC to meet with her (Forsythe and Essie were in NYC as well). We had a great meeting and Janet launched her line, Charni. I advertised Charni in *NAILS* and compared Charni to Essie. Business was fabulous. However, it turned out Janet had a greater love for her first baby than the nail polish line and eventually she closed it down in the early 1990s.

The second thing I did was launch my own nail polish line, Raku. It was brilliant. I copied Essie's square bottle, put the Raku logo on the cap, and came up with creative names. It was more upscale than Essie and I sold it for $1.40 a bottle. I had Forsythe make it for me, as they were not happy that both Essie and Charni knocked them off. Revenge would be sweet but short. Sales took off but when I reordered, many colors were not the same. Forsythe had terrible quality control and they would never overcome their issues. It was a disaster that would take both brands down and it would be yet another learning experience for me.

At the 1989 MAGIC trade show, one of our customers was in a restroom and found a bunch of business cards on the sink counter. The cards said, "Stop by the ESSIE room for the best show deals!" The customer gave me the card, and I was livid. I went to the room, and sure enough, there was Essie and her rep selling nail polish to my customers. Essie looked at me and smiled, "Hi Larry, you really know how to put on a great show!" I went to my Hyatt manager, and I was told there was nothing they could do. Once again, another lesson learned the hard way.

When OPI launched its infamous nail polish line in 1989, Essie would soon learn what real competition was all about. She hooked up with Max Sortino, who knew all about nail jewelry (you wouldn't believe how many gold nails we sold) but nothing about nail polish. However, Max had excellent business sense and would be the perfect partner for Essie who had the entrepreneurial sense. Max decided the only way Essie would compete with OPI was to open distributors. I flew once again to NYC and met with both Max and Essie, and we came to terms. I finally launched Essie in 1991 and Nailco would become their best-selling distributor.

But I would learn yet another lesson, and one I would take to heart in 2020 (don't worry loyal reader, we have a long way to go before we get there): Distribution sucks. Why? Because to grow your business, you are actually growing the businesses of your vendors and you aren't compensated for that. Max and Essie sold out to L'Oréal in 2010 for an estimated $135M to $175M. The company was doing less than $30M in sales at the time. On the day of the sale, Essie gave me a call to tell me the news. They made out like bandits while I was left with a brand that would slowly disintegrate to nothing in the professional industry.

LIFE LESSON TIP: If you are selling a product, decide early on if you want to be a retailer, distributor, or manufacturer. After being involved in all three types of sales, being a manufacturer is the most rewarding albeit the riskiest.

LESSON #31

Don't Take on More Than You Can Do

T here were moments in time back then that I often wondered: Am I a publisher selling products or am I a distributor that also happens to publish catalogs and magazines? Back then, there were no digital cameras or word processors. All copy was typeset, hand cut, and glued onto blank pages.

However, 1989 was the year color would make its debut in the Nailco catalog. I hired a professional photographer, and we had to bring all our products to his studio. He would then spend days photographing the products and go through hundreds of rolls of Kodak film. We would then have to go through thousands of photos and select the best ones for the catalog. It was both laborious and expensive. Nailco was the first distributor to come out with a color catalog, and sales exploded even more.

I also hired a professional designer to create our logos, set up the format of the catalogs, and handle all production. Jack DeWitt was talented and a great inspiration to me for learning to appreciate what it took to create attractive marketing tools.

It was also in 1989 that I decided to take *Nail World* and make it into a magazine to compete with *NAILS*. I gave the project to

Jack, and he opened an office in Birmingham to focus on both the catalog and the magazine. He hired Lisa Phillion, who would later become our lead designer for more than twenty years. *Nail World* was an instant success because our vendors knew the more advertising they did with us, the more business they would do. When they advertised with *NAILS*, they could only hope the ads would translate to additional sales because they had no way to track them.

In 1990, I got a call from Deborah Carver who wanted to buy *Nail World*. She already had a couple of other trade magazines in different industries and thought the professional nail industry would be perfect for her. It was a great deal for me because I really was a distributor, not a publisher. The ads paid the costs for production and mailing but were not a profit maker on their own. It was a great deal for Deborah because she got an instant customer base. We came to terms and shortly *NailPro* not only competed with *NAILS* but would eventually become the best-in-class magazine.

Business continued to boom. In 1989, we added 3,200 square feet, and in 1990, added another 3,200 square feet. I expanded into depilatory and paraffin waxes, which would pave the way for Nailco entering the spa market in 1993. In 1990, gels were launched by IBD, which triggered a huge expansion of the business. I also launched salon-merchandising displays, and I collaborated with *Inc.* to sell marketing and business books and videos to salons. Our creative business became so big that I launched an exclusive CND catalog in 1990 and 1991. Little did I know then that what would happen next in 1991 would shake my world like nothing ever before.

Teresa and I married on April 21, 1990, and moved into a new home. We had a nice wedding at a local Marriott, and I have to say Teresa was a beautiful bride. She still is to this day!

[Note: The United States experienced a recession in 1990–1991. That is when I learned that the beauty business is recession-resistant if not recession-proof. Clinton would become president in 1992 and the next eight years would be boom years that would ultimately lead to the dot.com crash in 2001. While plenty of political and economic events took place over the course of this book, I am not going to focus on them, as they did not play much of a role in TNG's evolution.]

LIFE LESSON TIP: An entrepreneur's mind never stops working. We have an insatiable desire to work hard, succeed, and do as much as possible each and every day. However, there are times that you have to ask yourself, "Do we really need to do this?"

LESSON #32

There Is Always Someone That Will
Have More Resources Than You Do;
Focus on the Resources That You Have

T he Barber & Beauty Supply Institute (BBSI) was the trade
association for the professional beauty industry (it would later
become the PBA), and they held an annual trade show for
beauty distributors. The shows were held in different major
cities across North America and featured everything beauty from
furniture and hair care to, eventually, nail care and spa. The 1980s
would be the best decade for the BBSI with the emergence of professional salon hair care brands and the booming nail industry all
happening at the same time.

The late 1980s would also see the formation of the almighty
full-service distributors. By definition, full-service distributors offered
everything a beauty salon would need to run their business. As you
recall, the likes of Paul Mitchell, Matrix, Aveda, and Redken all
needed distribution, and they didn't have the desire to hire their own
sales reps so they turned to manufacturer's reps who called on full-
service distributors. Those lucky distributors that got the major lines
became overnight rock stars because they had exclusive rights to sell

the brands in their state. Some distributors had two or more states. The golden rule was that distributors would never ship outside their territory. They all got rich and powerful. They had a monopoly, and business was booming. What could be better?

They attended the BBSI shows, which became biannual because so many new companies were getting into the game and so many new distributors were opening up. The manufacturers threw huge parties at night for their distributors; the food and drinks were readily flowing. Awards were handed out for highest sales and, naturally, the ones in California and New York typically won first, second, and third place. At the party, trophies would be handed out, photos taken, and the trade rags were all there to write big stories. It was a good old boys network and one that would last until the early 2000s. Cigars and fine single malts were on display like never before.

They all got into the nail business because, after all, they were full-service distributors. But they all hated the nail business. They had to stock hundreds of SKUs that sold for as little as a dollar. Dealing with individual manicurists was difficult at best because they all preferred to hang out with salon owners who placed big orders. And I quickly learned that they hated Nailco even more than manicurists. Nailco was a pain in their ass because in every meeting they had with the manicurists, Nailco was mentioned and they wanted the same prices, deals, and selection that Nailco offered.

I attended the BBSI's shows religiously because so many new nail companies launched each year. It was so much easier meeting at a trade show than them coming to visit me or vice versa. Like the hair care companies that were printing money, so were many of the nail companies including CND and OPI. OPI started giving away gold jewelry at its booth based on annual purchases. CND hosted its own elaborate evening party and went all out in decorations, food, drinks, and awards. At their first awards banquet in 1987 or 1988, the crowd went stone quiet when Jim and Jan announced that Nailco was number three overall. The same thing happened in 1989 and 1990. Truthfully, I think we were number one, but CND decided to tone it down and give us number three not to piss off their network. The full-service distributors and the full-service rep groups were pissed regardless. How could a little pip-squeak like Nailco possibly sell more CND products with no stores, no salespeople, and only a single catalog than the powerful distributors that had every resource imaginable? I was all smiles when I walked on the stage and accepted my trophy—at least Jim and Jan clapped for me.

LIFE LESSON TIP: Inherently, start-ups have less resources than established competitors. For that reason alone, focus on a niche category, disruptive technology, or a unique product that will differentiate your company from the rest.

LESSON #33

Business Is the Second-Most
Competitive Game in the World After
Politics; Be Prepared to Play at the
Highest Level or Don't Play at All

The year 1991 was one to remember. Magic, curses, and luck played a major part of the year. So much in fact, I have to give you the details in two parts.

The year had an amazing beginning. The 1991 catalog expanded to 108 pages and Nailco celebrated its five-year anniversary. Teresa became the operational manager, and for the first time ever, I created managerial titles as we grew to thirty-two employees. I expanded and now occupied half the building. I added yet another catalog for Christmas that featured gifts, gift baskets, candies, and much more. Remarkably, I noticed that tanning salons were ordering from us. I asked myself, "Why not sell them tanning products too?" The second part will talk all about the indoor tanning industry. The MAGIC trade show, *The Gay Nineties*, for the first time would feature tanning, clothing, and gift booths.

As 1991 progressed, a lightning bolt struck me in the most vulnerable place. CND sent a FedEx package to all their distributors. I opened mine and took out a huge binder that was labeled "CND Nail Advantage Program." I opened the binder. What I saw would resonate with me for the rest of my life.

Nail Advantage was a direct rip-off of the Nailco business model. It was divided into chapters with each chapter copying Nailco's strategy. One chapter was about catalogs and how each distributor had to make their own nail catalog, and our pages were shown. There was a chapter on doing a nails-only trade show; a chapter on doing nails-only education; a chapter on having nail techs as employees so they could answer questions; and so on. The entire program was designed to put Nailco out of business.

While no one ever told me how the Nail Advantage Program came to be, I can bet that the fucking sales reps and the powerful full-service distributors got together and likely met with CND and told CND it was either them or Nailco. They formulated a strategy, and Jan created the Nail Advantage Program for all CND's full-service distributors.

Shortly thereafter, I got a phone call from CND's VP of Sales who wanted to fly in for a meeting. I knew nothing good was going to happen from that. He came in and told me CND's new strategy would not include Nailco and that Jan wanted to meet with me in Chicago that weekend. John Caspole, a nice guy just doing what he was told, offered me a tip: At your meeting with Jan, do your best to change her mind. He knew that Nailco was the best-in-class distributor for CND.

I flew to Chicago and met with Jan. Gone were the smiles as she was all business. She said to me, "Larry, you are a dinosaur. Your business model is not sustainable long term, and we cannot stake the future of our company on it. In fact, as you know, I developed the Nail Advantage Program for our full-service distributors as I feel that is the future of the business." She went on to say, "I am terminating Nailco as a distributor effective immediately."

It was as if someone ripped my heart out of my chest. My body was going through the same shock as when I was held up at Cadillac Ace. I was speechless. There was no talking Jan out of this. My brain instantly filled with thoughts about the upcoming trade show, catalog, classes, and everything else tied to CND. It was the first time I was terminated as a distributor (I told you never to be a distributor), and I would later learn that it would not be the last time.

What does an entrepreneur do? Fight back and partner with a Sicilian. But first, you have to read about the indoor tanning industry.

LIFE LESSON TIP: If you are a retailer or distributor, limit the total sales of any single brand to 10-15 percent. If it exceeds 15 percent, do your best to get one-year auto-renewal contracts and at least six months' notice of termination.

LESSON #34

Never Stop Paying Attention to What Your Customers Want

Who would have known that while both the professional hair and nail industries were rocking in the 1980s that the indoor tanning industry would be doing the same? It was the trifecta with product innovation at its best. The main difference: Indoor tanning entrepreneurs were on steroids and nobody introduced new products and technology as quickly as they did. Also, tanning distributors were like Nailco; they had catalogs and could sell anywhere in the United States.

I considered myself an expert on tanning products because I sold the biggest brands at GAYNORS including Coppertone, Hawaiian Tropic, Banana Boat, and Bain de Soleil. Back then, SPFs were an afterthought and nothing sold better than Hawaiian Tropic because of its coconut fragrance. I quickly learned that being an expert in one industry means shit in another.

The early adopters were Swedish Beauty (1982), Australian Gold (1985, what a coincidence, same year Nailco started!), Body Drench (1986), and California Tan and Supre (1987). I called each of the companies, and they all opened Nailco with the exception of

Swedish Beauty (they were added in 1994). Little did I know then that our indoor tanning business would grow to more than $6M a year. I would also learn that the major difference between indoor and outdoor products was that indoor products were formulated not to harm the acrylic shields in tanning beds.

The first generation of products featured colorful packaging and were cheap, retailing for $10 a bottle or less. It was California Tan that revolutionized the business first with the launch of Tropical Fury in 1992, the first $20 price point for a tanning lotion, and then with Helix in 1994, the first $50 price point for a tanning lotion.

California Tan (Cal Tan) was owned by Don Crystal. The company was run by his lieutenant Terry Katz and his assistant Mike Brady. Terry was ruthless but made Cal Tan a powerhouse by focusing on basic retail principles (in-salon displays, posters, best packaging, and best formulations).

Body Drench was started by Rick Norvell, and his claim to fame was that he developed a moisturizer for bra wearers to use (his mother owned a bra factory). Body Drench Moisturizer would become the best-selling moisturizer for after-tanning.

Australian Gold (New Sunshine) was started by Trevor Grey and would become the biggest company in the industry before he sold out to Menard's. Trevor was the ultimate entrepreneur and was a bitter competitor. So much in fact, he put bulletproof glass in his office and had his own security. He was my favorite tanning entrepreneur; you will learn why later.

Bruce West started Supre because he saw an opportunity in an exploding industry. Bruce was more of a business guy than entrepreneur and tended to "borrow" other people's ideas. In 1995, Cal Tan sued Supre for copyright infringement and told its distributors that they could no longer distribute Supre products if they wanted to keep

Cal Tan. At the time, Cal Tan was the premium line every tanning salon had to have. All the distributors stayed with Cal Tan except one. Can you guess who the exception was? Right on loyal reader! Nailco became the go-to distributor for Supre, and eventually we got Cal Tan back, but it was a painful few years in-between.

Tanning lotion sales exploded in 1991, and believe it or not, tanning products were more exciting than nail products. We sold cases rather than "each'es," and I had a taste of what the full-service distributors were enjoying with hair care products.

As I said earlier, the Nailco catalog now expanded to 108 pages and we had thirty-two employees. Most impressive was that we had more than twenty-five thousand customers in our database.

LIFE LESSON TIP: There is a reason why major companies constantly send surveys to their customers: They want to know what their customers think about the product and/or service. Customer surveys and reviews are crucial not only for your continued success, but understanding what new opportunities you can offer. Do everything possible to get customer reviews. You will be amazed what you learn. For instance, hair conditioner is not just for hair, it is also amazing for tools, washing lingerie, and shaving legs.

LESSON #35

Every Industry Has Its Set Ways:
As an Entrepreneur, Learn Them
All as Fast as You Can

A s entrepreneurs, we love being exposed to something new, falling in love with it, and then going full blast ahead. Nailco was growing rapidly, and we were adding hundreds of new customers weekly. But there was something about the tanning industry that made me go head over heels, and I knew I had to seize the opportunity right away.

Four Seasons was the big shot tanning distributor. I will never forget the two brothers that started the company, Ronnie and Johnny Allen. They were first to the party and quickly established relationships with the lotion manufacturers. They had a big catalog and sold everything from lotions to equipment to retail products. My goal wasn't to be bigger than them but to get my share of the business. I would leverage my huge salon customer base and my competitive advantage, which offered both nail and tanning products. It was brilliant.

First off, I had to learn all about the industry. Like the nail industry, there were two trade publications, *Look Fit* and *Tanning Trends*. *Look Fit* was the best magazine, and they also did an annual trade show. I started advertising right away and attended my first tanning trade show. OMG!

This was nothing like any trade show I had ever witnessed. Attendees lined up by the hundreds before the show floor opened, and they all had roller bags! When the doors opened, they ran in and started lining up at tanning lotion booths. I ran in myself to learn that lotion manufacturers released their new products here, and to get tanning salons excited about their new products, they gave away full-size samples. WOW! Thousands of bottles were given away in the first hour alone and then the booths ran out. As a distributor, I was thinking about lost sales from the freebies; as an entrepreneur, I was thinking how brilliant this idea was.

The show had more than a hundred booths displaying everything tanning from equipment to lotions to accessories. However, I learned the real show was not until the evening. Forget about the BBSI parties, the tanning parties made the BBSI parties look like a one-year-old's birthday party. I walked into the Swedish Beauty party and there had to be at least three hundred people. There were giant bowls of shrimp cocktail, chefs carving beef tenderloin; there was a champagne fountain along with a full bar, all complementary. I then went to the ETS party, which was held at a restaurant, and they took the entire establishment over. It was over the top as well. Overall, it was a great experience, and not only did I pick up even more new lines, I sensed an energy that would endure for the next fifteen years.

Secondly, I added tanning equipment: Hex booths, Sun and Wolff beds. I added Wolff replacement bulbs. I signed up with the S.A.E. (Suntanning Association for Education). I hired a technical team to answer questions, install equipment, and service parts. I brought on a huge assortment of new brands that included Cocomo Bay, Sundays, Most, and Trevor Island. I added a full array of tanning accessories so any salon that wanted to get into the tanning business would only need to shop at Nailco. It was also my first time getting into the skin care business with Derma Magic and European Body Wrap (body wraps were a huge business in the 1990s).

Lastly, I added a full complement of fun products for salons to retail. These included matching tops and bottoms for women, bathing suits, t-shirts, dresses, and more than fifty styles of sunglasses. The 1992 catalog featured six pages of costume jewelry alone! I also added store fixtures for salons to merchandise clothing, jewelry, and other retail items. I even got into the personalization business and became ASI certified to offer mugs, frames, pens, and keychains with salon logos. The tanning and retail portion of the catalog was sixty-six pages.

How does an entrepreneur separate the two businesses so both nail salons and tanning salons would be primary to Nailco? I introduced the first flip catalog! One side was nails and the other side was tanning.

Now that Nailco sold nails, tanning, retail, and skin care products, I updated the logo to Nailco Salon Marketplace. If this wasn't enough to think about, I was getting restless not writing for my trade publications. I had sold *Nail World* to *Nailpro*, but I still had so much information to get out to our customers. That's when I decided to launch *Nailco News*, and it would soon turn into another trade magazine that would become even more successful than Nail World.

Oddly, I never took a liking to indoor tanning personally. Don't get me wrong, I loved the moment getting into the bed and feeling all warm and toasty. But when I heard that CLICK and the bed turned off, there was nothing worse. Teresa loved indoor tanning, and she was always tan. Just like smoking cigarettes after WWII was a big thing until it wasn't, we would find out that indoor tanning was not good for you either. For now, however, it was party time.

The catalog expanded to 166 pages. All the tanning growth created the need to expand the building to 19,200 square feet, and our employee count grew to forty-six.

LIFE LESSON TIP: There is no better way to get immersed into your business than to learn about your industry. Every industry has an association (you don't have to join to learn about it), trade shows, and magazines. Remember, virtually every company started out as you did: The quicker you climb the learning curve, the better.

LESSON #36

If You Come Up with a Crazy Idea, Run with It, Regardless of What Others Think: It Just Takes One Crazy Idea to Change Your Life

As an entrepreneur, you have to be obsessed with customer service. My office was directly across from the invoicing department. I outfitted this area with sliding glass windows, and the warehouse would pick up invoices for the orders here. I always had the windows open so I could hear what was going on and, more often than not, I would shout out the answers to any questions. Both Teresa and I frequented the warehouse to assist with picking and packing orders. I loved working in the warehouse, but my time was best spent innovating. And let me tell you, back then, my management style was way different from how it is today. Teresa could write a book on that alone. Entrepreneurs understand that passion and temper go hand in hand. They also know to hire the best HR talent to keep them out of trouble!

World-class customer service made Nailco … Nailco. I had to be in stock all the time and boasted a 98.7 percent fill rate. I established cut-off times to ensure that all orders placed by the cut-off would ship the same day (5:00 p.m. in 1993). Customers had to receive everything they ordered. If they called and said something was missing, we sent it out at no charge. If they had a question about anything, we had to have the answer. By now we had more than seven thousand SKUs and $2M in inventory.

In 1993, AT&T still had a monopoly on long-distance calls and we spent $.25 a minute for every call. My phone bill was in five digits each month, but I didn't care. In fact, I added more phone numbers: Client Services handled questions about orders and returns. Nailco News Hotline was a prerecorded loop message that mentioned our newest products and services. Tanning Technical T-Line was for customers that needed service for their equipment. Esthetician's E-Line helped estheticians with skin care products, and I hired estheticians to take the calls.

I created the Nailco Pledge of Satisfaction, which offered our customers a 100 percent guarantee of satisfaction, no questions asked.

I was also obsessed with having the best products and best pricing. I had a huge void to fill with the loss of CND and came up with the perfect solution to fill it: CLUB1 Warehouse Club. Price Club started in 1976 and would merge with Costco in 1993. While Costco would not open its first Michigan stores until 1999, I was so happy I decided to keep Nailco instead of GAYNORS because the warehouse clubs would be the death for all but one deep discount HBA chain. I still subscribed to *Chain Store Age* (I was a voracious reader of trade pubs and business books) and read all about warehouse clubs doing booming business and being the future of retailing. So what does an entrepreneur do? Steal the idea and use it for himself!

Tony Cuccio, founder and CEO of Star Nail Products, made all the CLUB1 products for me and the line featured every category of nail products at prices up to 40 percent less than name brands. I charged our customers a $25 annual membership fee. I took out full-page ads in both *NAILS* and *NailPro*, and the headline was "The Switch Is On!" I did a product-by-product comparison of CND and CLUB1 products and showed the difference in pricing. The 100 percent guarantee policy ensured there was no risk in trying the products. Customers loved it. CLUB1 was my second private-label brand and would pave the way for many other house brands. True or False? CND was happy with the ads? Entrepreneurs really do have the most fun when they are not being stabbed in the back.

Like tanning salons earlier, I learned that many spas were buying from Nailco. Spas decided to add nail services to their repertoires but the spa distributors were late to the game. So what does an entrepreneur do? Get into the spa business! Not as exciting as getting into the tanning business was, getting into the spa business was like listening to spa music. Boring! Little did I know, however, that getting into the spa business would later get me into the hospitality business. You see, the best spas were located in resorts. Unlike tanning salons, resort spas had first-class ambience. I was suddenly immersed in yet another whole new world.

I called the new section "Esthetics." This is what I wrote on the first page of the catalog: "America is aging. By the year 2000, the baby-boom generation will be in their late forties and early fifties. This is one generation that doesn't want to look old, and why should they." I could not know how right I was in 1993. Now I had to learn yet another new industry. What does an entrepreneur do? Spot on, my loyal reader, you knew the answer! Yep, there were two main trade magazines, *Dermascope* and *Skin Inc*. Both magazines held an annual trade show. However, selling skin care wasn't like selling tanning lotions: Education and training were intense, but worse, most estheticians in the United States were from Europe, and they used products in the spas that they used in Europe. I had to find a new U.S. skincare company that could compete with the European brands. I saw a full-page ad for the Repechage Four-Layer Facial in the trade magazines and decided to make a trip to New York City to meet with Lydia Sarfati.

Lydia was a Jewish immigrant from Europe and had a thick but lovely Polish accent. She was a skin care entrepreneur, and I was fascinated with her knowledge of skin care and her passion for products. The only thing I really cared about was selling her Four-Layer Facial. Repechage sold to boutique spas, and Lydia, like her peers and competitors, went door-to-door, and most of her customers were in NYC. Nailco would be her first distributor. I devoted six pages to her line in the catalog with one full page just for the Four-Layer Facial. Once again, I read the market perfectly and the Four-Layer Facial became an overnight phenomenon.

I also launched another house brand, COZ Cosmetics. The line featured cosmetic brushes and skin care applicators. I even got into spa equipment including hot towel warmers, steamers, electrolysis, facial beds, massage beds, flannel sheets, and stools. Business took off instantly, and soon we were selling to resorts such as the Four Seasons, Ritz Carlton, Canyon Ranch, and many others.

As crazy as all of this sounds to have happened in 1993, the craziest idea I came up with was The Nailco Tent Event. The last MAGIC trade show would take place this year as I had a new idea for a trade show in 1994. The Nailco Tent Event would be a huge flea market with live entertainment and complementary barbeque. I had installed a big-top tent in the Nailco parking lot and secured space across the street for customers to park their cars. I hired a trolley service to shuttle them back and forth. I took all the merchandise that was discontinued, damaged, or returned and put it on tables under the tent. We provided hand carts, roller carts, and shopping baskets for customers to fill up. We set up four cash wrap lines for customers to check out.

Remember what happened to me at my first trade show when I didn't bring the goods? This time we had the goods, and it was pandemonium. We had customers drive from all over the United States, some in campers, and they would arrive the night before and camp out in the parking lot. They wanted to be first in line. By the time The Tent Event opened, there were hundreds of customers waiting in line, and many brought their own carts and wagons. If you were there and watched as a spectator, you would have said it was better than watching a circus. By the end of the day, the tables were empty, the food was gone, the musicians slumped over from playing nonstop, and we were totally exhausted.

With esthetics added, the 1993 catalog expanded to 240 pages and Nailco expanded to 24,000 square feet. It was only a matter of time before we would run out of space. Something had to be done. And if you thought this was all I had to do in 1993, you would have been terribly wrong. I now had to select a location, work with an architect and designer, and plan on building a new 102,000-square-foot signature building.

LIFE LESSON TIP: Entrepreneurs love to reach milestones: the first $1M in sales year, celebrating five years in business, landing your first major customer, and so many others. The more milestones an entrepreneur reaches, the more the crazy ideas will appear.

LESSON #37

Be Prepared at All Times to Roll the Dice and Risk Everything

F ax machines and PCs were not only getting smaller but also getting faster. One huge competitive advantage Nailco had over its competitors in the early days was being 100 percent computerized. There was no other way the kind of growth we experienced would have been possible. Not only was it an exciting time for Nailco, it was an exciting time for salons. Overnight, beautiful full-service salons and spas opened. They offered hair, nail, and spa services. But to support their growth, salons too needed to be computerized. So, what does an entrepreneur do? Create N-Tech, Salon Technology Solutions.

The N-Tech Master System included a computer, color monitor, receipt printer, cash drawer, video card, hard drive, and Helios software. Helios was a pioneer in developing P-O-S software for salons. The system sold for $2,195 and I offered leasing. The software on its own was $495. I had computer geeks on staff to handle sales and installations.

I also launched the Nailco Miles frequent buyer program. I stole the idea from the airlines, and it would be the first program of its kind in the pro beauty industry. I harnessed the power of fax machines, and my goal was for every Nailco customer to own a fax machine to use as a business tool. With enough miles, salons would earn a free fax machine. Fax on demand services included: Material Safety Data Sheets (MSDS); education; Red Hot Fax Deals; new items and catalog changes; industry show calendars; and trade associations. Customers loved it.

Virtual reality (VR) made its first appearance in the technology industry in 1994. Who knew then that VR would still be a thing in 2023? As an entrepreneur, I was enthralled with the VR concept. I thought if you could visit a trade show virtually without getting on a plane, spending a night or two in a hotel, and walking miles on the show floor, how cool would that be! I launched VR '94, the first VR beauty trade show. I hired a professional developer, signed up vendors, and created the trade show on a VHS tape. I custom-packaged it with a show brochure, show deals, and fax-ready order forms. In addition, to mimic a real trade show, it was one-day only so "attendees" had to place their show order on that day to get the deals. I sold more than a thousand tickets for $25. It was a great concept, but it was one-and-done. I learned once again that people in the industry loved to touch goods before buying them and loved the social scene that a trade show provided.

I was happy that California Tan was back in the catalog. New categories included aromatherapy and pedicure spas that would revolutionize the pedicure business. Tanning equipment got more sophisticated, and we sold models for up to $40,000 a pop. However, the real action was in the low- to mid-market, and I collaborated with Sunal to become their main distributor. Wolff Systems introduced the Bellarium S, which would become the gold standard of indoor tanning lamps. Spray tanning was coming to fruition as well. St. Tropez started the craze before the sunless machines would be a fixture in tanning salons.

One of life's greatest experiences is building your own facility or home. Very few entrepreneurs get to experience this. I was very lucky to be one of them. It is also one of the scariest things an entrepreneur can do: Everything you own is suddenly at risk. Failure is not an option, but there is no crystal ball to look at or someone to tell you to do it or not. For an entrepreneur, it's all about gut instinct. My gut said to move forward, and I did. Comerica gave me the financing, and I had to sign over all of my assets in case of default. I could barely sign my signature on the papers I was so nervous. The building cost $5M to build plus another $2M that I needed for new software and warehouse systems. YIKES!

There is an adage when it comes to real estate: location, location, location. My first site selection was in Livonia, same city as my current building because I had a great relationship with the city and the mayor. But the location was not the best. Living in Farmington Hills at the time, I decided to check out locations there and found the perfect site right off a major highway and in an area that was ripe for growth. Now that I picked the location, I had to select a builder, designer, and warehouse consulting firm that did installations. So, what does an entrepreneur do? Open the Yellow Pages and get referrals.

There was plenty of land available for sale. The question I had to answer was "How big should I make the building?" We were now at 32,000 square feet, and I did not want to move ever again. I went BIG and bought enough land to build a 102,000-square-foot building that featured 80,000 square feet of warehouse space and 22,000 square feet of office space on two floors. I hired Scarcello & Associates to design the office space. Teresa and I selected everything.

The space on the first floor included: The Academy, one of the first permanent educational distributor spaces in the country, which featured a main stage and two classrooms; a top-of-the-line product showroom that emulated Service Merchandise at the time (Service Merchandise was the first retailer to utilize a showroom to sell their products); and a marketing department and photo lab (I bought the first digital camera, and it cost $25,000 but was well worth it— no more film!). Teresa and I had Jack 'n' Jill offices with our own bathroom and lunchroom and other offices.

The second floor was the call center with space for forty-eight stations along with offices, a lunchroom, and a conference room.

I hired the best warehouse consultant, and they designed an automated conveyor system that could hold up to three hundred order totes at once. I also had to install special logistic software and upgrade our database software. Trend was the latest and greatest software for distributors. It was robust and light-years ahead of our current system. However, it was so robust that we would all need weeks to learn it. I would find out, however, that the real learning took place after the launch.

The building went up, and it was spectacular. I spent a fortune on landscaping, installed flagpoles, and even had a Nailco flag made. In late December, we moved from Livonia to Farmington Hills, and it was a move I never wanted to make again. Boy, was I wrong about that.

The catalog expanded to 276 pages, the workforce expanded to eighty employees, and the next evolution would take place in 1995.

LIFE LESSON TIP: Cash is king when you're an entrepreneur, and you never have enough of it. Spend frugally. Always be mindful of your expenses. However, invest brilliantly in assets. Opt for the highest quality in everything that you buy as long-term costs will be far lower than buying something that is cheaper.

PART 3
THE EXPLOSIVE YEARS

1995-2002

LESSON #38

It's Amazing How Fast Your Business Will Change

D o you know the number-one fear most people have? Public speaking. Right behind that is going to the dentist. As an entrepreneur, going to the dentist is a treat compared to launching new database software. Not only did we launch Trend when we opened for business on January 2, 1995, we launched a new warehouse software system and a new phone system. Who does that? An entrepreneur who had his back to the wall and had no choice.

I was obsessed with customer satisfaction. It took a good six weeks to get all the systems working, and it was brutal. When we were running smoothly, there was no better warehouse operation in the beauty industry. Moreover, we had all the space in the world to expand.

Remember how Nailco got into the tanning and spa business. Note that there were plenty of hair salons buying from us too. At the time, nail techs were at the back of the salon and were an afterthought. Most hair salons were not into spa services. One thing I knew for sure, nails only accounted for 2 percent of the beauty business, professional and retail. Nailco was the number-one niche beauty distributor. The real money was in the hair industry, home of the powerful full-service distributors. Speaking of which, CND's Nail Advantage Program was a total flop and only a couple of distributors kept it going.

I had the space, I had the line of credit, and I had brass balls. So, what does an entrepreneur do to get into the hair business? Make an acquisition. Beauty Direct was based in Pennsylvania and had a nice catalog operation. I hopped on a plane to meet with the owner. He was tired of the business and wanted to sell. His operation looked like Nailco in 1989, and I could see that there wasn't any entrepreneurial spirit left. I bought the business for $1.5M. I shipped the merchandise to Farmington Hills and shut down the business in Pennsylvania. I renamed the business Hairco and launched the Hairco catalog later in the year.

Let me give you the backside of the hair care business. Full-service distributors focused on exclusive brands that salons could both use and retail along with hair color. The other side of the business was based on open line brands that could be sold by any beauty distributor. That was Sally Beauty's main focus, and they would become our newest competitor. The biggest open line brands were hair color. Beauty Direct had distribution rights to Wella hair color but not Clairol. Both brands were must-haves if you were in the business.

Luck came my way once again. The VP of Sales for Clairol was Paula Jacobi. Yep, the same Paula that worked at CND and opened me up when I was at GAYNORS. I told her that I bought Beauty Direct and was going to make Hairco as big or bigger than Nailco. Paula loved my story and gave me the line.

I focused on products that full-service distributors did not. Salon tools were a big thing because big hair was a big thing. Most distributors focused on one or two brands. I focused on every brand. The catalog was filled with hair dryers, flat irons, hair trimmers, brushes, combs, capes, and accessories. The full-service distributors hated me when I was Nailco; now they would hate me even more.

Trevor Gray, CEO of New Sunshine, was the smartest tanning entrepreneur as I mentioned before. Australian Gold Accelerator was the number-one SKU in the industry. Trevor decided to get into the equipment business and make tanning beds. It was a brilliant idea and we instantly added them to our catalogs. They sold like popcorn. Trevor was also the first in the industry to target consumers with home tanning beds. He advertised in the classified sections of newspapers. It was another brilliant idea. Then I thought, what the heck, if Trevor could do it, so could I. I launched Sunco, the first tanning catalog exclusively for consumers. I bought mailing lists and mailed ten thousand to start. It was a great idea, but I forgot my life lesson from the GAYNORS days: Dealing with consumers is a pain in the ass. Sunco only lasted a couple of years.

I decided to do another trade show and launched the Nailco Conference & Expo. It was more business-themed than show-floor-focused and did well. By then, trade shows were not as exciting and something else caught my eye that would change the world forever: the internet.

Amazon.com launched in 1994. I knew then that the internet was going to be the next big technology boom and would eventually replace catalogs and fax machines. If Nailco was going to stay the industry leader, it needed to be the first online distributor. I hired a website firm and launched Nailco.com later in the year. It was a fantastic idea and one that would keep Nailco number one. Full-service distributors didn't even think about going online because of their exclusive territories that would soon become a burden instead of a benefit.

One day, I got a call from Sam Leopold, CEO of Styling Technology. Sam led the first roll-up in the professional beauty industry and called me for a meeting. He flew in from Arizona and arrived in a stretch limo. He had already made major acquisitions including Body Drench and Alpha 9. Now he wanted to buy Nailco. He was an arrogant son-of-a-bitch; he had plenty of funding and thought he would leave the meeting with a deal. I told him to fuck off. It was one of the smartest decisions I made as his company eventually went broke. While Sam was the first one to try to buy Nailco, there would be plenty more suitors to come.

OK, let's talk new products because new product innovation was still my favorite subject. Aromatherapy was doing great, and I learned about the Natural Food Expo that showcased all natural foods and beauty products. Teresa and I attended, and what an eye-opener that was for both of us. There had to be five hundred booths, and it was packed with buyers from supermarkets, health food stores, and supplement shops. The food section was awesome as every booth sampled their food (yum!). The beauty section booths sold natural personal care products, loofahs, soaps, health supplements, weight-loss cookies and supplements, reflexology products, herbal products, books, VHS tapes, and detox products. Herbal teas were a thing too, and this was also the time yoga started to take off. It was overwhelming—and I loved it.

The 1995 catalog had a new section, Well-Being, and it would become one of Nailco's most successful category launches. Altogether, in 1995, we produced more than 600 catalog pages! We exceeded one hundred thousand customers for the first time. Employee count grew to 125, and we blew past $20M in sales.

[Sidenote: Teresa and I had nicknames for each other all the time. We were happily married and best friends too. That was a good thing especially since we were together day and night seven days a week. One day I called her "Bubby" and over time that got shortened to BUB. Eventually we started to call each other BUB instead of our first names, and we still call each other BUB to this day, although the BUB is also the QUEEN! Moving forward in the book, I will refer to Teresa as BUB.]

LIFE LESSON TIP: Your business will evolve constantly, and you have to be cognizant of change at every opportunity. Like the hundreds of filters on a workout app, you too have to filter through the opportunities and decide which ones are best for you. It's OK to say no if the timing is not right for you.

LESSON #39

As an Entrepreneur, There Is Nothing Worse Than a Monkey on Your Back; Too Many Monkeys Will Bring You Down So Get Rid of Them as Quickly as You Can

---

You might have wondered what was going on with my mother and father during this time. Life was good for them. They had their home in Boca with a country club membership; they bought a condo in Charlevoix, Michigan, and added a pleasure boat and another country club membership. They still had their West Bloomfield home and decided to join a third country club. They were living the good life because of the 25 percent equity I gave them in Nailco.

Not only was I in debt for the business, I had to pay them off each year with income distributions. Let me give you an example. We did $20M in sales in 1995 and earned $1M in net profit. Not bad, you might think, but I needed to make a lot of profit just to pay the interest on the line of credit along with monthly mortgage payments on the building. When it came time to pay income taxes in April, I would have to borrow more money because there was no positive cash flow. It was a vicious cycle that would go on for more than twenty years.

I called for a meeting with my father and told him that I could no longer afford to pay his annual 25 percent distribution. He understood the situation. This was the one fucking time that being a minority shareholder in a closed corporation actually worked out. I proposed a buyout. He agreed to it.

As an entrepreneur, you quickly learn that there is an expert for everything. Sure enough, the Yellow Pages featured plenty of companies that did company evaluations. I hired one of the best. The results were shocking, and once again, I learned that being a distributor sucks. But on the other hand, I was joyous. Distributors were valued at the lowest level because they had little proprietary value. I also learned that minority shareholder valuation was much less because they had no voting rights. I was even more joyous. After two weeks of research, the firm came back and told me my father's 25 percent interest was worth $1M. Not a bad return based on a $25,000 investment.

I wrote a check for $1M. It was going to be an exuberant moment for all, or so I thought. I remembered it was on a Sunday because I had the kids, and we went to their country club for lunch. We were at the bar waiting for a table when I brought out the check and gave it to my father. Now mind you, he knew his shares were worth $1M but to see an actual check for $1M with your name on it for the first time ever is a moment for the history books. He was shocked, thrilled, and happy all at the same time: a trifecta rarely witnessed. He was so happy that he said that we were going to the pro shop and he was going to buy new clothes for everyone.

My mother was pissed. The reality was that they were no longer part of Nailco. She could no longer brag that they owned Nailco to her friends, to her nail tech, to anyone that would listen to her. She also knew the annual distribution checks would be no more. More so, she knew that the business relationship between her husband and her son was over.

For some reason that I would never understand, my mother was cheap and selfish. I loved her father and would go to California once a year when I was a kid for a week. His favorite hobby was supermarket coupon clipping, and it would take most of the day to redeem them all. However, my grandfather was not cheap, he was thrifty. My mother owned three residences and was a member at three country clubs, but that did not matter.

My mother yelled out at the bar, "We certainly aren't going to the golf shop to buy clothes! Just take the check and put it in your pocket." The hostess came in just at that time and told us our table was ready. True or false? It was an enjoyable lunch?

LIFE LESSON TIP: There is an old proverb: "There is no such thing as a free lunch." Invariably, entrepreneurs sign up with someone because they have something they need. It's all good in the beginning, but eventually, it ends up all bad. That's when you need to get the monkey off your back, regardless of what it takes. Mistakes are costly, but not correcting them can be deadly.

LESSON #40

When Launching Something New, Start Small; That Way You Won't Lose Big When Making Mistakes

I knew early on that the real money to be made with hair care products was with exclusive brands. Beaute Craft and Maly's had most of the major brands in Michigan. They were friendly competitors as they shared only one brand, Redken. Times were still good, and there were plenty of new brands getting into the market so my timing was right. I decided to hire outside sales reps to call on salons and would start with ten. My first two lines were Brocato and Ecoly. Both lines were tiny and the big boys didn't want them. I had to start somewhere.

Luckily, for the reps, they had the catalog to sell too. With more than twelve thousand products, the main catalog was getting too large. I decided to combine the Nailco and Hairco catalogs and then make four separate catalogs: tanning, furniture, spa, and hair extensions. Hair extensions was a new category and became hot overnight. The reps struggled with Brocato and Ecoly but did a brisk catalog business.

I will never forget getting Tammy Taylor products that year. Tammy had a cult following and did not sell to distributors. She did live education events throughout the United States and nail techs loved her. Her husband, Darrell Mitchell, was her business partner and hated CND and OPI. He also hated distributors. Some would say that he was scarier than Tony Cuccio, and they might have been right. For whatever reason, he liked me and after a very long conversation, he agreed to sell the line to us. I was elated and couldn't wait to bring Tammy to our Academy.

The day the advertisement came out that Tammy was coming, tickets sold out. Here is what I will never forget: Tammy was on stage and was a natural entertainer. Perfect sense of humor, command of her audience, and smart. Then she said, "Write this number down, 1-800-xxx-xxxx. Call us anytime to place your Tammy Taylor product orders." I was floored. I reminded Tammy and my customers that Nailco was an authorized distributor and to buy all her products from us. Tammy was never invited back.

Nailco Miles continued its success as a loyalty program, and I added a new Platinum level. Platinum members received free shipping on all orders, free CLUB1 membership, their own 800 number, and 50 percent bonus miles. I also contracted with Northwest Airlines (soon to become Delta) and gave airline miles away.

I renamed The Tent Event to The Beauty Industry's Biggest Sidewalk Sale. It was pretty much the same event, but now we had virtually every beauty product to sell. It remained wildly popular with our customers.

Compared to years past, 1996 was easy-peasy. That was a good thing because 1997 turned out to be one hell of a year.

We now had 140 employees and did over $25M in sales.

LIFE LESSON TIP: You never know when someone is trying to undermine you: another employee, a vendor, a consultant. Always pay attention to what is going on around you and be curious.

LESSON #41

Trees Don't Grow Overnight: All
It Takes Is One Seed but It Has to
Be Watered and Nurtured for a
Long Time to Become a Tree

etiring the Nailco logo was one of the hardest decisions I made. We were far more than a nail distributor; we were a distributor and manufacturer for nails, tanning, hair, and spa. We were the industry source for our customers, and they trusted us more than any other distributor. I decided to rename the company: The Industry Source. I kept the Nailco logo on the cover of the catalog to make it an easy transition. Our customers loved the new name and still called us "Nailco."

I was obsessed with customer satisfaction and knew that our customers wanted to receive their orders faster. Customers in the Southeast received their orders in three to four days and customers in the West received them in five to six days. Because so many products we sold were flammable, two-day shipping was not an option. Opening a second warehouse in Atlanta was.

There is an expression, "Go big or stay home." I went big. We flew down to Atlanta and settled on a nice 20,000-square-foot facility. Not only would our customers in the Southeast now receive their orders in one to two days, but it relieved stress on our Farmington Hills warehouse that was suddenly getting to capacity. It also reduced our shipping costs. However, it increased our overhead, and now we had to place vendor orders for two warehouses.

Everything was going great until I got a phone call from George Schaeffer, CEO of OPI. Let me backtrack for a moment. OPI polish became all the rage because George had the brilliant idea to advertise OPI polish to consumers in fashion magazines such as *Elle*, *Glamour*, and *Cosmopolitan*, and state explicitly at the bottom of the ads that OPI was only available in fine salons. He spent more than $1M advertising annually, and he could afford it because he gave his distributors lousy margins and never put his polish on deal. The advertising campaign worked, and consumers flocked to salons requesting OPI. George had another brilliant idea: come out with seasonal collections. Every spring and fall, OPI would launch twelve new shades in a jazzy colorful display. We sold thousands. George's other brilliant idea was that he called it OPI Nail Lacquer. Anyone could sell polish, but only OPI would sell lacquer.

Demand for OPI Nail Lacquer soared in the 1990s. So much, in fact, that even the lazy full-service distributors started selling a lot of nail lacquer. Selling nail lacquer was easy, as education was not required. The pre-packs were a sales consultant's dream come true.

When Nailco SE opened in 1997, the SE full-service distributors were pissed. They contacted George and set up a meeting. They made a plea to George: You have to cut Nailco off; otherwise, we can't support your brand anymore. Recall, George was a shrewd business guy and an entrepreneur. He had a tough decision to make. In July, he made that fateful call to me. I was livid. Those fucking full-service distributors won once again. I vowed to get even. On the flip side, CND learned about this and I got a call from them. They agreed to bring Nailco back for the SE states. However, losing OPI was a bitter pill to swallow.

LIFE LESSON TIP: Business is a cutthroat game. When you expand to gain market share, always remember that you are encroaching on someone else's business, and they will do everything possible to stop you. Try to line up key suppliers ahead of your expansion.

LESSON #42

Niche Brands Often Become National Brands: Identify Which Brand You Want to Manufacture, Distribute, or Retail— and Be Relentless in Growing It

Hairco needed a professional hair color line. Windsor Beauty Supply was located in Farmington Hills and was a small boutique distributor. They had a hair color line, Schwarzkopf. It was made in Germany and had a great reputation. I called their VP of Sales, Mark Weber, and it was perfect timing. Mark was not happy with Windsor's performance, and he was looking for a new distributor. Mark flew in from Denver to meet with me. I gave him the nickel tour of the building, and he was totally impressed. I will say giving tours was a highlight for me, and everyone who took the tour was impressed. I gave him my strategy for Hairco, including hiring more reps and opening stores. He loved it and we came to a verbal agreement. I was elated.

A couple of weeks later, BUB was getting her hair cut at a local salon. They used Schwarzkopf color. BUB told the hairdresser that was great because Hairco would be carrying the line. The hairdresser told the salon owner who called Windsor who called Mark. Guess what happened? You guessed right. Mark changed his mind and stayed with Windsor. It turned out to be a blessing in disguise. I still needed a hair color line, and I knew just whom to call.

Paul Sharnsky, if you recall, was the VP of Sales at Peau. He moved on and became the VP of Sales at L'Oréal Professionnel (LP). LP was a division focused on professional hair salons and had its own brand, LP. At the time, L'Oréal also owned Redken. They would buy Matrix in 2000, ARTec in 2002, and Pureology in 2007. Beaute Craft was the LP distributor in MI, and it was their worst-selling hair color brand. Redken was number one. Paul had no love affair for Beaute Craft, and he came to visit. I gave him the nickel tour, and he loved how Nailco grew and was excited to give us a start with LP. I was ecstatic. Little did I know at the time that selling hair color to salons would be the most difficult product to sell. And little did Beaute Craft know that LP wouldn't be the only brand we took from them.

For the LP launch to our sales reps, Paul came in and I had all the reps wear yellow rain jackets. I gave Paul an umbrella. He loved the concept. He was also hungry for business. If anyone had resources, it was L'Oréal. They were the biggest beauty company then, and they still are today. L'Oréal had the best talent in the industry and my first strategic move was to bring that talent to Michigan. We premiered LP at the Salon Conference & Expo. I gave them a separate meeting room that seated three hundred, full stage, provided models, and Paul brought in the talent. Only six attendees visited during the show. It was a complete bomb. But Paul was my cheerleader, and he told me, "Larry, don't worry about it. Next year we will fill the room." And we did.

LIFE LESSON TIP: When developing your niche brand, make sure that you are protected. If you are the manufacturer, apply for a trademark. If you are a distributor, make sure you have a contract favorable to you. If you are a retailer, ask for a protected territory and at least six months' notice of termination.

LESSON #43

Pay Close Attention to Culture

The Vietnam War ended April 30, 1975, after lasting nearly twenty years. When the war ended, many Vietnamese citizens immigrated to Southern California. They all needed a job and money to live on. Most barely spoke English. They quickly learned that the nail business was starting to boom, and there was a tremendous need for manicurists. Those that could afford it got their licenses. Others were self-taught or learned while they were in Vietnam. The first generation opened nail salons and offered cheap prices to get business. They often slept in the salons because they could not afford to live elsewhere. Since they had nothing else to do, they were open seven days a week compared to other salons that were closed on Sunday and Monday. They also opened earlier and closed later. They did a booming business with women who worked nine to five and had no other time to get their nails done.

The 1980s would see a proliferation of Vietnamese nail salons open in California as more and more immigrants came over. Manicure schools in Vietnam flourished and Vietnam started manufacturing their own implements. Vietnamese manicurists learned to do manicures in thirty minutes and charged $10 or less. The 1990s would see Vietnamese salons expand into major cities in the United States. Almost overnight, strip centers would feature a nail salon, tanning salon, Blockbuster store, fast-food franchise, and even a hair salon.

Immigrants never forget their past. The second generation of Vietnamese salons was opening in the 1990s, and they would be far different from the first generation: They featured pedi spas, bright lights and windows, made sure proper disinfecting took place while still doing manicures in thirty minutes and at the cheapest price. The second generation also spoke English but still spoke Vietnamese in the salons. Vietnamese nail distributors opened, and they offered generic brands at cheap prices. They too flourished. But when OPI Nail Lacquer got hot, the Vietnamese wanted in. At the time, George didn't sell to Vietnamese distributors. It was a golden opportunity for me. So, what does an entrepreneur do? Open a Vietnamese division.

I printed a catalog in Vietnamese, hired three Vietnamese sales reps, and focused on OPI, CLUB1, and our other items that we could sell at cheap prices. It would be the first of many adventures for me selling to the Vietnamese market. After all, it is a known fact that the Vietnamese took over the majority of the nail salon business to get in on the ground floor. The division didn't last two years. However, my next foray lasted longer than I dreamed.

LIFE LESSON TIP: Every culture and ethnic group is different. That is why companies such as L'Oréal have different brands for different countries. If you are selling a product targeting a certain culture, make sure you fully understand the idiosyncrasies of the culture.

LESSON #44

When You Are Thrown a Curveball,
It's OK to Step Away from the Plate:
Most of the Time, It Won't Be a Strike

N ow that we were getting close to two hundred employees and operating two distribution centers, it became clear to me that quality control would be the lynchpin to staying successful. Being located in Michigan and the heart of the automobile industry, I was well aware of companies being ISO-certified. Even though not a single company in the beauty industry was ISO-certified and our customers could have cared less, I hired an ISO firm to get us certified. It was a grueling process but well worth it and was the start of what would become part of our continuous improvement campaign that launched in 2004.

When OPI cut us off in 1997, it opened the door for yet another company to cut us off, IBD. Lorenzo, who believed in me in 1985, suddenly shifted gears and decided that IBD was better off with full-service distributors. We made IBD's Softlight Light Gel an overnight success, and now he wanted to expand his business like OPI and CND did. We were allowed to keep 5-Second Nail Glue and the open line nail tips, but the business was in gels. It was another threat to our existence, and yet only made The Industry Source stronger.

I had to make a decision about how to recoup the lost business. We didn't have the top brands in the nail business, and yet were still the largest nail distributor. Once again, I picked up a Chance card and it read, "Launch your own upscale brand." What does an entrepreneur do? Launch an upscale brand. It was the birth of FPO, short for "For Professionals Only." I decided then that the future of my business would be on brands that I controlled. I already had CLUB1, which was doing great, but it was FPO that changed everything.

FPO was the master brand for: Pinnacle (upscale line that competed against OPI); For Pro Professional Use Only (nail files and accessories, which would eventually become ForPro Professional Collection and replace FPO); Cosmopolitan Glass (competed against Backscratchers); Lightbox (competed against IBD); and Tableware (our proprietary collection of counter and wall displays). I had Tony make most of the application products and expanded third-party manufacturing with lotions, crèmes, and oils. One of the top nail file manufacturers made our files.

For the Pinnacle launch, I hired professional models and did beautiful full-page ads in trade journals that highlighted the advantages of Pinnacle and Lightbox over our competitors. I had the same professional models at our trade shows, and I hired FPO educators. Pinnacle became an overnight success, For Pro nail files became our bestsellers, and Lightbox replaced the lost IBD business. Nevertheless, I needed a polish brand and after Raku, I did not want to launch another line. As luck would have it, Essie decided to launch MAX, an upscale polish line to compete against OPI, and the timing was perfect. Nailco became their first distributor, and I launched full-page ads comparing MAX to OPI. George sued, and it was my first major lawsuit. Fortunately, I had Dykema on my side, and the case was quickly settled. Unfortunately, for MAX, specks started showing up inside the bottles and ruined the nail polish. Essie couldn't figure out why and before you knew it, MAX was discontinued.

Given that I had L'Oréal hair color, I needed to add a designer hair care line. David and Carmen owned a boutique Michigan distributorship that sold TIGI, founded by TONI & GUY. The products were bland and packaged in black and white bottles. In 1996, TIGI launched Bedhead Wax Stick. Little did anyone know then that Bedhead would become a huge brand. The key differentiator for the brand was education as TONI & GUY were two of the best platform artists. I bought the brand from David and Carmen for $200,000, a little less than their actual sales. Eventually Hairco became the number-one distributor by state and did more than $6M in annual sales until we were cut off, which is yet another chapter.

I also decided now that I was a full-service distributor in Michigan, it was time to open my first outside store. The best location would be Grand Rapids, home of Maly's. That proved to be a smart choice as the store did very well and I would eventually open twenty-nine more locations.

While all this was happening, product innovation continued and we added more than a thousand new products. The proliferation of new products was such that we could not keep up with catalog production. The annual catalog was outdated shortly after publication. So, what does an entrepreneur do? Produce a second catalog! The new cycle started: January–June for the first catalog and July–December for the second catalog. Both catalogs were nearly four hundred pages. Our marketing team grew to more than twenty employees with a full-time photographer and expanded web team. The corporate intranet was launched so we no longer had to publish internal documents for our employees. It was also the final transition from Nailco to The Industry Source. Our customers didn't blink an eye.

LIFE LESSON TIP: Why did most of the smaller fast-food chains open near McDonald's? McDonald's was the biggest, and they wanted to attract their customers. However, Arby's, Burger King, and Wendy's are still distant competitors to McDonald's. When you start out, it is best to target the number-one competitor. Eventually, a new brand will roll out and target your brand. That is the perfect time to step back and review your packaging, brand promise, ingredients, and marketing strategy.

FOR THOSE WHO KNOW

LESSON #45

A Company Mission Statement Is Very Important: Make It Short and Sweet If You Want It to Be Effective

Everyone has an uncle in the furniture business, but I was fortunate enough to have an uncle in the commercial real estate business instead. Living in California, Sammy was always a wheeler-dealer and was married to my mother's sister, Teddy. I loved spending time with Sammy when I was a kid, and he spoiled me rotten. When I made the fateful decision to open our third distribution center, my first thought was to give Sammy a call.

Sammy found us a great building in Santa Fe Springs, about thirty minutes from Los Angeles. With the new location, our West Coast customers received their orders in one to two days. Additionally, it put us right in the middle of the action. Conversely, it also put us in the worst state to do business in, and we would learn that operating in California was like no other state.

The indoor tanning category was still booming, and sometimes the best way to grow even quicker is through acquisitions. Unlike the Beauty Direct acquisition in which I acquired new brands, the acquisitions of Look Fit Supply in LA and Summertime Distributing in

Minneapolis were about customer lists and salespeople. I closed down both businesses, kept the best salespeople, and added their customer lists to ours. Each acquisition cost between $300,000 and $400,000, and in the end, acquiring distributors without exclusive brands was not the best idea.

Discount mania came to the nail industry as both *NAILS* and *NailPro* launched special rates for black and white ads at the back of the magazine. Several distributors took advantage of this and soon sold nail supplies at cheap prices. To compete with this, I started NailSmart, which expanded our private-label product offerings, this time, with no brand name. Once again, Tony supplied the bulk of the products. Eventually, NailSmart became BeautySmart as we expanded to hair and spa products as well.

Local distributors throughout the United States were plentiful, and they were referred to as "cash-and-carry" distributors. They had a single store, perhaps one or two salespeople, and offered a full range of open line products. They were eager for brand names as well, but they were too small to buy direct. Remember diversion? It was a big business when I first started and was still a big business in 1999. So why not become a wholesaler to distributors? What does an entrepreneur do? Open Beauty Direct, a catalog operation that sold exclusively to local distributors. I hired salespeople, and it was an instant success.

Our spa business was growing quickly too. I noticed that many fitness clubs ordered from us so I started yet another new division, Club&Spa Direct. I hired salespeople that exclusively called on spas and fitness clubs. This would eventually start our hospitality division, but I am getting ahead of myself once again.

We got into the charity business this year as well. Always a believer in giving back, I thought that sponsoring a local charity would be great morale for our employees and customers. This would be the beginning of offering 100 percent customer success to our three Cs: internal customers (employees), external customers, and communities. For the inaugural year, the BUB and I selected the St. Vincent & Sarah Fisher Center, a Catholic organization that took care of abused kids. We donated $25,000. We also supported Forgotten Harvest and gave them more than five thousand pounds of food.

Hairco was growing quickly, and we opened three new stores. To attract A/A+ salons and top hairdressers, I launched Evening of the Stars, a spectacular night that featured food, drinks, and the best education, all complementary. It too was an overnight success, or was it? You'll learn more about customer goodwill or lack of it in later chapters.

There were a host of other changes that took place in 1999. I changed the corporate name from Nailco to The Nailco Group, since we had many divisions. The catalog became THE BEAUTY BOOK and N.C.C.E. became TheAcademy.

Last but not least, I added our first mission statement, which I later realized, was way too long. When it comes to mission statements, if your employees can't remember it, it's too long. Our mission statement would later become "100 percent customer success." Additionally, I implemented a company motto each year and produced a corporate video and theme song to go with it. Did I tell you about the company holiday parties? Damn, I totally forgot, so let me tell you all about them in the next chapter.

LIFE LESSON TIP: The mission statement is a critical piece of the company culture; it is only important to the employees. It needs to be short so every employee remembers it. Once you settle on your mission statement, display it proudly throughout your office space. And always remind employees about it at company meetings and internal memos.

LESSON #46

Splurge on Your Employees: The Cost of Splurging Is Nothing Compared to What You Get Back in Return

The beauty industry was one giant party. I already told you about the parties at the BBSI and tanning shows. What I have yet to tell you about were the national trade shows that catered to salon professionals. The biggest were: IBS Long Beach, IBS New York, Premier Orlando and Chicago. These shows were raucous events that attracted thousands of hairdressers and nail techs. All the big brands took huge booths and did live demos on their main stage. However, what got me most was that alcoholic beverages were sold on the show floor, and there were always lines to buy them. It was one giant party after another.

We often exhibited at these shows. I recall one year at an IBS New York show, we took six booths and created one huge store. We brought in $75,000 of merchandise and ran out after the second day. Yet, we still lost money as you quickly learned doing trade shows is a racket. Between outrageous union fees, drayage costs, hotel and entertainment costs for employees, transportation, theft and booth costs, it was a nightmare. For the attendees, it was a party. They brought cash and were always thirsty. Looking back at the more than fifty shows we did, I doubt any of them were worth it. I recall handing out hundreds of catalogs at each show only to find many of them in garbage cans at the end of the exhibition. Why? The attendees' suitcases were so stuffed with goods, they didn't have room for catalogs.

One thing the trade shows did teach me was how to throw a party. No one knows how to throw a party better than me. To keep employees in-the-know of all the things going on at the company, I held quarterly meetings. They would take place on a Saturday morning. This is where employees learned about new products, new divisions, new store openings, company sales and profits, charity events, and anything else new. I started the "Employee of the Quarter" award and gave away gold stars. Each meeting would feature several employees based on the department they worked in. Additional special awards were also created. After three years, employees would earn a solid gold Nailco necklace or a ring for the guys, after five years a diamond was added and after ten years, it would be diamond encrusted. I also launched incentive trips: after ten years, a free trip to Vegas or Disney for four days, three nights, and after twenty years, a free Caribbean cruise for two. I remember back to 1997, the longest tenured employee was Gary Lincoln, and he had been with the company for six years. No way did I have to worry about giving away cruise trips. Who knew then that I would give away more than twenty-five.

The last gathering of the year took place in December, and it was our annual meeting. The first of these took place where we held our trade shows, the Hyatt Regency Dearborn, and then later moved to the Ritz Carlton Dearborn. These parties were spectacles. The meeting started Saturday morning at eight; the breakfast buffet was bountiful and held in the large ballroom. I hired cheerleaders from Dearborn High School and their marching band to start the meeting (you'll learn how I incorporated all the invaluable intangibles I learned at MSU to TNG in 2001). The cheerleaders did routines and the marching band played a couple of hits as well as the National Anthem. We had a TNG employee who was also a veteran present the National Guard for an official flag ceremony. It was awe-inspiring.

I even had Nailco dancers who would perform on stage to our annual theme song, and I would share our annual video. The meeting would start with the same presentation as the quarterly meetings after which we would then break for an awesome buffet lunch. After lunch, I hired the best guest speakers (well, some were better than others) and they would speak about motivation, health, wellness, engagement, and other topics. There would be more awards passed out and the meeting ended at four in the afternoon.

Then the party. Employees were allowed to bring their spouse, and we paid for their room. The party commenced at seven that evening, and I would alternate the theme each year: one year formal and the other year festive. One theme I will never forget was Mardi Gras. My party team decorated golf carts like floats. I bought thousands of beads. With everyone seated inside the formal Ritz ballroom with crystal chandeliers, we drove four golf carts into the ballroom and tossed the beads in every direction. Everyone went wild, and I'm not sure how many chandelier bulbs we blew out. People stampeded over each other to get more beads and hurricane glasses emptied out quicker than expected.

Dinners were spectacular five-course feasts. The drinks and wine were free-flowing. Everyone was on the dance floor as the best bands played. Those who weren't, I dragged out, and there were people who danced for the first time in their lives. What a thrill! One of the high-lights of the evening was my toast. Every evening event I sponsored had to include a toast. Now mind you, everything was on the house for the employees, but they insisted on buying me drinks. My go-to drink then was Chivas on the rocks with a twist. It was the ultimate party that ended at midnight.

One party I remember succinctly. I was ready to present my toast and three Ritz servers came on stage, each carrying a Chivas on the rocks. Now I'm no David Copperfield, but I did my best to hold all three glasses while I made my toast: "The first toast is to good health, because without your health, nothing else matters." That has always been my first toast and always will be. My second toast was all about my belief that you have to work hard and play hard, "This toast is to a fucking good time! And if you aren't having a fucking good time, there is the exit door in the back and be my guest!" Of course, no one even thought to leave.

The next morning, we had à la carte breakfast in the dining room. Everyone was wiped out! These parties would continue for years until we outgrew the Ritz. Part 4 will highlight what I did next.

Now you may be wondering about a few things in regard to these parties. Such as, were there any incidents? To be sure, yes. There was the occasional fistfight in the parking lot. There was the time when I received a phone call from Ritz security at three in the morning asking if I knew who "x" passed out in the first-floor bathroom was. However, I would say that the incidents were well contained. I always made sure that if alcohol was involved, employees had to stay overnight. If they wanted to leave the party and go home, they could not drink. And it was important for the hotel to monitor guests at the bar.

You might also wonder how much these parties cost. No expense was spared from the dinner selection to band to decorated themes to handing out red roses and doing custom invitations. The average cost was $500 per person, $1,000 a couple. Yes, a lot of money, but well worth it. Here's why: You can hand out a $1,000 bonus check, which nets out to about $700 after taxes. The bonus check will be quickly forgotten. The party memory will last a lifetime.

LIFE LESSON TIP: There are many ways to splurge on your employees. What I have learned most over the past fifty or so years is that they love experiences over money. Better yet, a little of both. Early on, I learned the value of a $100 bill. Amazingly, the value of a $100 bill today is just as powerful. Here is a tip guaranteed to work for your business: on a Friday, do a pizza lunch with ice cream cones for dessert and afterward, pass out one $100 bill to every employee. Tell the story of your choice when passing out the money and you will be amazed at the reaction you get.

LESSON #47

You Are the Boss: Never Forget It

The worst part about being an entrepreneur is that you're also the boss. Your mind never stops thinking. You are always looking behind you to make sure no one is going to leap in front of you and steal your business. You are always wondering what the competition is going to do and what start-up technology can disrupt your business. Moreover, you are always thinking about cash flow, profits, investments, and FOMO. And as the boss, you have to deal with employees.

December 31, 1999, 11:59 p.m. If you were alive and over the age of fifteen, you knew all about Y2K. Our entire business was on computers; there was no manual option available. My tech team did everything possible to prepare, but no one knew really what to prepare for. The only thing we knew was that when January 1, 2000, came, it was going to be business as usual or total chaos. The entire world was on alert. We had everything backed-up and ready to move to new servers if needed, but that was the worst-case scenario. Luckily, it turned out to be all for nothing, and the world breathed a collective sigh of relief when January 1 came without a glitch.

March 2000 was the start of the .com crash. Long before that though, when I was eighteen years old, I first started trading stocks and options. Back then, you had to call your broker to enter an order and then wait a few seconds for the order to be executed. The only way of knowing what your stocks were worth at the end of the trading day was either to call your broker or get the night edition of your local paper.

Entrepreneurs have a love–hate relationship with the stock market. Why? Because the market represents a secondary way of making or losing money. Owning your own business is the first, and for me, that would always take precedent. However, there is nothing like the thrill of picking a winning stock or option, and the side hustle was almost as tantalizing as gambling in a casino. My investments into the stock market were to max out my 401(k) and invest up to 10 percent of my annual salary in stocks. I will tell you my loyal reader that looking back, the best investment is to buy an index fund and to put the same amount of money into it each and every year (keep pace with inflation and increase it as needed). I did that with Fidelity Templeton, and it was the best investment I made outside of starting Nailco.

By now, you have read everything that I have accomplished since 1985, and even I am impressed. However, it was the ultimate risk putting everything on the line, working unimaginable hours, being in charge of the lives of more than 200 employees, and being in debt for more than $5 million. The NASDAQ started its crazy ascent in late 1999. It hit 3000 November 3, which was its first milestone. Then it hit 4000 December 29 and exploded to 5000 March 3, 2000. Vegas was placing bets as to when it would hit 6000.

My father and Steven were fully invested. All my friends could talk about was the NASDAQ and how much money they were making. My employees were talking about it and buying stock. You could not go anywhere without stocks on everyone's mind. *Everyone was making a killing*, and here I was working my ass off, deep in debt and wondering why I was fully invested in The Nailco Group and not the NASDAQ. It was times like this that tested your nerves being an entrepreneur.

March 10 the NASDAQ hit its peak at 5048. The .com crash ended in October 2002: The NASDAQ dropped 78 percent to 1114.

Most of the investors/gamblers were wiped out. Hundreds of companies went bankrupt. In fact, my middle brother's broker committed suicide with a single bullet to his head. My friends were no longer bragging about their profits and didn't talk about their losses (it is amazing how gamblers only talk about their winnings) and conversations everywhere shifted back to sports and politics. In the meantime, The Nailco Group had a record year in 2000 surpassing $50 million in sales. I was vindicated in being an entrepreneur, and I never forgot that lesson.

LIFE LESSON TIP: Remember, you started your own business to be an employer, not an employee. As the boss, always focus relentlessly on your business, not outside investments that can distract you.

LESSON #48

Priority Number One Is to Make Money

itting $50M in sales was a huge milestone for me, so this is a good time to address financials. When you own your own business, you always wonder how much money your competition is making or losing, what their margins are, what their debt level is, and their quick ratio. That is one reason why I always follow public companies related to my industry, such as L'Oréal, Sally Beauty, Ulta, and Amazon. I love listening to their quarterly conference calls, especially the part when the analysts ask questions. Best of all, the calls are free and are an amazing way of getting relevant information.

The most important thing to remember when you own your own business is that priority number one is to make money. The reason for the .com crash was that none of the online public companies made money. You need to make a profit to pay employees, pay the bank back, invest in assets, and continue as a going concern.

In 1999, we did $40M in sales, and in 2000 more than $52M, so you can see the growth that we were experiencing. Wages were 12.5 percent of sales, more than $6.5M. Catalog expense was $1.3M and advertising in trade journals was $600K, so I spent nearly $2M on

167

advertising alone, about 4 percent of sales. Our net margin was 7.5 percent, very respectable, which came in at nearly $4M.

On the balance sheet, there was no cash, but we had inventory valued at $6.6M. Total liabilities were $7.8M, and that didn't include the $4M mortgage on the building.

This is where cash flow or should I say negative cash flow makes a difference for an entrepreneur. The tax liability on $3.9M was $1.5M and was due the following April 15. Worse, based on annual income, you have to pay quarterly tax deposits to the IRS equal to 80 percent or so of your previous year's income, which came to $300,000 each quarter. That meant I had to come up with $1.8M in cash to pay taxes for April 2001. Fortunately, the business was mostly C.O.D. and credit card, so cash flow was good enough to pay the taxes. However, as the company transitioned toward N30 terms for its biggest customers, cash flow turned negative, and I would have to borrow money to pay the fucking taxes.

Business was so good; we were running out of space in our Farmington Hills location. It was a good thing I had warehouses in GA and CA. In 2000, I decided to add another one in New Jersey. (Another fateful decision as I would close it down in 2005.) I knew the timing was getting closer and closer that I would have to build yet another new building and move again.

For twenty-four employees, the year 2000 was one to celebrate, and they did not care about the .com crash. Why? Because in 1994 at our annual meeting, I announced a very special incentive to keep employees motivated and to stay at the company: If Nailco hit $50M in sales, they would get their choice of a new car or $10,000 cash. Of the twenty-four employees, ten opted for a brand-new Ford car.

Here we were at the Ritz Carlton at the big formal party. It was a remarkable sight because all the guys were wearing suits or tuxedos and the girls were wearing dresses and donning heels. It was amazing how different everyone looked, and it was spectacular to witness. I recall back in the day "fancy" restaurants had a dress code with gentlemen having to wear at least a sports coat. Personally, I think we need to get back to those days as we have gone too far in the other direction.

I was on stage doing my toast and afterward, I brought the ten employees on stage who opted for the car. They were excited but had no idea why they were on stage. I brought the BUB up and we talked about hitting $50M in sales. Then I took out a bowl and we handed each employee their car keys. They were speechless and didn't know what to do.

When the party started, I had the Ford dealership drive the cars and park them in front of the Ritz ballroom parking lot. I then said to the employees, "Are you excited?" And they screamed "YES!" I then yelled out, "OK, then let's go take a look at your new cars. They are right outside the doors!" Suddenly, everyone got out of their seats and ran to the doors. Mind you, it was snowing outside and about twenty-four degrees. But no one gave a fuck. The ten employees unlocked their cars, got inside, and started them up. All the employees were so excited for them. Horns were honking, glasses were clinking, and it was a winter wonderland. We ended up being outside for a good twenty minutes and most amazing, no one was cold or had a coat on. That tells you what adrenaline can do for the body. It was a magical night to remember.

LIFE LESSON TIP: There is nothing better than giving away money, gifts, and awards to employees. But first you have to be profitable. All too often companies in their early stages "expect" losses and think eventually those losses will turn into profits. This is another reason so many companies fail, they never realize profits. Early on in your company, focus on being profitable and make that a relentless focus.

LESSON #49

There Is Nothing Better Than Team Spirit, and It Costs Little to Implement

Growth steadily continued in 2001. We opened five new stores bringing the total to ten. FPO took on new distributors. I added sixteen thousand more square feet to the building. The upper level became the headquarters for FPO and the lower level became the space for the marketing department.

My oldest son, Michael, turned twenty this year and was at Western Michigan University. Daniel, now eighteen, was just starting at that little university in Ann Arbor. Mark was a freshman in high school. I thought it was the perfect time to buy season tickets to MSU football. I took the kids when MSU played U-M, and back then, it wasn't much fun to watch State get crushed. However, it was not the football game that got me motivated, it was everything else. After all, the last time the Spartans won the national championship was in 1966. What got me motivated was watching the marching band, cheerleaders, pumping fists during the fight song and screaming when Sparty, the most famous college mascot, took the field. Of course, colleges all understood this and that is why all those elements were part of the college football experience and still are today. So what does an entrepreneur do? Steal the best ideas.

My first act of business was to create a company mascot and the Rebel was born. I had my design team come up with the costume, and it was perfect. Dan Mace, one of our longest tenured employees, would be the Rebel during company meetings. I hired Yessian Music to write the fight song, and it was all rah-rah-rah. I came up with purple and white as our company colors when we were designing the building and kept true to the theme. We recruited employees to be cheerleaders and bought them costumes and pom-poms. They would get the team excited before every quarterly meeting and partner with the high school cheerleaders at the annual meeting.

The frosting on the cake was the annual yearbook, complete with headshots of every employee and photos of all of the events that took place throughout the year. We passed the yearbook out to everyone at the annual meeting. The entire campaign strengthened our team spirit, and everyone became a TNG Rebel.

Now that we were in the hair business and the business of raising money for charities, I came up with yet another concept, DREAMS. DREAMS would be a sit-down charity event with a runway show, live auction, and feature a selection of our best salons. The salons would use their top hairdressers and recruit models. They were responsible for doing their hair, nails, and outfits. The competition was intense and awards won by the best were given out. I sold tickets for $100 and invited our vendors and sales reps to buy tables and participate in the live auction. It was a tremendous success. This coincided with the American Cancer Society (ACS) launching STRIDES and TNG became the flagship sponsor. In 2001, DREAMS raised $175,000 for the Sarah Fisher Home and $115,000 for the ACS.

Ernst & Young has sponsored the Entrepreneur of the Year contest since 1986. My Comerica banker sponsored me in 1999, and I was a runner-up. She sponsored me again in 2000 and the award ceremony was held in 2001. The BUB and I got all decked out and I bought a table of ten for some of my top employees and my banker. The Marriott ballroom was packed. There were ten different industries that would win the coveted award along with a couple of non-profits. The competition was always fierce. I was in the retail/wholesale category. The award ceremony started, and I knew this year would be my year. Then again, an entrepreneur is always thinking of winning, never losing (actually, we never lose, we just learn more). They were now going to present the award for my category. Third place was announced, then second place, and then the announcer said the name of the Entrepreneur of the Year: Larry Gaynor! I suddenly felt the excitement going through my body and knew what it felt like when an artist won a Grammy or Oscar. I made it on stage and my table yelled like crazy, as I made my acceptance speech. It was quite the achievement. The contest is still alive and well in more than fifty countries so if you are an entrepreneur, I highly recommend you check it out.

LIFE LESSON TIP: Work culture has changed so much since the pandemic. Happiness in America is at its lowest level in history, which coincides with lack of trust of politicians, media, and CEOs. As an entrepreneur, you have to filter through the noise and focus on your company culture and make it superior. Adding team spirit costs little, and you will be amazed at the difference it makes.

LESSON #50

If You're Not Growing, You're Dying

We sold tons of manicure tables, pedi carts, and foot baths. However, that was nothing compared to the potential of selling hair equipment. In 2002, the big brands were Takara Belmont and Belvedere. Both sold styling chairs for $500 to $1,000 each. I knew there was an opportunity to offer similar chairs but at lower price points. So, what does an entrepreneur do? Launch TISPRO. I knew nothing about Chinese factories at that time, so I partnered with a Chicago-based manufacturer. They imported a few styles from China, and we launched them. Additionally, I got into the high-end market by becoming a distributor for Gamma, who made quality products in Italy. I would learn soon enough that Italy would become my next source for products.

I do have to back up just a bit because I was negligent in telling you about our Salon & Spa Design Studio. This launched in 2001 by chance. A well-known salon and spa designer had to move back to Michigan from California to be close to her husband's family. She needed a job and contacted me. Leslie McGwire had a great resume and knew all the sources in the design business. I asked her what she needed to get started and she told me AutoCAD. I said to her, "What is AutoCAD?" She replied that it was the premium software brand for design firms. All I knew is that it cost me an arm and a leg. But what the heck, it was only money, so I hired Leslie and bought her a Mac loaded with AutoCAD. Hiring Leslie would later turn out to be yet another fatal mistake but the ride was well worth it along the way, as you will learn in the next few chapters.

Hairco was going gangbusters. TheAcademy was among the top academies in the United States, and we sold out classes every week. L'Oréal hair color was getting into more A and A+ salons, but I needed another hair color line that was easier to use and more affordable. I learned about Alfaparf, an Italian hair color line making its way to the United States and looking for distributors. I made contact with them in Miami, and they came to Michigan to visit. As always, when a manufacturer came to visit us and took one look at our building and distribution center, they were sold, and we became a distributor. Stylists loved their hair color, and next thing we knew, classes were booked well in advance.

This was still the golden age for trade shows. No one did trade shows like we did. This year we did our first Grand Rapids hair show, Progressive. I loved doing the show in Maly's backyard. Now we were not only "the annoying nail guy," we were the "annoying hair guy" and taking plenty of their business. We still did the Great Lakes Beauty Show, Fringe with Evening of the Stars, The Biggest Sidewalk Sale, and also launched the FPO Symposium.

FPO was gaining momentum selling to U.S. distributors as well as distributors in sixteen other countries. Pinnacle was on fire, and we barely missed CND and OPI. The FPO Symposium brought in guest nail artists from all over to talk about the business of nails. Nail techs loved it. And speaking of the business of nails, I also launched The Business of Nails for The Industry Source customers. For this event,

I brought in select vendors who talked about the nail industry and how nail techs could continue to evolve their business. This was the period in which the nail section in salons moved to the front of the salon from the back. Also, stand-alone nail salons continued to open in record numbers. Doing all these shows was exhausting especially when I had a thriving catalog business that didn't require any of the work that shows did. Sometimes an entrepreneur's brain does not know when to stop.

> ## We opened four new stores and now had 275 employees.

LIFE LESSON TIP: Growth is the equivalent of blood flowing through your veins. Profit is the equivalent of breathing. Entrepreneurs need both. When it comes to growth, always prioritize and focus on profitable growth.

PART 4
THE PEAK YEARS

2003-2009

LESSON #51

Niche Businesses Have Higher Chances for Success

2003 was one of the craziest years being in business and truthfully, I have no idea how I pulled it off. The Nailco Group was the largest national distributor and involved with every category in the pro beauty industry, and yet, we were just scratching the surface. Opportunities came to me constantly and always in the back of my mind was the thought: If I can do this much business in a niche beauty category, how much business could I do if I sold directly to consumers?

I was intrigued with the furniture business. Unlike selling nail files, nail polish, and tubes of hair color, styling chairs and wash stations were high-ticket items and salons spent tens of thousands of dollars to open a new location. One day I was reading *Modern Salon*, the number-one trade journal for hair salons at the time, and noticed the ads at the back of the book. One of them was most interesting, Equipmentforsalons.com. They sold styling chairs and wash stations at deep discount prices. They were located outside Boca Raton in Florida. I called them up and spoke with the owner, Eric Ryant. What does an entrepreneur do? Get on the plane and see his operation.

Surprisingly, Eric had an enormous showroom with about a hundred pieces on display. He also had a huge TV to show design drawings to his customers and a small warehouse. The most shocking thing I learned from my visit was that Eric bought most of his furniture directly from China and that was how he was able to offer cheap prices. Suddenly, I thought about TISPRO and getting all the TISPRO equipment from China and the numbers started clicking in my head.

They say that timing is everything. Eric wanted to get out of the business and right there at the meeting, we came to terms. I kept the Boca showroom open through the lease, shipped all of the inventory to Farmington Hills and retained Eric as a consultant to deal with the Chinese factories. It was one of my best $400,000 investments.

John Heffner was a seasoned P&G executive but wanted to work for a small company where he could eventually own a stake in the business. John left P&G to take over as CEO of CND. John was the first true business guy to work for a pro nail company, and he quickly learned how quirky the industry was. For John, it was always about the bottom line. When he learned that the biggest nail distributor wasn't selling CND products, he hopped on a plane and made a visit to Farmington Hills. Like others before him, he was very impressed, and we relaunched CND in July. John could work relationships like no other. (To this day, I don't think anyone has more LinkedIn contacts than he does.) And to celebrate the launch, I devoted a special twelve-page section in the catalog. We once again quickly became one of their top distributors.

NAILS and NailPro had become more biased as to what products and companies they would feature in their magazines. It was annoying to say the least and I was spending more than $500,000 a year advertising. You already know that I sold my first publication to NailPro and that I continued to stay active in the publication business. But now I was at a crossroads and it was time to pick another Chance card. This time it read: "Sorry, but you have to start another magazine, sooner rather than later." So, what does an entrepreneur do? Start *NailBiz.* It was an instant success because after all, I owned distribution and my vendors had no choice but to advertise with me. We produced more than a hundred unique ads each year, and *NailBiz* was the perfect vehicle for us to showcase them in.

Our website business was growing quickly but even so, we were running out of room in the call center. In 2002, we had more than forty licensed professionals answering calls and we averaged more than twenty-five hundred calls daily. However, that did not stop me from fulfilling yet another goal of mine: sell to consumers. Yep, you got it; I started a consumer division, bebeautiful.com. Sunco never panned out because the margins for distributing tanning beds were terrible, and there were too many liability issues. This time, the focus would be on professional beauty products in consumer sizes.

Daniel graduated from U-M in 2004 but worked for us during the summer months in 2002 and 2003. Long story short, Daniel wasn't like me when it came to the hardware store where I had to learn everything. Daniel only wanted to learn about what he was interested in. It turned out to be bebeautiful.com. That was perfect for me since it was a brand-new division, and Daniel could do his thing. Bebeautiful.com would heat up in 2005 after Daniel graduated and he focused full time on it. Stay tuned for the rest of the story.

No one offered free shipping in 2003. We now had four DCs and had the lowest shipping costs in the country compared to our competition. Why not turn up the heat? I was first to introduce free shipping on all orders, $99 and over. Customers loved it! They ordered even more products from us and it pissed off the full-service distributors even more. The smart ones (there were very few) matched our shipping policy. But in the end, we were first and never looked back.

LIFE LESSON TIP: Nails account for less than 2 percent of total beauty sales. Few pay attention to this category for that reason. TNG's success was in part because it was able to become the leader in the niche category with superior customer service and product innovation. Sometimes it's best to look at the industry you are in and focus on the bottom 2 percent that no one else cares about.

where America shops for beauty solutions®

LESSON #52

You Can't Buy Customers

As an entrepreneur thinking about starting your own company, try to find an industry that is not filled with "good old boys." I was an outsider when I started Nailco in 1985 and remain an outsider to this day. And that is 100 percent A-OK with me. One of the key lessons as an entrepreneur is learning how to deal with the insiders: Their sole objective is to keep you from succeeding.

The indoor tanning business was going full blast when the government started getting into the fold. Indoor tanning was not healthy, and they were on a mission to get rid of it. However, just like smoking, gambling, prostitution, and all other sins that man loves, the government never really does away with anything. It is true that over time, fewer people tanned indoors, and the industry downsized significantly, but for now, we were in the moment and it was time to enjoy every single one of them.

Like the fucking full-service distributors in the beauty industry, indoor tanning distributors hated Nailco. Simply put, we took away their business because their business case was weak. They thought we took away their business because salon professionals were buying indoor tanning products at wholesale prices from us instead of buying them at tanning salons. It was a ludicrous thought. For years, they fought with our vendors to prohibit Nailco from selling to beauty salons and through our stores. The vendors ignored them until one day they didn't. Due to antitrust laws, I never got the answer as to why they changed their minds, but I suspect it was Four Seasons Tanning flexing their muscle. They remained the largest distributor (and even tried getting into the beauty business with their own beauty catalog but the division never took off). At the end of 2002, California Tan, Swedish Beauty, and Australian Gold told me I could no longer sell tanning products in our catalogs or stores.

So, what does an entrepreneur do? Start CTS (Complete Tanning Source). I hired a fantastic sales manager, Frank Hutton, who was better than any used-car salesperson you ever came across. He was energetic, enthusiastic, and so full of shit that everyone loved him. The first CTS catalog was oversized and featured a mostly naked model on the cover. He inherited our salespeople in California and established a Tennessee office where Four Seasons was located. He hired six of their best salespeople. Game on, Baby!

Already having TheAcademy, I established the CTS training center where we provided education and displayed tanning equipment in an 1,800-square-foot area. Programs were established for salon employee certification, products, and business owner classes. We held an annual trade event called the Beach Party and sold out every year. Best of all, California Tan, Swedish Beauty, and ETS loved the concept and were the lead lines in the new catalog. Thank you, Four Seasons!

I have to share a sidebar story that took place at the Looking Fit trade show in 2005. CTS took a huge booth, and I hired a designer to create a maze inside that attendees had to walk through. The maze had a roof so it was dark inside other than glowing black lights. It was so cool. The theme to the booth was Mardi Gras and we all wore beads. At the end of the maze, we displayed a $20,000 tanning bed and we were giving it away on the second day of the show. To enter to win, the attendee had to walk the maze and at the end, they received a numbered ticket and a set of beads.

It was unfucking believable! The lines were long to get in and soon everyone on the trade show floor was wearing our beads. Even exhibitors came to our booth begging for beads. At the night parties, we brought more beads and people were hysterical for them. But mostly, they wanted to win the tanning bed. I will never forget the moment. On day two of the show at 2:00 p.m., we held the drawing. The show manager turned down the lights on the show floor and gave me the microphone. Suddenly, the activity on the show floor stopped and the more than a thousand attendees rushed to our booth. The thoughts going through my head were many, but the one that came to the forefront was that a beauty distributor stole the excitement from all the other tanning companies because of a $20,000 tanning bed. Frank had the tickets in a huge bowl, and I picked the winning ticket and announced the number. The winner shouted out.

Unfortunately, the moral of the story is so sad and certainly one of my biggest life lessons: You cannot buy customers. The attendee who won the bed was located in Ohio and bought from an Ohio tanning distributor. One of our sales team delivered and installed the bed and never got an order for products. The customer stayed loyal to the local distributor and that was the last time I gave away a tanning bed. But hey, it was fun while it lasted!

LIFE LESSON TIP: We have a tendency to think as entrepreneurs that our product is so good that if we just get it into consumers' hands, we will be wildly successful. Hence the reason for free samples, giving away promotions, and hiring influencers. But rarely do those tactics work. Your product has to be good enough that people want to pay for it.

A division of tng worldwide

LESSON #53

Never Stop Looking for Ways to Kill Your Competition

Hairco was doing $6M a year with L'Oréal Professionnel hair color, and we were their number-one distributor by state. These were incredible numbers, and I understood why the full-service distributors were so protective of their business. Recall, Beaute Craft didn't even bother selling this line when we took it on. We were doing more business with a single hair color line than either CND or OPI.

For this chapter, it is important to talk a bit about L'Oréal. L'Oréal is the world's biggest beauty company and among other things, they invented hair color. L'Oréal has always been the leader because they have always had the best CEOs who understood one thing and one thing only: relentless focus on their customers. I will never forget Paul Sharnsky telling me one day, "Larry, you are not our customer. Our customer is the hairdresser." I would learn sooner than later that he was right.

L'Oréal understood best that its future in the professional beauty industry would not come from internal innovation but from outside acquisitions. It also kept a keen eye on what *Sally Beauty* was doing, as Sally was the leader in professional hair care sales. L'Oréal's claim to fame was Kerastase. Their first acquisition was Redken in 1993, and they made Redken into a powerhouse brand. In Michigan, both Beaute Craft and Maly's distributed it. Pat Parenty was the GM in charge of Redken. I became very friendly with him because I wanted it for Hairco. We got along well, but Pat always told me to be patient and if and when the opportunity came, he would be in touch. He never did.

L'Oréal acquired Matrix from Bristol-Meyers in 2000 and, at the time, it was the biggest professional hair care brand for both hair products and hair color. Beaute Craft was the exclusive Michigan distributor.

Matrix was the perfect brand for Hairco and would put us over the top. After the acquisition, L'Oréal brought in a new GM, Francesca Raminella, whom I quickly got to know. She made it clear that she was not happy with Beaute Craft's business and told me to make a proposal. So, what does an entrepreneur do? Write a book.

Winning in the 21st Century was my first book. It was forty pages and hardcover. It had a print edition of three. It was brilliant. Each chapter outlined strategy that would make both Matrix and Hairco winners in the twenty-first century. I sent the book to Francesca in 2001. She got back to me and told me that Beaute Craft's contract ended in 2003, and we would get together in 2002. I had to wait patiently.

In 2002, I made the trip to 575 5th Avenue and met with Francesca. This was my second time to 575 (they have since moved to the Hudson Yards). One thing I will not forget from my first visit was their executive dining room. It was outfitted exactly like a five-star restaurant with a menu and food quality to match. The lowly nail distributor actually got the opportunity to enjoy lunch in the dining room. It was sublime.

There was no lunch on this visit as we met in her office. She was very intrigued and wondered if I could pull it off. The investment was huge (more so than I even imagined). But like so many others before her, she loved my energy and enthusiasm. She saw Beaute Craft as a "good-old-boy" distributor that was milking the brand. She gave me co-distribution rights in 2003 and then based on our sales, exclusive rights in 2004. Total sales potential was $10M a year. I walked out of her office and flew home with all smiles on my face. It was the highlight of my career in the haircare business.

Then came chaos. You know how much inventory you need to sell $10M a year? The number of Matrix SKUs alone was over five hundred. SoColor, the best-selling hair color then, had more than two hundred, and you had to be in stock on all of them. There was no way that we had enough space in our Farmington Hills warehouse to manage the business. Oh, I forgot to tell you that our TIGI business grew to $6M a year too. So, what does an entrepreneur do? Buy another warehouse.

Unlike Farmington Hills, I had no time to plan and build so I had to buy something already built. I found the perfect location in Wixom, just twenty minutes away. I got it outfitted with racking and conveyors and it was operational by November. All our Hairco products moved over and we were ready to launch Matrix. Another $3M in debt for the mortgage. But wait, we opened five more stores this year and eventually the store count would get to thirty, all because of Matrix.

I launched Matrix with a stealth marketing idea: I created a Matrix mailer to look like a FedEx envelope. Inside the envelope, content included information about TheAcademy (we now had three locations); FRINGE hair event; sixteen stores with ten more opening in 2004 and 2005; Club Hairco; Business Development Specialists (BDSs, we didn't have fucking sales reps); and business management programs. It also included coupons for all Matrix products and a contest for five grand prize winners to be flown to NYC for the grand opening of the Matrix Academy (I paid for everything). I mailed this to every salon in Michigan. The response was immediate.

Beaute Craft didn't know how to respond and the following year, we won the exclusive rights for Matrix. We hired most of Beaute Craft's salespeople and not too long afterward, they went out of business. BAM!

> Sales hit yet another record, $70M, total debt exceeded $10M, and we boasted three hundred employees.

LIFE LESSON TIP: Never stop paying attention to your competitors. I love looking at their websites weekly and spotting their best-selling products, new offerings, and close-outs. There are plenty of clues to learn their weaknesses that you can capitalize on.

LESSON #54

Never Stop Monitoring Expenses

Hairco was on a roll in 2004 having Matrix exclusively for Michigan and Northern Ohio. Consequently, it took most of my attention. The nail industry entered a mature stage and would stay that way until 2010 when CND introduced Shellac. It was the perfect time to focus on Hairco.

In addition to all the classes held at TheAcademy's three locations, events and shows became even more important to Hairco's growth. Or so I thought. We already had the Great Lakes Beauty Show, and now hair was a major part of it. We also had Fringe and the Tiffany Awards. Let me tell you more about them.

Fringe was a special event that was held at the coolest places in Southeastern Michigan: the Royal Oak Music Theater, Masonic Temple, and Rock Financial Showplace. It featured a top celebrity hairdresser; the most famous one I brought in was Frederic Fekkai. He cost me $25,000 for a one-hour performance plus expenses. I vividly recall the time it was at the historical Masonic Temple in Detroit. I always did the best catering for Fringe and gave attendees drink tickets. (The event was completely free but salons had to qualify based on their annual purchases.) Fekkai was ready to go on stage so I walked outside to the balcony where many hairdressers were smoking and enjoying cocktails. I told them that Fekkai was getting ready to start his set and to go inside. They looked at me as if I was a schoolteacher on a playground telling the kiddies to go back inside to their classroom. Most stayed outside. It was then that I realized I was paying all this money for nothing. Hairdressers wanted to hang out, and if they wanted to be educated, it would be on their terms.

There was not a single distributor that held an event like Fringe. Now I knew why. I stopped doing Fringe and focused on The Tiffany Awards. The Tiffany Awards was a first-class gala in which salons all over Michigan competed in three categories: hair color and style, haircut, and fantasy hair. The awards were actual Tiffany crystal trophies. First-, second-, and third-place trophies were given out for each category. Each year I had three judges review all of the entries to determine who would be the finalists for each category. The finalists had to compete live on stage in front of the guest judges. To cheer on the finalists, salons would buy tickets for their entire staff. The competition was fierce. We always sold out: more than five hundred tickets. I tied in our charity fundraising at this event too. But did the event produce long-term goodwill? Not really.

As if Fringe and the Tiffany Awards were not enough, I also hosted Evening of the Stars in January. At first, the event was held at the Ritz Carlton, and it was produced at the same level as our holiday parties. Later on, I moved it to The Capital Grille. I took over the entire restaurant. At a cost of $200 per person and RSVP required, it was amazing how many customers didn't show up (at least 10 percent). When I later asked them why they didn't come, their response was always the same, "something else came up." Like Fringe, I stopped doing this event after four years. However, during these years, the salon community knew that no one threw a party like Larry.

At the Soaring Eagle Casino & Resort, I held our one and only Matrix trade show, Celebrate-a-thon. The highlight was that I gave away a brand-new Mini Cooper at the end of the show. Amazingly, the excitement of the contest was the same as giving away the tanning bed at the tanning show, and unfortunately, the results were the same too. The hairdresser that won was a booth renter and didn't even use Matrix products. Such is the life of an entrepreneur; you never know the outcome until you experience it firsthand, and you always pay the price when you fail to learn a life lesson.

Regardless, business was soaring, and we won over virtually every A and A+ salon in Southeastern Michigan. Grand Rapids proved to be the ultimate challenge because salons there were entrenched with Redken. Little did anyone know then that Maly's would be gone by the end of 2009 so it didn't matter. We had more than twenty-five BDSs in the field along with twenty-one stores. It was an incredible investment but one that would not be long term.

The best thing was that we were raising a lot of money for charity. That year we raised $158,000 for the Gail Purtan Ovarian Cancer Research Fund and the same amount for ACS.

I was enthralled with continuous improvement. In-between doing everything else, I found time to read business books and loved Seth Godin (*Purple Cow*), anything Tom Peters (*In Search of Excellence* and *Re-Imagine* were my top favs), and Malcolm Gladwell (*The Tipping Point*). During the ISO-9002 process, I learned more about continuous improvement and Kaizen. Kaizen is a Japanese term for continuous improvement, and Toyota made it famous. Ironically, *The Toyota Way* was written by Jeffrey Liker, a U-M professor. I read his book and decided afterward to implement Kaizen at The Nailco Group.

I hired a team of Kaizen experts, and it was a jaw-breaking experience. I won't bore you with the details (speaking of boring, I hired

Jeffrey to be a guest speaker at one of our annual meetings. Within twenty minutes, the entire room was snoring). However, I will tell you the coolest thing about Kaizen was 5S, which included: Sort, Set, Shine, Standardize, and Sustain. Everything was based on this premise. The three principles of Kaizen are: Housekeeping, Eliminate Waste, and Standardize. Let me give you an example.

The consultants walked around the call center and noticed each employee had a holder filled with pens, pencils, and markers. I can't tell you how much we spent in office supplies a year, but I know Quill could have sent us 500 pounds of M&M's and have still made money. The consultants asked me how many pens, pencils, and markers did each employee need. I told them a couple colors of pens and markers and one pencil. They put a giant box on the call center floor and made an announcement, "Pick the two pens, two markers and pencil you want to keep and then put the rest of them in this box." It was amazing; the box was full and had more than a thousand pens, markers, and pencils. We did not need to reorder them for months. The same concept was carried out throughout the entire company. The savings were immense. In 2005, we added more processes such as the A3 sheet, employee suggestions, and process improvements. Here again, I could write a book just on Kaizen.

For us, 2004 was the pivot year for bebeautiful and The Nailco Group: Bebeautiful.com integrated on the amazon.com platform. We were the first pro beauty company to do so and that would prove invaluable over the next nineteen years.

> Sales hit yet another record, $79M and we had 325 employees.

LIFE LESSON TIP: It's far easier spending money than making money. A good rule of thumb is to spend about 4 percent on advertising and promotion each year. These are discretionary expenses and can rev up or down each year based on new product launches, events, and competitive activity. However, don't believe in the premise that the more you spend in this category will eventually pay off and sales and profits will roll in.

LESSON #55

The Only Way to Make Money Is to Take Risks: Be Prepared to Accept Risk at All Times

The Nailco Group was light-years ahead of its competition when it came to technology, continuous improvement, employee motivation, speed of delivery, fill rates for orders, and product selection. Even with all that, full-service distributors did much more business than we did because they had several states to sell high-demand hair products and color in. I knew then as I knew back in 1985 that I had to innovate nonstop to stay ahead of the competition and sustain the business long term. Not a single full-service distributor that I was competing with in 2005 is still around in 2024. You will learn why in the next few chapters.

The Center for Industry Excellence (CIE) was another one of my concepts that brought next-level technology to salons and beauty professionals. CIE was the most comprehensive consulting firm for the salon industry. I utilized every TNG core capability and extended them to our customers. Services included: Design & Marketing Solutions (business cards, brochures, invites, menus, and more); Financial Solutions (payroll, business insurance, financial statements, financing); e-Strategies (website development, intranet, appointment scheduling); Employment Solutions (employee benefits, liability insurance, front desk training, hiring and firing); New & Existing Business Development Solutions (business plan creation, design services, menu creation, and spa development); and finally Business Training Solutions (intensive boot camps, business plans, on-site staff training, and retail merchandising).

CIE held its inaugural Cruise of Champions in 2005 and featured our top consultants for a three-night cruise. Tickets were $599 per person, and we sold more than a hundred tickets. We also held CIE events at major trade shows and had consultants do classes at TheAcademy. We even sold their books and CDs. Now you might ask did I make any money with CIE. The easy answer was no. However, entrepreneurs don't always exclusively focus on profits. They also focus on what their customers' needs are before customers know they need them. As it turned out, CIE was over their heads and lasted only a few short years.

Daniel was working for the company full time and ready to take bebeautiful to the next level. Working with our marketing team, he launched the first bebeautiful catalog. Little did he know then that consumers were not demanding professional beauty products in consumer sizes. They wanted niche, trendy, and cool beauty products. Remember, Amazon was just getting into beauty so mail-order beauty catalogs were still the rage. Daniel hired a buyer and soon enough, the catalog was filled with the products consumers wanted. We were one of the first Spanx retailers and self-adhesive nipple covers would be the best-selling SKU; StriVectin became our runaway best-selling skin care line as they took full-page ads in beauty magazines, and specialty makeup products took off. We even launched our own makeup line, BePro.

Overnight, catalog production went to seven catalogs a year. Each catalog mailing was up to 100,000 pieces and up to 1M for the holiday issue. Business was good. Then we made the fateful decision to open the first bebeautiful store in Strongsville, Ohio. Why Ohio you might ask? With nearly thirty TIS stores in Michigan, I didn't want to create customer confusion and bebeautiful had to stand on its own. The store location was decent and right next to David's Bridal Store. We spent a small fortune on outfitting the store and even created a spa area in which customers could receive hand and foot massages. The store was a bit ahead of its time. It opened to great fanfare and press, but it would close the following year. The focus turned to the catalogs and website.

The Farmington Hills warehouse was at capacity even with all the remote warehouses. The Wixom location for the Hairco products had plenty of space but was inefficient. We had to ship Hairco products from Wixom and all other products from Farmington Hills so our customers received two shipments. Further, it cost us double to process orders. So, what does an entrepreneur do? Build a new building.

The BUB and I narrowed down the search to two locations: Romulus, just down the road from the airport, and New Hudson. New Hudson at the time was mostly farmland but it was right off I-96, one of the main freeways in Southeastern Michigan. We decided on New Hudson. We found the perfect lot and bought it for $2.5M. We found the perfect builder, Quadrants, and we used the same designer as Farmington Hills, although we would not build-out the office area until 2011.

This time, I decided it was going to be the last building I was ever going to build (and it was). I decided on 175,000 square feet with the option of adding another 40,000 square feet if the time came. With landscaping and all the bullshit, it came in at $12M. Comerica was very happy to give me a mortgage. Now I had the mortgage on the Farmington Hills and Wixom buildings and drew on the line of credit to build the New Hudson building. Even after selling the Farmington Hills and Wixom buildings, my total debt was $27M. As my banker always told me, "Larry, its only money!"

I hired the best contractor to install a state-of-the-art pick-to-light picking system, best-in-class conveyors, and automatic box-taping machine among other improvements. I also bought the best stand-up lift trucks and the best software to tie into SAP (you'll read all about that in 2007 when the building opened).

> Sales hit the all-time record of $86M and we also peaked at 365 employees.

LIFE LESSON TIP: Of all the moments that define being an entrepreneur, perhaps none are as memorable as those moments when you sign your name on a document that is inherently risky. It could be your first line of credit, mortgage for a new building, or company acquisition. Just remember that when signing the document, you and only you are responsible for its contents.

LESSON #56

There Are Two Sides to Every Coin

I just want to say "thank you" loyal reader for getting this far into the book. You have already read that I started Nailco in 1985 with two employees and now we are up to 365 employees twenty years later. I know you are wondering about the tail side of the business. If you are an entrepreneur or thinking about starting your own business, the tail side is the side that can get you in trouble. The more you can learn about dealing with the tail side, the better. It is also a good time to talk about management and leadership style, which I will cover in the next chapter.

There are two sides to every coin. I love to do research and I dug this up online from grammarist.com:

Heads or tails refers to the two sides of a coin. When a decision must be made with two equally viable answers, or two people disagree and must find an equitable way to choose between two answers, a coin may be flipped. As one person tosses the coin in the air, the other person calls either heads or tails. Heads refers to the side of the coin with a person's head on it. Tails refers to the opposite side, not because there is a tail on it, but because it is the opposite of heads.[2]

At The Nailco Group, I'm the "head." After all, I am the founder, CEO, and president. BUB (Teresa) is the "tail." She is the VP and in charge of HR.

Entrepreneurs love to build companies and invent products and solutions. What we hate to do is the tail side of the business. The worst two initials you can mention to an entrepreneur are H-R. There is nothing worse for an entrepreneur than the head of HR coming into your office and closing the door. Oh wait; there is one worse thing: when your CFO is behind the head of HR.

Now I might be the CEO and president but a long time ago, my CFO gave me a Post-it. Let me share it with you (see bottom left).

When I left off with the BUB, she was a buyer and in charge of HR. As Nailco grew, buyers were hired and BUB took over HR full time. Now you might be asking, "How is it working with your spouse in the business?"

I have three golden rules to share with you if you decide to work with your spouse. Rule 1: Create totally opposite roles in the business. Rule 2: Give autonomy. Rule 3: Make sure your spouse is your best friend. And one bonus rule: Don't bring up work issues at home.

women are always right

---

2   https://grammarist.com/idiom/heads-or-tails-and-cant-make-heads-or-tails/.

I was a fan of Jack Welch's management style and loved his book, *Winning*. Welch preached that 20 percent of his workforce was the cream of the crop, 70 percent was the middle and could reach the top, and 10 percent was the bottom and had to be eliminated each year. It was the 10 percent that the BUB and I fought the most over.

I understood that employees made mistakes, some worse than others. But to an entrepreneur, certain types of mistakes are unforgivable. For instance, an important customer had to receive an order via FedEx overnight and the shipping clerk sent it through ground instead. Or an employee shipped twelve cases of a product instead of twelve pieces. Mostly, it was employees who were not paying attention or engaged in their work. I wanted those employees fired but HR always won out, "we have to follow procedure." Unless it was a termination violation in the employee handbook.

The employee handbook for the first few years was a piece of paper, front and back. I don't remember everything that was on it but there was a code of conduct, dress code, being on time (I hated employees who showed up late), and all the legal mumbo jumbo. I don't recall anything about benefits because who had time for them?

Vacation time? The BUB and I did not take a vacation together for the first ten years of the business other than to splurge on the boys during Christmas season and take them away on a trip for a week. What BUB and I did do, a few times a year, was to take an overnight trip and sometimes even an entire weekend away.

Sick days? Are you kidding me, who got sick in your thirties?

Health insurance? Who could afford that?

Like everything else in business, you learn the hard way. Our employee handbook went from two pages to seventy-two pages in a deluxe binder. The HR team grew to include coaches and trainers, interview experts, and a Dykema HR attorney. His name was Bob

Duty, and we used him so often, I knew his phone number by heart and I wasn't even in HR! We played golf and dined together, all the while he billed us hundreds of thousands of dollars in legal fees. However, he was worth every dollar and this is one of life lessons from this chapter: Hire the best damn HR attorney sooner than later.

At the quarterly meetings, I introduced new employees. It would not be unusual for twenty to thirty new employees to come up on stage at any one of the meetings. In fact, we had so many new hires I often could not remember their names and would have an HR person next to me to help remind me.

Anyway, have no fear, 100 percent customer success extended to our internal customers so HR developed the best benefits. I learned quickly that health insurance was the most important benefit and selected Blue Cross/Blue Shield from the onset. Yes, it was the most expensive, but it was the best, and employees to this day appreciate it. Over time, we developed personal days that employees could use how they wanted. The number of days given were based on tenure.

Other benefits that we introduced included: Fitness club reimbursement; Weight Watchers; college tuition reimbursement; quit smoking programs; birthday off with pay; and many others. I also loved the intangible benefits we offered: Birthday card with $100 Nailco dollars (they could be used for any Nailco products) and Anniversary card with a $100 restaurant gift card, both signed by the BUB and me.

We also started doing company lunches. Every summer, we grilled outdoors for the company. May featured Chick-A-Doodle-Doo; June, Cheeseburgers in Paradise; July, Hot Diggity Dog; August, Mexican Fiesta; and September, LG's Steakhouse. These were wildly popular with the employees, and we still do them today.

Overall, we offered the best benefits in the business and it was one reason why we had the best employee retention rates and won so many awards for being the best company to work for. The other reason was that we had the best fucking HR department, and women are always right!

> **LIFE LESSON TIP:** Make sure you have the best HR department, best HR attorney, and let HR do its thing. Every time I got involved with HR, it never ended well. This lesson alone will save you thousands of dollars and hundreds of wasted hours.

LESSON #57

Manage Smart, Lead Smarter

N ow you know that we had the best HR department. But that was only one department of many. As an entrepreneur, you must learn how to manage and lead people at the same time. It's not easy, and that is why I recommend reading as many management and leadership books as possible. Let me share what I considered to be best practices up until this point.

Departments are groups of employees (we have always referred to employees as "talent") engaged in performing a similar function to support both internal and external customers. Our departments in 2005 were: HR, Financial Solutions, Purchasing, DC (Shipping & Receiving; operations), Marketing & Web, Technology, Call Center, Outside Sales, Stores, Salon & Spa Design, FPO, CTS, and Beauty Direct. Each department had an executive in charge.

There were two teams that reported directly to me: Leadership and Sales. The leadership team was comprised of the executives that ran the business. We met every Monday, and an agenda was required prior to each meeting. If anyone on the team wanted to partake in the meeting, they had to send an agenda item to me for approval. This happened because meetings were often too long and unproductive.

The purpose of the meetings was to get everyone on the same page for future projects, continuous improvement initiatives, company challenges, and other pertinent happenings.

The sales team encompassed the executives that ran the sales side of the business. We met on the first Tuesday of each month. Topics included sales to forecast, growth initiatives, competitor activities, new product ideas and launches, upcoming trade shows, and customer feedback.

I was an avid reader of the *Harvard Business Review*. There was an article that came out in 2005 that stopped me in my tracks, Developing First-Level Leaders (you can buy it online). The article highlighted the importance of developing First-Level Leaders (FLLs), and I thought it was the best idea since sliced bread. So, what does an entrepreneur do? Develop FLLs!

There was no one better in the organization to lead this project than Dawn Kuhn, the company CFO. Dawn is an "includer" and ranks high in empathy. Sorry, I am getting ahead of myself because the next chapter is all about Gallup®, but you have to know entrepreneurs typically rank at the bottom for both "includer" and "empathy." If there was anyone in the company you wanted to lead a new important project, it was Dawn.

FLLs are non-executive employees and can be salaried, hourly, or commissioned. They are highly regarded within their respective departments. More importantly, they are the most aware of the "gossip" within their department. Let me sidestep for a moment. Gossip is the curse of all companies. Gossip is HR's worst nightmare, and as the CEO, I was always the last one to find out about anything "gossipy" at the company. Anything you can do to reduce or stop gossip is worth doing.

Dawn selected the FLLs from each department, and they met monthly. Like all our other meetings, minutes were published and shared with the executive team. It was amazing the type of information the FLLs shared together and how simple issues were resolved or prevented.

I will also tell you that having an internal intranet is crucial for employee satisfaction and awareness. We use it for everything HR (handbook, holidays, meeting dates, job postings), phone numbers, safety data sheets, UPS tracking, employee directory with photos and start date, message from the CEO (I write a monthly message and have been doing so for more than thirty years), and my blog. I strongly recommend this for all companies of any size.

The last topic I want to mention is employee reviews. To an entrepreneur, employee reviews are like going to the dentist, a necessary evil. I much prefer to tell my direct reports "Do your best job and if you need my assistance, let me know." But of course, that is a NO-NO! HR demanded written annual reviews for all employees, and more often than not, I would get gentle reminders from HR that one or more reviews were late.

The next chapter changed everything when it came to employee reviews. But up until now, we did them religiously, and there is truth that employees appreciate the time taken for them. Another thing we did was rate employees on a scale of 1.0 to 4.0 with 4.0 being the highest rating. Rating 4.0 employees were outstanding in every area with no write-ups in their file; 3.5 employees were excellent but tended to make non-critical mistakes; 3.0 employees were on the brink of staying employed with the company and tended to make too many mistakes, have attitude issues, called in late or missed days. Those were the employees I had the most issues with and rarely did they elevate back up to 3.5.

Employee ratings were significant because that determined their annual bonus. I gave employees our sales numbers and profits at the annual meetings. I reminded them that the purpose of being in business was to make money and from the beginning, I awarded annual bonuses when the company was profitable (we have been profitable every year except for two). Bonuses ranged from 10 to 20 percent of the total company profits, and after figuring in all the costs of the holiday parties and quarterly meetings, the BUB and I gave away up to 25 percent of the profits annually. Employees with 4.0 ranking received the highest share and those with 3.5 ranking received 20 percent less. We did not bonus 3.0 employees.

I have to brag, and I will confirm it wasn't because HR tilted the results; we always had an extremely high percentage of 4.0 talent. It was nothing like the 20/70/10 formula Jack Welch bragged about. It was always closer to 75/20/5. Little did I know then that it would make a big difference when it came time to launch our next huge initiative, Gallup®.

LIFE LESSON TIP: Under fifty employees, entrepreneurs can be hands-on in most company meetings. With 51-150 employees, carefully select meetings that you need to participate in. Over 150 employees, an entrepreneur should only participate in meetings that they lead. Post-pandemic, the fewer layers of management, the better. And FLLs work best when you don't have off-site employees.

LESSON #58

The World Is Filled with Unexpected Surprises: The More You Read, the More Surprises You Will Find

One of the all-time best-selling business books is *Strengthfinders 2.0* (you have to buy it if you haven't already). The book is published by Tom Rath and Gallup®. If you are like most folks, you've heard of the Gallup® Poll. While that has made Gallup® famous, it only accounts for a fraction of their total revenue. Most of their revenue comes from the book and all the training offered as a result of the book.

My view of Gallup® is a pretty good one considering how much money I have invested with them. Gallup® scientists have identified thirty-four strengths that people can possess. The top-five strengths are the most important ones to focus on. I like to refer to strengths as talents because most people are born with them. There are two ways to make your top-five strengths better. But how do you find out what your top-five strengths are to begin with?

When you buy the book, you will receive one online Strengthfinders test. The test will ask you a series of questions. Once you complete the questionnaire and click "submit," your personal top-five strengths will be returned to you. The book defines what each of the thirty-four strengths means. Just by reading a person's top-five strengths, I could tell you so much about that person.

When I met with new employees, I always told them that, "TNG is a Gallup®-trained organization and soon you will learn your top-five strengths." They were so excited to find out what they were. I then asked them, "How do you think Tiger Woods gets better?" I would get all kinds of answers, and inevitably, I would get "practice." I said "Yes!" Tiger would practice six-foot putts and he would have to make a hundred in a row. If he missed, he started over until he made a hundred in a row. What is the other way? This answer was more difficult for them so I piped in, "Coaching." I then asked, "How many coaches does the MSU football team have." They knew about the head coach, but they had no idea about the assistant coaches. I told them "eleven," and then asked, "Why do they need eleven coaches?" I explained that each position on the team had unique areas that needed personalized coaching attention. That is the reason why we had full-time coaches on staff.

Here is the most brilliant part of Strengthfinders: It focuses on what individuals do well, not what they do poorly. I told the new employees another story. "Remember when you were in high school and came home with your report card? Let's say you had three A's and a C. What did your parents say to you?" They always said the same thing, "What's up with that C?" Typical of human behavior, the parents didn't recognize the three A's, they were only concerned with the C. However, what the parents failed to recognize was that their kid's strengths were in the A subjects and not the C subject. Bolstering the A subjects will be far more beneficial. The A's (strengths) can infinitely develop but the C's (weaknesses) may never develop.

Strengthfinders is just the tip of the iceberg of what Gallup® offers organizations. I was so intrigued; I gave them a call to find out more. Sure enough, Gallup® offered a multitude of programs. I enrolled in Gallup® University and got on a plane to Omaha for my three-day journey. It was one of the best journeys of my life.

I met with my coach, Mary Pat Loos, and she introduced me to others that I would be working with. She gave me the nickel tour, and I will say their building and campus is beautiful. I learned about the second floor that housed the critical Gallup® Poll computers and how no one had access except for a few employees. I took the test again and learned detailed information about each of my thirty-four strengths. Here are my top five: Competition, Focus, Ideation, Maximizer, and Strategic. One added benefit of taking the test through Gallup® is that you learn the exact order of all your strengths. I found out that "includer" and "empathy" were near my bottom. Gallup® also made it crystal clear to never focus on weaker strengths; it was a waste of time. Another reason why it is so important to know your talents at an early age.

At the end of the program, Mary gave me my "diploma," which included her professional assessment of my Gallup® strengths. Let me share her findings with you:

"Going far beyond the call of duty, doing more than others expect...for you, this is what excellence is all about. It comes from seeing the larger picture, striving to innovate, looking for the best solution, and always going the extra mile. Excellence means doing your very best, in everything, in every way, contributing to the larger effort. The critical measurement that drives you is 'successful' customer experiences. Day-to-day you sophistically handle the 'what ifs' that arise, study the options, and set a strong course to resolution. If there's a way to do it better...you will find it. Your inquisitive mind keeps raising the bar for yourself and the organization. Therefore, for those around you, they must be ready to execute your visions. Take time to understand each team member's unique talent and how they best can contribute to meeting these new challenges. This combined knowledge about your people and the inner working of your organization will enhance the organization's capacity. Take time to strategically select partnerships that will spur growth within yourself and others. When others come to you for help, partner with them to not only learn from each other, you're better together."

I also learned other key Gallup® measurements, Q12 and C11. Q12 is a twelve-question survey that your external customers take to measure their level of engagement with your company. C11 is an eleven-question survey your internal customers take to measure their level of engagement within the company. Gallup® is most accredited for coming up with the term, "employee engagement." Most companies have less than 32 percent engaged employees. When I hired Gallup® to administer both Q12 and C11 surveys, TNG came back in the top 90 percent percentile of all Gallup® companies surveyed. Fully engaged employees were the ultimate outcome of being a Gallup®-trained organization, what they would refer to as the Gallup® Path.

The last take-away was the Gallup® Four Keys. The Four Keys to employee engagement from bottom to top: Confidence, Integrity, Pride, Passion. Unlike an annual review, this was a document that had to be completed by the manager and direct report quarterly. All the questions were engaging, and managers learned the levers that motivated employees to perform their best. HR replaced annual reviews for all leadership employees. The goal was to create fully engaged employees that had passion for their own success as well as that for TNG.

The Gallup® Path became an institution at TNG. I bought the book for all existing employees and all new hires. HR posted the top-five strengths for all employees on the intranet. I sent the entire leadership team to Omaha and enrolled them in Gallup® University. It forever changed our culture, and to this day, we are still a Gallup®-trained organization. I even brought Gallup® to salons and brought in the CEO to speak at one of our company meetings.

A sidebar story that I have to share is that the Ritz Carlton at the time was a huge Gallup® customer. They went a step further than most companies go and developed their own credo card. It contained the Gallup® Four Keys, mission statement, and other key engagement levers. Since I was a huge Ritz Carlton customer, I asked for my own copy of the Ritz credo card and got it. So, what does an entrepreneur do? Make his own credo card! Since 2006, I have kept the TNG credo card in my money clip and still have it today.

LIFE LESSON TIP: Reading books is the elixir to continuous learning, pumping up the brain, and getting new ideas. Take the time to read at least one business book a month, and you will be amazed at how more ideas come to mind that you can implement effectively.

LESSON #59

Recognize Failure Early, Then Reboot

For an entrepreneur, there is nothing like building something from the ground up. Typically, it is a business, but I was fortunate enough to also build and design not one but two buildings. The Global Logistics Center (GLC) was my biggest undertaking.

Howard Emmer was a good friend, and we hung out on the golf course. He was the one that hooked me on Friday night martinis (although Howard indulged more often and preferred gin to vodka). Howard was a self-made business guy who owned two homes and two black Mercedes. I will always remember two of his sayings to me, "I've been both rich and poor, being rich is a whole lot better," and "It's important to enjoy life every day because when you are on this side of the ground, you are alive and it sure beats being dead." Howard made his money in real estate, and he taught me early on that it was always better to be the landlord instead of the lessee.

It was that lesson that allowed The Nailco Group to survive tumultuous economic times, especially the housing crash in 2007–2009 and the pandemic in 2020–2022. There is nothing better than paying rent to yourself. The downside of designing and constructing your own building is that it is very time-consuming, and you have to come up with a lot of money for the mortgage and build-out. Not only do you have to run your business, you have to spend hundreds of hours with designers, contractors, and various trades.

When the GLC opened in September 2007, we desperately needed the warehouse space as we combined both Farmington Hills and Wixom locations. Moving was no picnic, and I was very happy this would be the last time we had to move. The entire move had to be completed over a single weekend so we could open for business on a Monday and not affect customer orders. We weren't ready to move offices, TheAcademy, or store, so the office staff stayed in Farmington Hills. This meant I had to commute back and forth as necessary (we would move in 2012). The opening was seamless and prepared us for the next round of growth, or so I thought.

Massage therapy was booming, and I noticed that a lot of chiropractors were ordering massage supplies from us. If this theme sounds similar, you are spot on loyal reader. So, what does an entrepreneur do? Launch a chiropractic catalog, thechirobook. The catalog featured treatment tables, equipment, and supplies along with a full array of massage products. However, I quickly learned the industry was small and did not need many supplies. The catalog didn't last two years.

The Industry Source (TIS) was the largest national beauty distributor, and our Michigan customers were sometimes confused as to what to call us if they dealt with both TIS and Hairco. TIS was national while Hairco was Michigan and Northern Ohio. We did more business with TIS than Hairco, and if I was going to expand into other states with exclusive hair distribution, I thought about what the division should be called. I decided to leverage the TIS name, retire the Hairco name, and rename the exclusive division, The Industry Source Exclusive (TISE). Both our customers and BDSs loved it.

Sales were $81M, and we had 315 employees.

LIFE LESSON TIP: It's OK to fail. No team goes undefeated. The key as an entrepreneur is to know that failure goes with the territory, to recognize it early, and cut your losses. If this involves closing your company, then so be it. On the flip side, you have to take that experience and get back into the game. Never stop trying.

LESSON #60

Decide What Your Core Competency Is and Stick to It

I would be remiss if I didn't talk about Sally Beauty in this book. It is worthy of an entire chapter because Sally Beauty is the predominant reason for the demise of the professional beauty business. Worse, Sally bought and stole away the entrepreneurial spirit that defined the industry.

There are those that believed Mike Renzulli, the executive who worked for Alberto-Culver and was brought on to start Sally, to be one of the smartest guys in the business. Alas, Mike was not an entrepreneur, he was a business guy. Renzulli made a fatal mistake in 1985 (same year Nailco started) that doomed Sally and the industry. This was the year he bought Victory Beauty Supply. It was a fatal mistake because Victory was a distributor, and Sally was a retailer.

Sally Beauty hit a thousand stores in 1991 and eventually grew to forty-eight hundred stores. But when Ulta opened its first five stores in Chicago in 1990, Renzulli didn't pay attention. At first, Ulta floundered and it would take them ten years to move in the right direction. Ulta's secret sauce: They were a beauty retailer and a salon operator, which allowed them to sell professional hair care products to consumers at full list price. Ulta stores were supersized compared to Sally stores.

Sally differentiated itself from mass beauty retailers by offering professional hair color, perms, and ethnic products. Sally never opened supersized stores to compete with Ulta because of their decision to buy Victory, and they couldn't compete with their own customers because Victory sold to beauty salons.

Renzulli continued acquisitions of full-service distributors buying Heil (1999), Davidson (2000), Armstrong McCall (2001), West Coast Beauty (2003), and Aerial (2010). The division was renamed Beauty Systems Group (BSG), and their store division was renamed Cosmoprof. But BSG was a distributor, and they were at the mercy of the manufacturers they bought from having to deal with 40 percent distributor margins. Sally on the other hand was a retailer and could sell products at any prices they wanted. They could also dabble in private-label products. Sally margins were in the high fifties.

Renzulli and his successor, Gary Winterhalter, thought they could own the professional beauty industry. Winterhalter started in 2006 with big aspirations but little did he know that his following year would be a shocker. The reason: BSG's aggressive growth in distribution began to worry L'Oréal. They were apprehensive that BSG would become a monopoly and start to dictate terms to them. Not only that, but the days of professional hair companies owned by entrepreneurs were quickly ending as large multinational companies saw tremendous profits in hair care.

Henkel bought Schwarzkopf (1995) and added Alterna, SexyHair, and Kenra (2014). Kao bought Goldwell (1989) and added KMS (2002) and Oribe (2018). P&G bought Wella (2003) and Nioxin (2009), and Unilever bought TIGI (2009). All these companies bought in to compete against L'Oréal. None of them would come close.

Sally went public on the NYSE the same year Winterhalter started. Sally has been one of the worst-performing public stocks since it went public. In 2023, Sally's total sales were $3.7B and had a $1.1B market cap. Ulta, on the other hand (they went public in 2008), had sales of $10.2B and a market cap of $23.2B. Ulta has been one of the best-performing stocks since it went public. Over the past few years, Sally has been closing stores and getting rid of sales reps while Ulta has kept opening new stores and signed a deal with Target to put Ulta stores inside Target stores.

Sally buyers kept a close eye on TNG and would constantly match prices. I didn't see them as a key competitor because their stores only sold open line products and BSG mostly sold brands that we didn't with the exception of CND and OPI. However, as you will read in the next chapter, their flawed strategy was the beginning of the end for many distributors, and for TNG, the reawakening.

LIFE LESSON TIP: Restaurants and caterers are two totally different businesses but still involve food preparation and service. Being a retailer, distributor, or manufacturer are totally different businesses but still involve many of the same characteristics. Decide what your core business is and stick with it.

LESSON #61

Don't Put All Your Eggs in One Basket

Paul Sharnsky gave me a call in the spring and said I had to go to NYC to meet with the L'Oréal executive team. I asked him what the purpose of the meeting was and all he could tell me was that I would be happy and he would be joining me.

David Craggs was the CEO of the L'Oréal professional division and called the meeting. David and I were on good terms and I always asked him to persuade Pat Parenty to give me Redken. Craggs was one of the good guys so I thought the meeting could have been about us getting Redken. Why not? We were kicking ass with LP and Matrix.

I got to 575 5th Avenue and was taken to one of their conference rooms. As I walked in, I noticed ten guys with suits on including Sharnsky and Craggs. I did not see Francesca (Matrix CEO). I said to myself, "There is nothing good going to happen here, and I am certainly not getting Redken." Craggs thanked me for coming and introduced everyone in the room. Right away, one attorney put some papers in front of me to sign, an NDA (non-disclosure agreement), and I was told that the meeting was confidential. Another attorney put some papers in front of me and I was told it was a non-binding purchase agreement. I signed the papers because I was the lowly distributor, and L'Oréal was the $218B powerhouse company.

Craggs opened up the meeting and told me that the industry was in a transitional period and that L'Oréal had to take a new strategic direction. It did not like what Sally Beauty was doing with distribution and the company had to maintain its leadership within the industry. What he said next was the shocker: "We are buying all our distributors. You will be paid $.80 on the dollar for every L'Oréal product sale you made last year and $.60 on the dollar for all other product sales. You have until September to make a decision. If you do not sell to us, you will lose all distribution rights for our brands starting in 2008."

There was no emotion in the words he was saying; it was all a matter of fact. This is how the French did business. Just then, what Sharnsky told me years ago resonated, "TNG was not their customer, the salon was." He was right all along. Craggs was eager for me to say "yes" right then but said to take my time and think about it over dinner. Dinner? Are you fucking kidding me? Who could eat? I went to dinner and with Sharnsky sitting next to me, he whispered in my ear, "Larry, don't worry, I can get you $1.00 for your L'Oréal sales."

I was doing $16M with their two brands and $64M with the other brands. I valued the company quickly: $16M for L'Oréal brands and $38.4M for the other brands with a total valuation of $54.4M (yep, that is $54,400,000!). Here I am in NYC, fifty-two years old, and I was just offered $54.4M for TNG. This was by far the biggest Chance card that I had to draw. What would you have done?

L'Oréal had the same meeting with each of its distributors. Now mind you, for virtually all of them, their sales with L'Oréal products were 50 percent or higher and they had few fallback options. More than 80 percent of their distributors sold out in 2007. Only four said no, and three of them relented and sold to L'Oréal eventually. The only one that didn't eventually sell to L'Oréal was TNG. I picked up the Chance card and it said, "Fuck L'Oréal, go to Italy and write your next chapter of the business."

This was by far the biggest decision I made in my business life. I could have retired and become a beach bum and listened to "Margaritaville" 24/7. But I already knew then that after a week on the beach in Mexico, I was ready to get back to work. I was shocked, disappointed, thrilled, and delusional all at the same time. I bled for L'Oréal; they were the biggest beauty company, and we were the biggest national beauty distributor. And I still wanted Redken! But now, it would never happen. Craggs thanked me for my time and awaited my answer.

After heading back to Michigan, I had to make a quick decision on what to do next. So what does an entrepreneur do? Head on a plane to Bologna, Italy.

The biggest beauty trade show in the world was Cosmoprof (no relation to BSG stores), and it was held every spring in Bologna, Italy. I knew about Italian hair color as we already sold Alfaparf, but I needed a universal brand to compete against both LP and Matrix. I did plenty of research on Italian hair color brands and understood after my research why Italian hair color was so good: the Renaissance period. The top-three artists were Leonardo de Vinci, Raphael, and Michelangelo. They all used Italian paint, back in the 1500s, and to this day, it is still regarded as the best paint primarily due to the pigments used. Italy was known for its rich soil, and it made a huge difference. I decided that if Italian paint was good enough for the masters, it was good enough for hairdressers.

Kemon was founded in 1959, and I met with the Nocentini family, which was second generation. They shared the same values as TNG. Better yet, they made three brands of hair color, all of which were compatible with LP and Matrix. At the time, Kemon had very limited business in the United States and was looking for a new partner. The family loved my story, and we signed a long-term contract contingent on the outcome of my test study.

I had ten A+ customers that purchased $50K or more of LP hair color a year. I invited them to my office for a meeting. They sat down, and I gave them NDAs to sign and told them this was a very exciting meeting and one that could be a game-changer for their careers. I gave them Kemon's history, heritage, and culture. I went on to tell them that Kemon was located in Tuscany, Italy, and made their own hair color and products. They had their own Academy. My customers were curious. They wanted to know more.

Here was my plan: Eight out of the ten customers were in and I flew them to Kemon's headquarters all-expenses paid. There they spent three days with the Kemon education team to use their hair color. They did half heads with Kemon and half heads with L'Oréal and saw for their own eyes which hair color was best. They learned; they indulged in pizza, pasta, and red wine; and they came back home hungry for more. By the end of year, they converted to Kemon, and our team would be busy converting our other customers. Our customers not only loved the hair color, they loved my program, Kemon Owner's Circle. Since TNG was the direct importer, I offered Owner Circle members distributor prices for all Kemon products. Overnight, they saved 40 percent on their hair color. Not only were they using superior hair color, they were making record profits.

When September rolled around, I met with Sharnsky and I presented my plan. I would not sell my company. However, because of our 2004 acquisition of the Matrix business in Michigan and Northern Ohio and opening thirty stores, I wanted store distribution rights for five years. They knew that stores were a big part of the business, and it would take them years to get stores on the ground. L'Oréal accepted the plan.

I gave up $56M in cold hard cash (OK, minus capital gains tax of 20 percent) to place a bet on an Italian hair care company. While the bet turned out to be a good one, it would take years for me to forget about the cash. There was no going back.

In 2008, L'Oréal opened Salon Centric, its first distributor network across the United States and converted all the distributors it bought to its new brand. The world's biggest manufacturer was also now a lowly distributor. What I originally thought was this: They would distribute their owned brands through Salon Centric. It made sense. Not only would they earn double margin, but they would also secure the rights to their brands by never selling their brands to BSG. However, that's not what happened. Salon Centric was hell bent on stopping BSG in their tracks and they became a full-service distributor just like everyone else. That would be Craggs' biggest mistake. He was forced to retire in 2009.

Meanwhile, two public companies now owned 75 percent of salon product distribution. It would have been more but John Paul DeJoria (Paul Mitchell) never allowed his products to be sold by either company. And this my loyal readers was the kiss of death for the industry. L'Oréal never acquired another professional hair care line after Pureology in 2007. Only two hair care brands were introduced from 2008 to 2022 that made an impact: Moroccanoil in 2008 and Olaplex in 2014. It was the end of entrepreneurial hair care brands, and while full-service distributors still exist, the business has been in decline for years.

LIFE LESSON TIP: If you are a retailer or distributor, try not to have any one company be more than 15 percent of your business. I have reiterated this earlier in the book, but this is a very important life lesson to protect your business.

LESSON #62

Bite the Bullet on Key Initiatives

I t is every entrepreneur's worst nightmare: The need to upgrade your enterprise resource planning (ERP) system. TNG was using Trend, but Trend could not keep up with TNG's growth. The nightmare was that there were only two ERP programs worth considering: Oracle and SAP.

Julie Szostak was our senior technical executive, and she knew software. I made her the lead for the project. Dawn and I were also involved. We all met with the teams from Oracle and SAP. After consideration, we went with SAP.

Unlike launching Trend, SAP was a beast. While SAP had every module known to humanity available to us, we had to configure each module to our best business practices. For instance, manufacturers use SAP much differently from distributors. Worse, TNG was a hybrid company in which we did both manufacturing and distributing. What we later learned was that TNG was also a retailer with its thirty stores and that created yet another conundrum: We had to hire a third-party software company to tie in with SAP.

Bottom line to launch SAP: We had to hire a team of consultants that lived at Farmington Hills for six months. They worked diligently with Julie and her team. It was the project from hell; building the GLC was a piece of cake compared to this. Somehow, we were ready to go live January 2008 and, like launching Trend, it was one of the most miserable periods being an entrepreneur: totally helpless and dependent on a team you had no control over. In the end, launching SAP cost more than $3.5M, by far my biggest expense being in business. In addition, to keep SAP current, we had to pay more than $200K annually for licensing fees (now you see why profits are crucial to a company's success). In case you are wondering, yes, it was the best choice and we are still running SAP today.

Now that most of the inventory had been moved from Farmington Hills to the GLC, I had a lot of warehouse space available. Our furniture business was booming, and we had three full-time designers. So, what does an entrepreneur do? Launch The Pavilion. Let me quote Walt Disney, "If you can dream it, you can do it." The Pavilion was my concept of giving salon professionals their own "Disneyland."

Opened on September 9, The Pavilion featured "The world's largest furniture and equipment showroom." I had collaborated with two of the biggest European furniture companies, Olymp and Beauty Star, while at Cosmoprof. The Design Center at The Pavilion included a massive reference library. S.P.A. at The Pavilion was the largest educational center for spa training. TheAcademy was updated and enlarged, and the TIS store expanded in size. The Pavilion was over 40,000 square feet and quite the spectacle.

A couple of years back, George Schaeffer (OPI founder) called John Heffner from CND and made him an offer he couldn't pass up. John accepted and became George's right-hand guy and CEO. George wanted to get into the professional hair color business and needed John's expertise at the company. When I found out, I was elated.

John would be my conduit to getting OPI back after all these years. It didn't happen overnight, but John reassured me it would happen.

At our annual meeting in 2007, Santa Claus came to visit and brought with him a huge bag of gifts. Our employees were all smiles because this Santa was special, and they wanted the gifts that were in the bag. What were the gifts? Holiday sets of OPI Nail Lacquer. Santa Claus was George in person, and he made the grand announcement that OPI was back with Nailco! OPI made the cover of the 2008 catalog. It was a fantastic way to end the year, and what a year it was. It was also the year that TNG became CND's largest distributor.

> Sales were $82M and we had 295 employees.

LIFE LESSON TIP: Entrepreneurs have to look at spending money in software, R&D, and facilities as an investment, not an expense. Investments offer long-term benefits and are amortized. Always invest at the right time; more often than not, it's the right decision.

LESSON #63

Customer Loyalty Is Fleeting: It Can
Go Unhinged on a Moment's Notice

T
he year of 2008 was that of Kemon buzz on the streets. Many
of our A+ salons converted and loved the results. The BDSs
were busy making appointments with salons to launch Kemon
and schedule conversions. To support the demand, I created
the Kemon Academy USA and the Kemon National Artistic Team.
However, Kemon was truly an Italian company, and only the CEO and
sales manager spoke fluent English. While they had great educators,
they only spoke Italian. When they came to the United States to
teach classes in the Academy, they needed interpreters. It wasn't ideal.
And for whatever reason, Kemon would never train English-speaking
educators, which hindered the brand's growth. Our peak sales hit
$2M, well shy of the $6M we did with LP.

L'Oréal countered our strategy sending their sales team to
Michigan to offer salons discounts up to 40 percent based on volume.
Our pricing was still better but they fed on the hairdressers' egos.
Instead of hairdressers asking L'Oréal why they suddenly offered
discounts, they were enamored that the biggest beauty company
wanted to do direct business with them. For me, it was disappointing

because of all the events we held exclusively for them. Many of our customers went direct and that would be the beginning of the end of our customer appreciation events.

Wendy's Wigs in Livonia, Michigan, was the place to go if you needed a fashion wig or you were a cancer patient (they have since closed). By now, TNG raised more than $1.2M for the ACS. The ACS partnered with Look Good Feel Better, which provided beauty advice, and techniques to help people with cancer face their diagnosis with greater confidence. One aspect of this was wigs. I thought this was the perfect tie-in for salons to collaborate with Look Good Feel Better and provide custom wigs for their clients undergoing cancer treatments. So, what does an entrepreneur do? Open the Raquel Welch Wig Showroom inside The Pavilion. The showroom featured more than a hundred different wigs, and it was beautiful. Our BDSs presented the program to their salon customers, and we all thought the response was going to be terrific. To our dismay, most hairdressers did not want to get involved with the program and yet another great idea went down the drain.

Luckily, for an entrepreneur, not all great ideas go down the drain. My next idea was a game-changer that completely transformed TNG. Now that we had both CND and OPI back, it was apparent that the demand for FPO professional use products including Pinnacle and Lightbox was going to be short-lived. However, what FPO continued to excel in was professional accessories including nail files, implements, pedicure tools, carbide drill bits, towels, and disposables. I had the brilliant idea to change FPO to ForPro Professional Collection and came up with a new logo. It was launched in 2008 and is now the number-one selling accessories brand in the beauty business.

On October 7, 2007, the Dow hit its high of 14,164. All was good until Lehman Brothers collapsed September 14, 2008. Stocks dove, and the government stepped in with a bailout on September 19 and the Dow rose to 11,483. Then all hell broke out and on October 10, the Dow hit its low of 7,882. The housing bubble and stock market crash were official, and home prices declined all the way through 2011. It was a hellacious time to be an investor, business owner, or banker.

It was a double-whammy for TNG. This was the first year without LP and Matrix except for the stores but at least we picked up the lost OPI business. But unlike previous recessions and the .com crash, consumers were spooked and cut back. For the first time in history, we had to let employees go and cut expenses. Our CFO at the time, Shawn Peralta, scheduled a special company meeting and outlined his plans for the layoffs. It went better than I expected and allowed us to cut underperforming employees. Still, it was an eye-opener. The annual meeting and party were already scheduled at the Ritz Carlton but it would be our last event at the Ritz. For the next five years, the event was held at our corporate headquarters.

Blogs were becoming a thing in 2008, and I decided to launch my blog, larrygaynor.com. It was the first blog in the professional beauty industry and would become the number-one blog over the years. It has been a great tool to inform my readers about TNG and the industry at large. I have posted nearly a thousand blogs covering people, companies, and products.

Sales were $66M, and we had 260 employees.

LIFE LESSON TIP: I always thought customer rewards programs were the best way to ensure customer loyalty. But I was wrong. The best hospitality brands include Four Seasons Resorts, Aman, and Rosewood. None of them offer loyalty programs, yet, they are leaders in the industry. Best tip: Offer products and/or services consumers want and they will be loyal to you. Everything else is just noise.

LESSON #64

Surveys Are Invaluable: Just Be Sure
You Are the One Conducting Them

ompany name changes are difficult at best. Since 1985, I used Nailco Manicurist Centers, Nailco Salon Marketplace, and TIS for the catalogs. I used both Nailco and The Nailco Group for the company name. At least the name of the catalog stayed consistent: thebeautybook. I thought about the business, who our customers were, and decided in 2009 that the company name needed a global presence. I still loved our tagline, "the beauty experts," and decided to change the company name one more time to TNG Worldwide (to this day, people ask me what "TNG" stands for, and yes, it stands for The Nailco Group).

The 2009 catalog debuted with the new TNG logo on the cover along with thebeautybook logo. Inside the front cover, I reviewed our company history and explained the changes. I even launched the latest version of our customer loyalty program, Nailco Gold, to keep the Nailco name fresh in our customer's mind. However, I was ahead of my time. Customers and our BDSs were confused and wondered what happened to TIS. It was a fight not worth fighting and the following year until the pandemic in 2020, the catalog reverted to TIS.

Nailco Gold was a membership-only program. Registration was complementary and available online only. Benefits included free shipping on orders $150 and over; free subscription to TNG Worldwide magazine and monthly e-newsletter; monthly discount codes and coupons, and free samples. However, the program only lasted a couple of years, and I renamed it Nailco Rewards in 2011. One thing about being an entrepreneur, you can never let things stay stagnant.

Windsor Beauty was a small local distributor that I mentioned earlier in the book. Moroccanoil came out in 2008, and Windsor Beauty got distribution rights. Moroccanoil launched with one product, Moroccanoil Hair Treatment. The product was an immediate success, and Windsor got greedy: They diverted it and got caught. I got a call from Moroccanoil asking me if TISE wanted to be a distributor and it was a slam-dunk decision.

I vividly recall that they wanted all orders to be a minimum of one pallet. The product was made in Israel, and they had high shipping costs plus long lead times to get the goods to the United States. Not knowing what sales were going to be, we agreed on half-pallets for the first few months. Then they launched their first shampoo and conditioner, got celebrity reviews, and next thing I knew, we were ordering pallets. We quickly did over $1M in sales the second year and would hit more than $2M in sales shortly thereafter. It was a great story.

The company held a distributor summit in Israel, and I happily attended. It was my first but not my last visit to Israel. Moroccanoil was thinking of launching a hair color line. They wanted feedback from their distributors. The meeting was loud and obnoxious with distributors vehemently telling the company not to launch hair color because the last thing anyone wanted was another hair color line. That is when I really learned that most distributors were clueless (feedback only made the company more valuable in a buyout), and they would learn their lesson in the next few years. Moroccanoil decided not to launch hair color but instead, decided to open multiple distributors in each state. Not only that, they later launched the entire line in Sephora. That was the one and only distributor trip.

Sales were $58M and we had 215 employees.

LIFE LESSON TIP: I have spent a lot of money on customer surveys. Remember the clipboards at GAYNORS? They were nothing more than an in-store survey about what customers wanted. Make surveys an integral part of your business strategy. Not only will you learn how you can improve your business operations, but you will learn which competitors you should focus on.

LESSON #65

When It Comes to Due Diligence, Never Do It Half-Assed

D amn the housing bust and damn the stock market. That was just noise. And here is a bonus life lesson: Drown out noise and focus on your own business because no one else will.

In 2010, TISE was still going strong regardless of losing Matrix and LP on the street. But I needed more brands and more growth, and an opportunity came my way. Salon Source was based in Houston, and the owners were contemplating selling. They had great brands: Davines, Nioxin, Joico, and Eufora. They had a few stores, decent sales team, and were doing around $5M in sales. So, what does an entrepreneur do? Get on a plane to Houston and meet with the owners, JD and his wife, Linda.

I got the nickel tour, visited a couple of their stores, talked strategy and numbers. I came back to Michigan and told my CFO to do due diligence. This was going to be my biggest acquisition to date and $5M was a lot of money. He did his due diligence and told me it was OK to proceed. JD and Linda came to Michigan, and I gave them the nickel tour. We then went out to dinner to review the final numbers, timing of the sale, and the launch date.

Their building was old and not worth buying. Besides, we had all the catalog items to sell to our new Texas customers and needed a bigger warehouse than what Salon Source had. So, what does an entrepreneur do? Open a distribution center in Dallas. The warehouse opening coincided with the live launch. I flew down to Houston and met with the sales team. Both JD and Linda were in the meeting. I announced the acquisition and that they would become TNG employees, they would be able to sell everything in thebeautybook and that they would make more money than ever. They were thrilled. We then went out to dinner and opened bottles of Dom Perignon. It was a celebration that wouldn't last long.

The next day I asked Linda for a sales report for their top-100 customers. I knew that my CFO already reviewed all the reports, but I wanted the most up-to-date one. Linda paused at my request and I wondered why. She ran the report. I reviewed it and was shocked to see such a high concentration of sales to a few customers. Usually, the 80/20 rule is a good one, but this was more like 90/10, and I was concerned.

Within a week, I found out that JD diverted most of his sales, especially the Nioxin brand. I also learned that JD did not have long-term contracts for most of his brands. This was not good news. I asked JD to get on the phone with the vendors to get the contracts extended. He was not successful. I tried too, but I had no relationship with the vendors. For the time being, we let business go on as usual.

Events were part of my early strategy to gain new salon business. I held a Fringe-type event at a downtown music theater. Complementary food and drinks were served. It was a huge success until the CEO of Eufora got on stage and made an ass of himself. We had to escort him off the stage. It put a damper on the entire night.

I also held an exclusive event for Salon Source's top customers at the Four Seasons Dallas. I offered complementary education during the day and a really nice sit-down dinner poolside at night. The party got rowdy later on. The sales manager for Davines ended up in the pool with his clothes on, and he egged me on to join him. I was new to the Texas scene and didn't know what to do, but I knew I wanted the brand in Michigan too. I jumped into the pool. It was all in good spirits, but the sales manager was a real jerk and our relationship was never the same afterward.

Long story short, I didn't buy Salon Source to divert professional goods, and the real business wasn't enough to justify the buyout. Vendor contracts were not renewed and my CFO failed miserably in doing his due diligence. However, I was on the hook for $5M and ended up suing JD for fraud and misleading documentation. We settled in mediation and closed the business and warehouse in 2012. It was yet another painful lesson to learn.

LIFE LESSON TIP: Even when you have experts working for you or hired, always be part of the due diligence effort when doing an acquisition or making a major investment. I made many acquisitions before this one and I wrongly depended on someone else to make the final decision.

LESSON #66

When Others Are Struggling and Cutting Back, Move Forward

In 2010, IT'S A 10 Leave-In Conditioner was a big seller, and Tony Cuccio worked with a factory that could knock it off for me (kind of like Costco does with the Kirkland's brand). I thought about it and knew being a manufacturer was the key to long-term success. I've done well with ForPro, why not try hair care? So, what does an entrepreneur do? Launch Black 15-in-1. If I was going to compete, I had to have a better product and I came up with fifteen benefits. It was a 3.3 oz spray leave-in conditioner treatment, and it retailed for $20. Packaging was black and magical, and it was boxed as a premium item. I put the same manager as FPO in charge to sell to distributors.

I quickly learned that launching a premium hair care product was expensive, time-consuming, and risky (all the favorite buzzwords entrepreneurs love). The manufacturer came through as Tony said they would and the product performed. I hired a private testing company to test for the fifteen claims. They did a test with a hundred users over a thirty-day period. The test results came back perfect, and we were ready to launch.

But first, I needed a marketing campaign. I researched the best PR agencies in NYC that specialized in beauty products. I hired Shadow PR and put them on a $10K monthly retainer. They recommended that I hire a professional photographer and use professional models so they could use the photos to create magazine ads and use for their beauty editors. I hired one of the best and spent $25K on the photo shoot.

Then I thought that I needed another hook for consumers to buy the product. Competition was fierce and Black 15-in-1 was a new brand and a new product in a crowded field. I came up with the idea of contacting Good Housekeeping and getting the Good Housekeeping seal on the product. It was an extensive process, but what I later learned is that you had to advertise in their magazine to get approved. I thought that if the scheme worked for giant companies like P&G, why shouldn't it work for Black 15-in-1? I signed up with them. The product was approved for the seal, and my PR firm loved the idea. However, spending $85K for a quarter-page ad was painful.

The product launched at the BBSI show. I spent more than $50K for an elaborate booth and it was all decked out in purple and black, the colors for the product. My manager and I were ready for action. My lead designer at The Pavilion, Leslie McGwire, was friends with Jonathan Antin. He was the celebrity hairdresser on Bravo's show, *Blowout*. I loved the show; there was no cooler hairdresser than Jonathan. He launched his signature product "Dirt" on the show, and it became a bestseller. There he was at my booth and it was the first time I ever met a TV celebrity. It was kind of cool, and his persona was the same as on the show.

He checked out the product and told me that together we could make lots of money. His pitch was that he knew the producer at Shop NBC, which was a competitor to QVC. With Jonathan as the lead stylist for Black 15-in-1 and going live on TV, what could have been better? So what does an entrepreneur do? Sign Jonathan up.

Now here is yet another life lesson for entrepreneurs: There is nothing worse than dealing with celebrities. Jonathan had an agent, complex contracts, and I needed my Dykema attorney to review everything. Jonathan's fees were $50,000 and a piece of the action. But hey, I was hooked and Jonathan was convincing.

I distinctly recall flying to Minneapolis and meeting Jonathan at Shop NBC. It was the first time I saw a live TV production set and we met with the producers. He arranged for a model call, he picked two, and went to work in the dressing room. He was impressive to watch styling the models and they were gorgeous. We had a five-minute live segment. The set producer came into the dressing room and said we were going live in ten minutes.

We were hoping to sell a thousand units or more (I would need to sell more than five thousand units to break even). I sat behind the set and watched Jonathan put the finishing touches on the model's hair. It was electrifying. But alas, we didn't even sell five hundred units. Although I knew Shop NBC was a distant third to the QVC and the Home Shopping Network, I didn't know how distant it was until that day. If we were on QVC, it would have been a smash success. But Jonathan thought Shop NBC was best. In the end, he got paid and I lost my ass.

If you thought this was enough for one entrepreneur in one year, you would be wrong. Damn the housing bust and falling stock market. Here is yet another life lesson: When others are struggling and cutting back, move forward. It has always been this way in the stock market. Once all the retail investors sold their stocks, the pros came in and made a quick 20–30 percent.

I got a call from EV. EV worked at Ready Care Industries, and they were sort of a competitor. They specialized in locker room products and sold some accessories. EV wanted out and to come work for TNG. I flew him out and we had lunch at J. Alexander's (EV's name is Ed Verbeke, but I always called him EV). He wanted to start a hospitality division at TNG. We were already selling treatment room products to spas but not locker room supplies. His argument was that if we offered both treatment and locker room products, spas could buy everything from TNG. His argument was compelling.

EV was a talker and to tell you the truth, a real pain in the ass. But in-between bites of his cheeseburger, I could tell he was passionate about the hospitality business. Now mind you, if you asked me what business segment was my favorite at TNG, I would have told you spas. I love spas. I love getting massages. I love relaxing in the spa lounge with a comfy robe and cup of hot chamomile tea. I love spa locker rooms with their hot tubs, steam rooms, and saunas. I love the fresh fruit and nuts and ambient music. I love the amenities in the sink area from mouthwash, to ready-to-use toothbrushes, and all the personal care products. Resort spas were the best (and still are), especially five-star properties such as the Four Seasons, Ritz Carlton, Canyon Ranch, and Rosewood. Vegas's claim to fame when it moved from being kid-friendly to adult-only was in part their investment in spas. Best of all, they were all TNG customers, and I thought EV might be right.

So what does an entrepreneur do? Hire EV and launch the hospitality division. This was really big news and so much in fact, I have to write an entire chapter on it.

> ## 2010 sales were $57M, and there were two hundred employees.

LIFE LESSON TIP: Chickens can't fly and retreat when things get tough. Entrepreneurs are soaring eagles and move forward when things get tough. Amazing opportunities always arise after a crisis.

LESSON #67

Recruiting Key Talent Is Crucial
for Continued Success

E V lived in NY, and he was anxious to get back all of his lost Ready Care business and then some. I was anxious to start the new division and invest whatever was needed to make it successful. So much so, in fact, I put it as the first section in the next catalog and devoted more than twenty pages to it.

The lead category for locker rooms was personal care products: shampoo, conditioner, body wash, and hand lotion. I was quite aware of the products from both Hairco and TIS (but none of the brands we sold focused on locker rooms). EV told me that we had to launch ten fragrances in one-gallon sizes and offer samples sizes of each product. In all my years at TNG, the most fragrances that any company offered were four to six. I asked him why we couldn't start with four to six and he told me, "Larry, you don't understand, I have many types of customers. Some of them are located in mountains and want a eucalyptus scent; some of them are located in beach properties and they want sweet scents like coco mango; and some of them are located in urban areas and they want relaxing scents like green tea lemongrass." Oh, we needed fragrance-free too.

Right off the bat, EV wanted 44 SKUs of gallons and sample sizes. But he didn't stop there. "Larry, we need two formulations. One formulation has to be spa-quality for high-end spas. The other formulation has to be for fitness centers and golf clubs, still good, but cheaper." I convinced him that we would start with spa formulation. Then he said, "Larry, I have to tell you, we will also need to make custom products for our best customers as they want their own blended fragrances." We were only thirty minutes into the meeting, and I was already getting dizzy.

EV went on to say that we needed to manufacture custom dispenser holders not only for showers but for in-room bathrooms as well (back then some hotels used dispensers in showers instead of small size amenities). I learned that we would need to make eighteen different models, some in plastic and some in stainless steel. But wait! We also needed bottles to go into the holders. We needed them in four sizes; we needed them in white, amber, clear, and frosted. We needed them in HDPE, PET, and aluminum. But wait! We also needed pumps, caps, and sprayers for the bottles. And if that wasn't enough, we had to silk-screen the bottles with the customer's logo.

Then came the locker room supplies we needed. Brand name products like Listerine, Colgate, Right Guard, Secret, and Barbasol; specialty products like Flossers, ReadyBrush, and LA Fresh Wipes; and our own branded mouthwash, shaving crème, hairspray, disposable shavers, brushes, and combs. We even had to bring in tampons and maxi-thins. It was like reliving GAYNORS all over again. In fact, I went back to the same wholesaler to buy these products. It was crazy.

EV also sold a lot of in-room accessories so I had to bring in loofah mitts, body brushes, shower caps, sewing kits, and plush slippers. We had to offer custom bar soaps, turn down sweets, vanity kits, and wet bags. And finally, for fitness centers, we needed gloves, disinfectants, wipes, and wipe dispensers. YIKES!

We met with a manufacturer to make our personal care products. But first, I needed to come up with a brand name. I already had ForPro Professional Collection, Pinnacle, and CLUB1 but none of those worked. I wanted a brand name that would resonate with high-end spas and consumers. The products had to be natural, contain essential oils, be botanical-rich, and free of bad ingredients. That is when I recalled taking my kids to Mayberry Farms in Northville. Mayberry had farm animals, gardens, nature trails, and was a great place to spend an afternoon. I also thought back to my Raku days when all the nail polishes were named after a flower. I then "Google-searched" exotic flowers and the ginger lily plant was one among many that popped up. I took "ginger lily" and "farms" and came up with the brand, Ginger Lily Farms. As much as a pain-in-the-ass EV was with all his needs and custom bullshit products, it was all worth it because of Ginger Lily Farms. While the division wouldn't survive the test of time, Ginger Lily Farms went on to become the number-one bestseller of one-gallon personal care products.

LIFE LESSON TIP: There is a reason why there are so many recruiters in business: they serve specialized needs for CEOs and entrepreneurs. Sometimes you need to hire recruiters to start a new division or to get into certain doors. They are expensive but worth the cost.

PART 5
THE GOOD, THE BAD, AND THE UGLY

2010–2019

LESSON #68

It's OK to Be Friends with Your Vendors, but Understand the Difference Between Business Friends and Personal Friends

Essie

5:45 p.m., Tuesday. I dial 1-800-232-1155 (don't ask me why I still know this number by heart),

"Essie Cosmetics, may I help you please?" said Essie with a lilt to her voice.

I said, in the same manner that Howard Stern imitates his mother, "Yes, I would like to order a bottle of Baby's Breath and Ballet Slipper."

Essie responded back, "Is there anything else you would like to order?" and I replied, "No."

"Would you like to pay by credit card or C.O.D.?" I told her C.O.D. She responded back to me,

"OK, the total comes to $9.24 and we will ship your order tomorrow." Essie didn't care that Nailco was her distributor, she still sold direct.

That's Essie in a nutshell. All her employees had already left for the day, but she was still in the office, and if a customer called to place an order, she would answer the phone and take it.

Her parents were European Jews that immigrated to NYC. Her father passed on early, but her mother would live well into her nineties. I already told you that she got her start in the beauty business working for Forsythe and then went on her own. Essie didn't invent nail polish; she didn't come up with the concept to sell unbranded bottles for $1; and she didn't even invent the idea of coming up with cute names for nail polish. As a matter of fact, Essie wasn't an entrepreneur or a businesswoman, she was a hybrid but mostly she was customer-centric and worked nonstop.

Essie was single most of her adult life, never had kids or pets, and her only passions outside of Essie Cosmetics were her mother and cooking. And she loved to hoard. I will never forget visiting her Malibu condo and opening up one of her kitchen cabinets. BUB loves Nespresso, and we always have at least ten sleeves on hand. Essie had more than a hundred. Instead of one Costco pack of toilet paper and paper towels, she had six of each. I won't even tell you the number of cans of tuna, olive oil and red wine vinegar she had. I asked her why she had so much of everything, and she told me, "Larry, you can never be certain when you are going to need the stuff; I just want to be prepared." Essie was always prepared.

Max

Max was raised an hour outside of Bologna, Italy, and came to the United States in his late teens with broken English, good looks, and a desire to become rich. More than anything, Max loved to have fun. Instead of heading to NYC like most immigrants at the time, he went to Southern California, the perfect place for beautiful women, beaches, and plenty of sunshine.

Max never went to college, but he was street smart like Tony Cuccio (while both were Italian, they could not have been more different). Max learned about the nail industry and went to a nail trade show in the late 1980s. This was the time nail art took off. I remember when we had more than twenty catalog pages devoted to nail art. We sold gold fingernails from Snails, rhinestones from Kami, and airbrushing equipment and paint from San Francisco Nails. Marlene owned Snails, and we did a lot of business together. Marlene was an entrepreneur and was always introducing new nail art designs and products. What she wasn't was a businesswoman. At the nail show, Max visited her booth and started up a conversation. That led to dinner that night and shortly thereafter, they got together and eventually got married and had twins. Max got involved with the business and it was renamed Snails Italian Jewelry. Max was the perfect business partner for Marlene, and the business grew.

Essie

Back in the 1980s and 1990s, there were three major beauty trade shows that I mentioned earlier in the book. There were also nail-only shows, spa shows that included nails, and my annual show. Altogether, there were ten shows a year that manufacturers had to do. Essie was at every single show. She brought her office staff and set the booth up, ran the booth during the show, and tore the booth down when the show ended. All the nail techs knew Essie by name because she was the one boxing the bottles of nail polish, doing the cash transactions, and giving out her business cards. At the NY show, her mother always worked the booth. She was a workaholic.

Essie needed a business manager to take her business to the next level. However, she trusted no one but her mother. Unlike most of the other vendors I dealt with, Essie kept to herself. She was never on the phone with the likes of Tony or George. She was a bulldog.

Max and Essie

Eventually, Max, now divorced, and Essie got together at a trade show and they started to date. Over time, they became more serious and eventually married in 2015. They could not have been more opposite, but they had one thing in common: They both loved business. Max moved to NYC and became Essie's business partner. That is when my relationship with both of them took off. Even BUB got involved since we had a lot in common. We both owned our own businesses. Max and I were divorced with kids. Max and I were a year apart. Essie and BUB loved to cook. We all loved to travel. What we didn't have in common was that they were a manufacturer, and we were a distributor. But for the time being, that didn't matter.

As Essie's business partner, Max opened domestic and international distributors. He offered a take-it or leave-it 40 percent margin. He told distributors to order what they needed because he didn't take returns. He called *The Industry Source* "The Industry Soup" and always made fun of my business model. However, I helped to make him rich. He never participated at my charity events nor would he advertise in my trade magazine. Yet besides all this, we became friends. In fact, I would call him several times a week on my way home from work, and we would talk industry bullshit.

In the 1990s, they invited us to Maui for an all-expenses paid vacation for a week. We stayed at the Four Seasons, and it was the first time we ever stayed at a five-star resort. It was amazing. Poolside, attendants came by with cold Evian water and sprayed your face. The service was perfect. It was my first taste of the hospitality business. I will never forget when we did the volcano sunrise bike ride one early morning. The tour company picked us up at three in the morning and drove us to the top of the volcano. It was foggy, cold, and drizzling. But the sun never rose. We took bikes down the mountain and had breakfast at this really cool restaurant halfway down. Max didn't want to get wet or cold, so he followed us in a bus. It was comical.

A few years later, they took us to Rome and Florence. We stayed at the best hotels, and with Max's ability to speak Italian, we learned many local traditions. But mostly, we learned about Fiore, pizza, gelato, pastries, and fine Italian red wines. It was a magical trip and we always got along. We were invited to his kid's Bar Mitzvah's in Miami and his son's wedding in San Diego.

I also got to see how a manufacturer lived compared to a distributor. As you recall, Essie's sales peak was $28 million and TNG's was more than triple that. However, their margins were triple, and they made serious profits. I loved their NYC "apartment" on Madison Avenue, two stories with fabulous balcony views. We had dinner at the fine Italian restaurant down the block at which they were regulars. I never knew pasta to be so good. I loved their Hamptons beach house (although it was a couple of miles from the beach). Complete with pool and Vespas, it was quite the getaway. And I loved their Malibu condo overlooking the Pacific Ocean.

One day in 2010, I got a call from Essie. "Hi Larry, it's Essie. I just want you to know before you hear it from someone else that we sold the company to L'Oréal." Before I could respond, she hung up. I was in shock. But I was in even more shock when I learned they sold the company for more than five times sales. Moreover, they were given positions at L'Oréal for seven years, and their compensation would go up based on sales growth over that period. Once again, I helped another company sell out and get rich.

It would be the start of the decline of the professional nail business. What L'Oréal did next was predictable, they took the line retail, increased Essie sales to $350 million, and ultimately killed professional sales. That sucked but what happened next was even worse.

LIFE LESSON TIP: Rarely do business friendships continue once you stop doing business together. It's amazing how fast you go your separate ways. It's OK to enjoy the friendship while it lasts but never stake your business on it.

LESSON #69

Entrepreneurs Often Help Others Get Rich; Don't Look for Your Fair Share

---

G eorge Schaeffer was one of a kind.

His story started out familiarly enough, his parents were Hungarian Jews who immigrated to New York City. After college, he went to work at his parents' garment factory in Queens. His ambition was to own his own company, and he waited for the opportunity. The opportunity came when his father's cousin wanted to get out of the dental supply business. So, what does an entrepreneur do? Buy Odontorium Dental Supply in 1981 and move to Southern California.

George needed a soul mate and went out on a blind date. He fell in love with Miriam, and they got married. Miriam had a sister, Suzi, who George thought would be a perfect fit for his company and hired her. It was a brilliant hire. You already know what happened next from Lesson #25, now it's time for the rest of the story.

I always called him "Georgie George" because he had such a lovable fat face, and I loved to squeeze it. He was a giant teddy bear and had a passion for everything: business, food, wine, money, and, mostly, himself. I never met a person who loved to celebrate himself more than George did. I will never forget his fiftieth birthday party at the BBSI show in 1997. There had to be five hundred people in the ballroom. He had a master of ceremonies roast him. He brought in celebrities and a first-class band to entertain everyone. He had *Nailpro* do a satire on him, "Where's George?" God knows how much money he spent on the party. No one spent money like him.

George was the ultimate entrepreneur and businessman. He had vision like no other manufacturer in the nail business. At the BBSI show, he took a huge booth that had at least eight meeting tables because he had so many distributors. He gave away gifts to distributors based on their purchase volume. I got gold and silver bars, a gold Mont Blanc pen, and BUB got her first and only gold Chanel watch. I remember that one year someone asked him for a hundred bucks and he took out his money clip and gave the person a hundred dollars. The money clip was made with a twenty-dollar gold coin. I loved it. "Larreeee, here, it's yours!" I still use it to this day. That was George, generous unlike anyone else. He even commissioned an artist to do custom OPI prints for his $1M distributors. He sent one every year for many years.

Nevertheless, he was shrewd. He gave distributors the barest 40 percent margin (Max learned most everything from him but would never admit it). He never offered deals on nail lacquer. There were no cash discounts. His terms were net thirty, and you best pay on time.

He was brilliant too. I remember coming to North Hollywood to visit his factory. I cannot say I was impressed because it was the oddest collection of buildings. One building had bulk nail polish, one building was pro products, one building was finished goods, and one building was offices and R&D. George told me he never wanted to move. When he produced his semi-annual collections, he had to store the pallets in the parking lot and pray for no rain. However, I was impressed with his inventory levels. I knew how much we ordered from him, and OPI had the highest fill rate. When I saw the inventory live, I knew why. He told me, "Larreee, you can't sell goods if you don't have them in stock." We were very much alike except for the fact that he was eccentric and a manufacturer, and I was a lowly distributor.

Nobody liked gadgets more than George did. When he took me to his office he pointed at the shower stall in his bathroom and said, "Look Larreee, I installed a built-in urinal in the shower so I can piss in the shower." I had never seen that before in my life and still haven't since.

I can't say that George was a mentor to me, but I learned a lot from him. He also opened my eyes to the finer things in life. He invited me to stay at his house in Beverly Hills; this was after we got back together to do business in 2007. His house was a gated mansion, and I was in awe. He started the tour in his garage. It was heated, had epoxy floors, a car wash, and something I had never seen before, a brand-new Rolls Royce. As I sat in it, he touted his embroidered initials on the front seats. Then again, he had his initials engraved in the front windows of his mansion too.

We then visited his wine cellar, which any five-star restaurant would have envied. I consider myself fortunate to have a mini cellar with two hundred bottles. His immense cellar had well over three thousand bottles. I asked him, "George, how do you plan on drinking all of them," and he told me, "Ah, I just like looking at them." The tour went on as he pointed out his private elevator, introduced me to his full-time housekeeper and cook, and then took me outside to the backyard. There was a swimming pool and another housing structure. That is where his kids lived. I then noticed all the furniture was covered and I asked him why, "The salt kills the finish so I just cover it to protect it." He never used the pool or the furniture.

Finally, he took me to my guest room and said to me as he opened up this enormous closet, "Pick whatever amenities you want for the bathroom." Inside the cabinet there had to be two thousand bottles of hotel amenities. George collected them from previous hotel visits; he too was a hoarder. I won't bore you with his art collection. George confirmed to me that being a manufacturer was the way to go, as that was where the real money was.

In a strange way, we had more than a friendship. He was eight years older than I, and we formed a bond. I think more than any other distributor he did business with, he liked me the best. He told me many times that when he cut me off in 1997, it wasn't personal, it was just business. When I asked him in 2008 at the BBSI meeting if it was OK for me to sell OPI Nail Lacquer on Amazon, he thought it over

for a few minutes and gave me the green light and the exclusive rights. He also made sure our orders were prioritized.

One last story about his vision. At the August 1999 BBSI show, George held a breakfast meeting for all his distributors (even the BBSI shows were all about George). After everyone feasted, he got on stage and said, "I am concerned about our industry's future, not just OPI's." He went on to say,

"No industry, including ours, is immune from paradigm shifts. We must be prepared to seize the moment." He presented his concept of the "Professional Beauty Center." He wanted full-service distributor stores to be divided: one section for pros that sold hair color, acrylics, etc., and one section for consumers and pros that sold retail products like nail lacquer and hair care. He saw what Ulta and Sephora were doing, and this was his solution. It never happened. If you asked George what his great failure was, he would have told you it was this.

One day in 2010, I got a call from George, "Hi Larreee, it's George. I just want you to know before you hear it from someone else that I sold the company to Coty." Before I could respond, he hung up. I was in shock. However, I was in even more shock when I learned OPI sold for nearly $1 billion, yes, that is, $1,000,000,000. Once again, I helped another company sell out and get rich.

With both Essie and OPI sold in the same year, the professional nail business would never be the same. Coty killed the brand and ended up selling it to KKR along with Wella, Clairol, and ghd.

In case you are wondering, George is alive and well. Not only did he get into the pro hair color business with the purchase of Aloxi, he bought an insurance agency in Florida that, at the time, was one of the top agencies in the state for property liability insurance. In 2021, George celebrated his seventy-fifth birthday and guess what? He brought in John Heffner as his master of ceremonies. George hasn't changed.

LIFE LESSON TIP: Business is a game and you need a lot of players to play. Some players get rich, some players go broke. Always stay focused on your business; as long as you are growing and profitable, that's the only thing that matters.

LESSON #70

Hairco On The Go: Instacart and Door Dash Before Their Time

Hairco was on a roll, but there was one category that we could not get traction: shears. Hairdressers love their shears and spent upward of $500 a pair and sometimes owned four to six pairs. I thought it was a great business to get into.

I went to many tradeshows and met with shear companies. However, most sold direct to hairdressers and didn't want to deal with lowly distributors (who could blame them?). The best-quality shears came from Japan, and after a lot of research, I found a fabulous company that would sell to us.

However, the secret sauce in selling shears is being able to sharpen them. Most companies provide a sharpening service for a fee; the hairdresser sends the shears to the factory, and a few weeks later, they get them back. But this was too time-consuming for most hairdressers. For that reason, there were local sharpeners who went from salon to salon to sharpen shears. They would pick them up, take them to their shop, and bring them back in a day or two. I contacted the top-two to partner with, and neither wanted to get involved with a lowly distributor.

So, what does an entrepreneur do? Open Hairco To Go! This was one of my craziest ideas ever, and once again proves that when an entrepreneur gets an idea, sometimes there is no stopping it from happening. Allan and Teresa owned a knife shop in a local mall that also did knife sharpening. I asked them if they could sharpen shears, and their answer was yes. Further, they wanted to get out of the mall and start something fresh. Bam! It was time for some excitement.

I learned about the best sharpening equipment for shears and bought it. But I had to come up with an innovative concept to attract hairdressers to our shears bypassing the existing shear factories and local sharpeners. I bought a truck and outfitted it with a generator, shelving, pegboard, and I made it into a store in the back and sharpening area in the front. It was genius.

Allan and Teresa drove the truck salon to salon. The truck not only offered shears and sharpening service but also offered hair color, accessories, capes, and supplies. Hairdressers could walk on the truck and shop. It was an amazing concept.

The truck cost $80,000, and with both Allen's and Teresa's salaries, it had to generate more than $200,000 a year in business to justify itself. The plan was to have a Hairco To Go truck in every major city in Michigan.

Alas, even with all our expertise in the business, we still couldn't sway hairdressers to buy shears from us and trust us to sharpen their shears that the locals have been doing for years. It was a tremendous disappointment and had to be shut down in less than a year.

LIFE LESSON TIP: There is an old expression, "If it ain't broke, don't fix it." Entrepreneurs hate that expression, but sometimes in rare instances, it really is true. It was another expensive life lesson to learn but wouldn't stop me from coming up with even more wild ideas.

LESSON #71

Always Trademark and Protect Your Brands

CND was cursed from the beginning when Dr. Nordstrom founded the company. As you recall, he was a dentist and figured out how to use dental acrylic for nails. He had two sons, Jim and Tommy, and one daughter, Jan. The three kids couldn't have been more different. They eventually sold to Revlon. Jan stayed on (and is still with CND as of this writing).

In 2000, Revlon sold CND, American Crew, and Revlon Professional to The Colomer Group for $315 million. They sold the company back to Revlon in 2013 for $660 million (as of this writing, Revlon is emerging from bankruptcy).

Now for the rest of the story.

CND launched Shellac in 2010. Shellac was the first gel polish that went on like nail polish but lasted for two weeks. CND launched with twelve colors and *The Industry Source* was first to get it. No one could have predicted the outcome of the launch, but suffice it to say, the launch of acrylic nails in the 1980s was pale in comparison. Nail techs loved it because it was the first new innovative service in more than a decade. Consumers loved it because they could go two weeks without having to change their nail polish, and they could work, swim, and exercise without worries of their polish chipping.

When OPI launched a new lacquer collection, we typically ordered 480 of each color. That is what we did with Shellac. We sold out instantly. We reordered 5,000 bottles of each color. CND could not keep up with production. Suddenly, Shellac classes were selling out as nail techs wanted to learn all about Shellac. One issue with Shellac was removing it. It wouldn't come off with acetone or polish remover. It had to be soaked off. It would take years to figure out the best way to remove it, but no one cared. All consumers could say when they walked into a salon was, "I WANT A SHELLAC MANICURE."

Unfortunately, they did not patent the product nor did they do proper trademark registration. Mind you, there are three main companies in the world that supply the stuff that goes into nail polish. All three companies are adept at knocking each other off when it comes to product innovation. Colomer didn't own any of the manufacturers; they only contracted from them. Nevertheless, they could have done more to protect the brand. OPI launched its competitive product, GelColor in 2013, so Shellac had the market to themselves for three full years. They were CND's greatest days.

Revlon saw what was going on with Shellac, wanted back in, and rebought the Colomer Group. It would be one of Revlon's worst decisions and help lead to their demise. By the time Revlon bought it, Shellac didn't have just OPI to compete against, it had the world.

Quick question for you: How many brand names can you list right now that are the same as the product name (these are called eponyms). I'll give you a few minutes to think (stop reading while you are thinking!).

Here are the most popular eponyms in no particular order: Kleenex, Band-aid, Jeep, Jell-O, Chapstick, Vaseline, Velcro, and Shellac.

Shellac was so popular that discount nail salons had to bring it in. At the time, they all had Essie and OPI nail polish and their own private-label brands. Unlike nail polish sold in a .5-oz bottle for a few dollars, Shellac was sold in a .25-oz bottle for $15.95. CND's pricing and bottle size were both brilliant. If they only had a patent. When OPI launched GelColor, it was .5 oz for $16.99 and instantly stole market share. Discount nail salons would pay up in the beginning, but once again, because CND didn't have a patent, discount nail salons would kill the brand in just a few short years.

Today, walk into any discount nail salon and the first question asked is "What can I do for you today?" The consumer mostly says, "I want a Shellac manicure." Instantly, the owner says, "Pick a color," and they don't even have Shellac in the salon, they have their own private label. Worse, consumers don't care; they just want gel nails that last two weeks.

This was such a sad story. CND sales went from $40 million to more than $100 million because of Shellac in three years. Shellac made CND relevant again. Jan was having the time of her life. The ending could have been so much different only if…. Let me repeat this life lesson: ALWAYS TRADEMARK AND PROTECT YOUR BRANDS!

Shellac was the last product innovation and helped to kill the professional nail industry.

LIFE LESSON TIP: You need a driver's license to drive. You need a passport to travel internationally. And you need a trademark if you are launching a new brand. Competitors and counterfeiters will attack if they see success in a new offering, so always be prepared.

LESSON #72

Sometimes You Have to Reach for the Top

This is a good time to talk about Amazon not because anything special happened in 2011, but it is important that you, my loyal reader, understand how Amazon became TNG's biggest customer and sales platform.

Amazon first launched health and personal care products in 2003 and added beauty in 2004. If you recall, TNG launched its first website in 1995. When Amazon added personal care and beauty, it was an excellent opportunity for TNG. As a catalog company, what technological segment was better than the internet? Now that Amazon was getting into our space, it would become the best of two worlds.

In 2005, I started to host a vendor conference at TheAcademy before the Fringe event, and I did these for three straight years. Most of my major vendors attended, and it was my time to sell them on my vision for the future, which was Amazon. Georgie George had it right in 1999 about being concerned for the future of the professional beauty industry. I was relaying the same concerns at my vendor conferences.

I told them that Amazon was the future of beauty, and we needed to sell our products on Amazon now. Remember, the bulk of the vendor's sales went to full-service distributors who sold them to salons, and salons resold the products to their clients. They could not sell direct to Amazon because it would have created a conflict of interest. I knew that, and it was the basis of my sales pitch to them, "Let TNG sell your products, and we will be the reseller on record, not you." It was brilliant.

I convinced some vendors to sign up right away. Others were hesitant because they weren't certain that Amazon would be successful selling salon products. And the rest didn't want to take the risk. In 2006 and 2007, I continued to hammer home that Amazon was not going away, and they had no choice but to sell their products on Amazon. In the end, they all agreed that there wasn't any other distributor they had that could do what TNG could do: sell to Amazon direct.

There are three ways of selling products on Amazon. The first is Seller Central (SC). SC is the simplest and least effective method: You list your products on Amazon and ship orders from your warehouse. Amazon takes their commission. It is the least effective method because Amazon Prime customers do not get one- to two-day delivery.

The second way is Vendor Central (VC): You sell your products directly to Amazon. They pick them up at your warehouse, ship them to their warehouses, and are responsible for selling and shipping the products to their customers. All VC products receive the Prime badge (Prime was launched in 2005). This was the primary method I used to sell our products and only used SC when VC ran out.

The third way is Fulfillment by Amazon (FBA): You ship your products to Amazon warehouses. Amazon is responsible for shipping the products to their customers and the seller is responsible for the sale. All FBA products receive the Prime badge. FBA was launched in 2006 and now accounts for 60 percent of Amazon's retail business.

TNG did not utilize FBA until Daniel came back to the company in 2020.

TNG was selling its best brands on Amazon including CND, OPI, Helen of Troy, Biotone, Star, Amber, ForPro, and Ginger Lily Farms, among others. By 2011, TNG sold well over $1M on Amazon. While we were doing this, none of the full-service distributors were paying attention and both Salon Centric and BSG couldn't do a thing about it. Even Sally Beauty, who did not launch their website until 2001, was clueless because they didn't want to lose in-store sales. I blazed a trail that would eventually take me to the pot of gold (I love books with happy endings!).

You can call me an "Amazonian," even though I am not technically one (you have to work for Amazon to gain that distinction). When Jeff Bezos launched Amazon in 1994, I was on board. The only difference between Jeff and I are a few 0's in net worth. Otherwise, we are the same: serial entrepreneurs. Here is another life lesson worth memorizing: In the scheme of things, there will always be someone ahead of you and behind you in everything that you do. This means there is always someone that makes more money than you do and someone that makes less money than you do. The point of this life lesson is not to get wrapped up in this and to focus on what you do best. Jeff will always be a mentor even though Andy now runs the company.

Speaking of Jeff, although he was once the richest man in the world and still worth more than $150 billion, his email address has always been jeff@amazon.com. I have emailed Jeff three different times, each time to express an idea that I thought would be great for Amazon. All three times he responded back to me within twenty-four hours (OK, not Jeff personally, but one of his assistants). Jeff was that kind of guy. In fact, I learned from Jeff that CEOs of big corporations are just guys and they want to communicate with other CEOs and customers too. I came up with the subject line: From One CEO to another CEO years ago. I have sent emails to the CEOs of Costco, Walmart, Delta, Four Seasons, Starbucks, and many others. Every time, they responded back to me, some within the hour.

One of my favorite books is *The Everything Store* by Brad Stone, published in 2013. I highly recommend it if you want to learn more about Jeff, how he survived the .com crash, and why Jeff is perhaps the most brilliant entrepreneur of all time. The year 2013 was also when Amazon launched premium beauty, and once again, one of the fucking rep groups was in part responsible for this and yet another reason for the demise of the pro beauty industry. More Amazon stuff to come!

> 2011 sales were $58 million, and we had 210 employees.

LIFE LESSON TIP: Never be afraid to contact the CEO of any company if you have a passionate reason for doing so. I know as a CEO that I would rather get an email from a passionate customer about an issue than to learn about it secondhand when damage control is too late. Conversely, I also love to read compliments so I can share them with my team.

LESSON #73

Make Sure Your Best People Have Signed Noncompetes

We ran out of office space in Farmington Hills, and we moved at the end of 2012 to the GLC, which I renamed TNG Global Headquarters. We hired Scarcello again for design services, and the new space was splendid. The first level had a call center with forty brand-new Knoll workstations and a lunchroom. The second level featured the marketing and web team, financial solutions along with BUB's and my offices.

Just down the street from our Farmington Hills building, a perfect location became available for us to create our new flagship store. I hired Davis & Davis to make it one of the classiest beauty supply stores in the business, much like Sephora. It was beautiful and featured all our products, and we added TheAcademy. It would stay that way for ten years until we finally shut it down and moved it to our headquarters.

Vince Davis was the VP of Sales for TIGI. TISE was one of TIGI's best-performing distributors and had the largest sales for a single state, more than $6 million annually. As you may recall, Unilever bought TIGI in 2009, and there were always concerns that they would hire their own sales team and get rid of the lowly distribu-tors. Those concerns came to fruition when Vince paid me a visit. I had known Vince for years, and he was a good guy, always traveling with his backpack (I was never a backpack type of guy). He supported everything we did. I thought the visit was to give us more territory.

He opened his backpack and took out a single piece of paper. It was a termination letter. He said to me, "Larry, I want you to know that I really respect you and want to thank you for all the business you have done with TIGI. But the company has changed its strategic path and I have no choice but to terminate you." I asked when it was going to take place as L'Oréal at least gave me a few months. "It's effective immediately," he said somberly, and he added, "I didn't want to tell you on the phone, that's why I made this visit."

We had just launched Brocato and Neuma, but neither of those lines even collectively came close to $1 million in sales. I asked him about the stores. He said it was a complete termination, no stores either. I would say that I was devastated, but by now I was used to ter-minations and was as calm as I could be. Unilever was a $50 billion+ company, and Vince was only doing what he was told to do. I asked him, "What compensation is Unilever giving me for the business I just lost?" He replied, "They don't do compensation but I will take your entire inventory back at full distributor cost." It really does suck to be a lowly distributor.

A couple of weeks later, my TISE sales manager and two of my top BDSs came to my office and resigned. They told me that TIGI made them an offer they could not refuse. So not only did I lose my top hair care brand, TIGI stole my best people as well. It was another fucking life lesson to learn: Make sure your best people have signed noncompetes. There was nothing we could legally do. Game over.

Speaking of game over, bebeautiful's strategy for selling unique beauty products was ending with Amazon's surge into beauty. Spanx cut us off, and other brands would not sell to us because we were too small or they could sell on Amazon. The division was doing $6 million a year but wasn't profitable due to heavy marketing costs. Daniel was being a bit rebellious, and it was time for him to move on. He decided to get his MBA at Duke and then took a position at Sears Holdings followed by a move to United Airlines. It would be ten years before he would make his way back to TNG, where he would find his true calling.

2012 sales were $55 million and we had 260 employees.

LIFE LESSON TIP: I can't tell you how many employees left TNG over the years to take a better position at another company. I am always thrilled when that happens as long as the other company is not a competitor. Noncompetes are only a legal tool, effective in some states and not in others. They send a message to your employees that you mean business and, in most instances, have intangible benefits.

LESSON #74

Never Get too Comfortable with Vendors;
Do Competitive Price Checks Annually

have always called Tony Cuccio "Tony!" He's my Sicilian friend
I wrote about in Lesson #35. The only thing the two of us have
in common is that we don't wear socks. Oh, and we are both
entrepreneurs. You already read that Tony! made CLUB1, many
Pinnacle products, and most of my private-label stuff. Now for the
rest of the story.

While Tony! started Star Nail in 1985, it wouldn't be until his
launch of Cuccio Naturale in 1999 that business would take off for
him. Cuccio Naturale was the first natural nail, hand, and foot care
treatment product line. His top-selling products were cuticle oil and
"Butter." He launched nail polish in 2011 and gel polish in 2013. His
goal was to beat CND and OPI, and he thought Cuccio Naturale was
going to be his winning ticket. It wasn't.

Tony! was street smart and relationship driven. Based in Southern
California in the heart of the nail business, he knew everyone. Not
only that, he knew everything that everyone did. I spoke with him
every week, sometimes two or three times, to learn the latest gossip.
He was intimate with the publishers of *NAILS* and *Nailpro* and would

get inside information from them. He knew who all the power players were and who made what products for CND, OPI, and the rest of his competitors. I was doing nearly $2 million in business with TONY!, and we became mentors for each other. We both taught each other plenty, but too bad for Tony!—he didn't listen to me when it counted.

There was no one cheaper than Tony! His mindset was the fact that both CND and OPI were overcharging salons for their products and that they should be buying his products instead. He had distributors in five to ten key countries, and he would take his seminar "How to make money in the nail business" to those countries. It was amazing that he did the same seminar for more than ten years with little change to the

format. It was even more amazing that he would attract up to five hundred to a thousand nail techs, many of whom were infatuated with him. What really got me is that he always flew coach. I said to Tony!, "Spend some money and fly first-class." He always responded, "WHAT! I'm not going to spend that much fucking money on a seat."

Tony! had more money than God.

He always carried a wad of cash in his pocket. He made more profits than any other nail manufacturer because he did everything cheap. While George and Essie enjoyed staying at the Four Seasons, Tony enjoyed the Red Roof Inn. At the BBSI show, he would rent a house and make his entire staff stay in the house with him. He bought the same generic black shirts, black pants, and black slipper shoes. One day I asked him why he didn't buy a decent brand name, "What the fuck for, Larry?" He always wore the same clothes regardless of the event.

His cheapness would bite him in the ass in 2013. We were buying a lot of disposable slippers from him, and the freight costs from his warehouse to ours was almost the same as a container from China to our warehouse. Tony always made me pay freight on private-label goods. I said to him, "You're making a huge profit on our private-label products; I need you to pay the freight." He didn't ponder the demand and said, "Fuck you. I'm never paying the freight." So, what does an entrepreneur do? Find a way to buy the same disposable slippers cheaper.

My second Gallup® strength is Focus. It was amazing the stuff I could find on the internet. While searching for disposable slipper manufacturers in China, I stumbled across the "magic website." This website gave me information about nearly every manufacturer, distributor, and retailer that bought goods in China. The information included the factory name and contact, container load quantity, and date of each order. I now knew where my competitors bought their products from, including Tony! It was awesome. So, what does an entrepreneur do? Start making contact with every factory for the products that I was buying from Tony! Not only that, I contacted factories for all my top-selling products. I bought massage sheet sets, foil sheets, esthetic wipes, red foot files, birch wood sticks, nail files, cotton rounds, and, of course, disposable pedicure slippers.

Best of all, my cost was 40–50 percent lower than what I was paying my vendors. Full and partial containers arrived later in 2013, and this was the start of the ForPro Professional Collection. I put all the products on Amazon as soon as they came in. They became bestsellers and still are bestsellers.

Who do I have to thank for my lucky website and incredible success? Tony!

LIFE LESSON TIP: Never stop negotiating best costs with your vendors. I can't tell you how much money we saved over the years switching insurance brokers, freight lines, FedEx over UPS and vice versa, packaging materials, and so forth.

LESSON #75

Four Out of Five New Product Launches Fail—It's the One Out of Five That Makes All the Difference

have to admit I was giddy after finding the magic website. It was time to create my first line of truly manufactured products. My marketing team designed a new ForPro Professional Collection logo. From this point forward, all ForPro products would have consistent packaging and be best-in-class. That is what helped ForPro Professional Collection become the number-one brand.

BePRO was also experiencing a period of great success and popularity. BePRO had a full line of makeup and accessories including brushes, applicators, and sponges. Out of nowhere, airbrush makeup came on the scene. When I went to trade shows, the airbrush makeup booths were jammed, and demand was insatiable. Every makeup artist wanted in on the concept. So, what does an entrepreneur do? Launch BePRO airbrush makeup and hire an expert makeup artist. It was an instant success. I brought in compressors and airbrushes, this time direct from China (using my magic website!). Andrea, my makeup artist, was booked doing classes in TheAcademy. Unfortunately, like airbrush nail art, it too faded away.

Black 15-in-1 was going strong, and I added shampoo and conditioner. Now I was ready to add an aerosol hairspray and my NYC PR firm had a recommendation for me: update the packaging. They wanted something more sophisticated, and they expressed that some of their editors thought the current packaging looked too whimsical. They gave me some concepts; we refined them and we relaunched Black 15-in-1 and added hairspray. While the new packaging was stunning, it did not have the magical aura that the original packaging had, and sales started to fall. Just a couple of years later, I would have to discontinue the brand. While this was among my greatest disappointments with a product launch, my ultimate letdown was with Stylist Water.

At GAYNORS, we sold lots of Evian water, and if you are not aware, it is purified water in an aerosol container. Hairdressers need water for styling hair and have always used water bottles and tap water. The problem with tap water is that it contains impurities and can clog hair shafts. That is why you have to descale coffee makers regularly and even soak showerheads. Not only did I use purified water, I added fruit extracts to enhance hair conditioning. At only $10 a can, it was an amazing value, and I targeted it toward A and A+ salons. Our BDSs could not sell it and told me "hairdressers don't care about water." It was then that I realized why so many hair care manufacturers went direct to retailers: You cannot create and sell innovative products just for hairdressers. Because the packaging was aerosol, it was difficult to dispose of. I ended up giving it away in customer orders and that helped to create a little demand for it. By that point, it was too late.

2013 sales were $53 million and we had 240 employees.

LIFE LESSON TIP: Expect your new product launch to fail, and if it doesn't, be pleasantly surprised. By now you have read that I launched both success-ful products along with plenty of losers. The thing is, every product launch has a reason, otherwise I wouldn't have done it. But the marketplace is fickle, and you never know how it is going to respond to your product. Write the losers off and move forward.

LESSON #76

Excitement with Retailers Is Usually a Short-Lived Experience

With social media gaining acceptance in 2014 and the rise of influencers, beauty brands that were early adopters started to gain traction. Two retail nail polish brands, both from the United Kingdom, quickly became rising stars and retailed their polish for $15 a bottle. It was also the year that Christian Louboutin launched its over-the-top nail polish at $50 a bottle. Suddenly, OPI polish at $10 a bottle seemed "boring" and some high-end nail salons started using retail-branded nail polish. This was not a good trend for the pro nail market, and it was very surprising since retail nail polish brands did not discount to nail techs.

To get in front of the trend, I struck deals with both Butter London and NAILS, INC. to be their exclusive U.S. distributor. Nail techs were now able to buy high-end retail nail polish at wholesale. Alas, it turned out that fewer nail salons than I thought wanted retail-branded nail polish, and I dropped both brands the following year.

Black 15-in-1 intrigued one of the rep groups that sold to Target. They were located in Minneapolis and just across the street from Target headquarters. I flew in and met with them. This was a new experience for me because it was my first product to be sold to a retailer. I know what you are thinking loyal reader, "This was so exciting!" You are right, it was so exciting, but excitement with retailers is usually a short-lived experience. Why? They dictate terms. As an entrepreneur with a retail product, you dream about getting into Target, Sephora, Ulta, and others. The fact is most companies fail miserably.

At my meeting with the rep group, I learned many things, and none of them were exclusive to Target. They wanted a high margin. They wanted an allowance for advertising and returns. In case the product did not sell, they wanted write-down funds. For instance, after ninety days on the shelf with sales not meeting forecasts, they expected a 25 percent write-down reimbursement. After 120 days, they wanted 50 percent. Moreover, after 150 days, they would return what was left. Payment terms were net 90 (in 2024, many retailers are taking net 120). This is what you must do if you want to play the game. So, what does an entrepreneur do? Roll the dice! And guess what, they came up snake-eyes. It was a terrible experience. Here is another life lesson worth remembering if you ever want to launch a retail product: Pick and choose your retail partner(s) carefully and read the fine print on any contract that you sign.

ForPro with the help of my magic website kept on rolling. I was buying all my nail files in the United States. One day the fucking rep group that represented my nail file factory called me and told me that I was getting a 12 percent price increase. I told him to have the CEO of the factory call me. He called and explained that his raw material and labor costs were going up and he had no choice. I asked for a thirty-day extension on current pricing and searched for a new nail file factory.

It was no secret that South Korea made the best nail files because they made the second-best sandpaper in the world, next to Japan. I quickly found a company that would make our nail files, and they are still making them for us today. Best of all, the quality was better and I saved more than 40 percent.

ForPro was a dream come true for many reasons. One, the brand was exclusive to TNG. I learned my lesson from selling Pinnacle to distributors. Second, I wasn't locked into selecting what our vendors decided was best for the market. I was free to come up with my own colors, patterns, and designs. For example, when it came to nail files, I could make them mini or jumbo; I could make them bulk or individually wrapped; I could make them in any color or pattern. Now, instead of boring red foot files, I offered purple, yellow, black, and cool gray. When one of our customers wanted three-ply masks, I was able to make them for her (wait until that chapter!). It was so much fun, and it kept ForPro products fresh and relevant. Even during the pandemic when manufacturers were cutting back with supply chain issues, I launched at least fifty new products a year.

Third, I could list them at any price I liked. Unlike most vendors who offered bimonthly discounts, I decided to make ForPro a value brand and never discounted it. I learned discounts did not increase the overall business, and they only gave up margin. It was a brilliant strategy and one that luxury brands have always used. Lastly, no matter what the category was, I could enter it at any time. Everyone told me that offering dishwasher rinse aid in a one-gallon size was a terrible idea. Finish was the bestseller, and it was offered in consumer sizes. "Everyone" was amazed that it took off. And who would have thought that a beauty manufacturer would have the best-selling tongue depressor on Amazon? Only an entrepreneur.

> **2014 sales were $49 million, and we had two hundred employees.**

LIFE LESSON TIP: New entrepreneurs are always confused where to sell their first product and rightfully so. Depending on the product, here are some tips. 1. Launch on your own website; 2. Launch on Amazon.com; 3. Sell to a few local retailers; 4. Exhibit at one major trade show and see what types of buyers your product attracts. When applicable, select one buyer to sell to and give them a 90- to 180-day exclusive. Learning is critical for your company's growth.

LESSON #77

Quickly Spot the Difference Between Trends and Fads

orPro's focus was professional salon and spa accessories, and Ginger Lily Farm's focus was personal care and locker room. Neither of the two brands were retail-focused. When opportunity came along to introduce retail products, I realized I needed a new brand. So, what does an entrepreneur do? Launch the Works brands.

Remember the konjac sponge? I recall going to a NACDS (National Association for Chain Drug Stores) show where we were first to market konjac sponges. While I was trying to sell nail files and blocks, all they wanted was more information on the sponges. Konjac Sponge Works was the first brand launched (konjac sponges proved to be another fad and would fade away).

Remember Clarisonic? The skin care brush tool launched in 2004 to great fanfare and was acquired by L'Oréal in 2011. One of my new Chinese factories came out with a similar model at a third of the cost. I named the brand Sonic Tool Works, and it took off immediately. I even did a private-label version for Walgreens. However, the market for skin care brushes crashed when dermatologists claimed the tool caused skin to break down. Sonic Tool Works stopped in 2018, and L'Oréal shut down Clarisonic in 2020.

Remember Korean skin care masks? I remember walking the Cosmoprof Hong Kong show in 2015 and could not believe the number of skin care mask booths there. I found three amazing factories and branded the products, Beauty Mask Works. Sales were incredible—but once again, it turned out to be just another fad. I will tell you, learning the hard way about what products trend over decades versus what products are fads sucks.

Winner, winner, chicken dinner! Some of the Works brands are still going strong. Paraffin Wax Works' claim to fame was the launch of a ten-minute paraffin glove for hands and feet that warmed up in a microwave. It competed with a product that was triple the cost. I am happy to say the product is still selling, now under the ForPro brand.

Pure Essential Oil Works brand includes aromatherapy diffusers and a complete range of aromatherapy oils. We sold more than 400,000 diffusers to T.J. Maxx during the peak from 2016 to 2021. Aromatherapy oils from lavender to eucalyptus crushed it as well.

Remember salt lamps? During the heyday period from 2016 to 2018, we could not unload full containers quick enough. T.J. Maxx sold more than 200,000 units. Pure Himalayan Salt Works still makes salt lamps, and I am sensing a resurgence over the next few years. For now, salt stones are doing well.

thebeautybook needed an update. I subscribed to *Wine Spectator* and loved the oversized look and feel of the magazine. So, what does an entrepreneur do? Make thebeautybook the same size. It was a brilliant idea and further defined the importance of the catalog business even as our online business continued to grow in double digits.

With thebeautybook oversized, I needed to update Nailco Rewards and renamed it TIS Rewards. The loyalty program now offered customers money-back coupons each quarter based on points earned. Customers received one point for most brands in the catalog. However, they received two points for our semi-exclusive brands and three points for our signature brands (ForPro, Ginger Lily Farms, and Works). The tiered point program further enhanced our customers' experience, and at the same time, we sold more of our branded products. More than 25 percent of our overall sales were now our brands.

[Sidenote: There is truth to antitrust claims when public companies buy out private companies and limit competition and innovation. The pro hair care industry was a perfect example. L'Oréal is still the market leader but has not purchased a company since Pureology and hasn't launched a new brand since Serie Expert in 2000. Even Olaplex, which went public in 2021, is struggling to gain new sales after it focused on retailers during the pandemic.]

> 2015 sales were $48M and we had 190 employees.

LIFE LESSON TIP: We're all guilty of this: hopping on the bandwagon when it's too late, especially when it comes to meme stocks. The "lemming effect" is both powerful and dangerous. It's nearly impossible to differentiate between trending and fad products. If you happen to be involved with a hot product because it appears on TikTok, don't overreact because demand will die as quickly as it exploded. Think of product investment like stocks, long term only.

LESSON #78

Always Know What the Best-Selling Products Are in Your Category

Lush Fresh Handmade Cosmetics opened its first U.S. store in 2003. Among their bestsellers were bath bombs. It was not until 2016 though that the bath bomb explosion would begin. One of my factories was already making fizzy balls for manicures and pedicures. Sure enough, they also made bath bombs. So, what does an entrepreneur do? Come out with Ginger Lily Farms bath bombs. The line consisted of eight-ounce fizzy bath bombs and a gift set of four bombs. Little did I know when I launched it that it would be one of our all-time best-selling fad items.

The launch was at the Cosmoprof (former BBSI) show in Vegas in 2016. I bought cute glass containers from Libby and merchandised bulk bombs inside them. At our twenty-foot exhibit booth, there were six jars, each featuring a unique scent. Scents included Cranberry Passion, Lavender Lullaby, Happy Hour, and Champagne Mimosa. It was amazing how almost every buyer who came to the booth was drawn to the fizzy bombs. We were the first beauty company to sell them, and they instantly took off. Between 2016 and 2019, we sold hundreds of thousands of bath bombs and kits. The warehouse never smelled so good. I thought for sure because of Lush, this boom would last a long time and would not be a fad. Alas, it too was a fad and even though we still sell bath bombs, they came and went like aroma diffusers.

Ginger Lily Farms was doing great in the locker room category, so it was time to break out and get into the body category. I launched body butter, sugar scrubs, body lotions, and gel masks. What stood out most for the launch was the introduction of fragrance-free products, which no one offered at the time (to this day, Ginger Lily Farms is still the leader in this category). Fragrance-free products allowed spas to add essential oils so they could develop their own signature scent. It also turned out to be great for consumers who were allergic to fragrances.

Depilatory wax was a big business, and TNG sold all the major brands. The story repeats itself; we were competing against other distributors selling the same brands. It was time to introduce our own brand of depilatory products. So, what does an entrepreneur do? Launch Too Naked Hair Removal products. One thing I learned early on was that while China was great at making many products, personal care products were not their sweet spot. Since most of the depilatory companies were European, I decided to collaborate with the best Italian factory to make Too Naked. It was a brilliant idea, and to this day, the brand is being used at the finest spas and retailers in the United States.

Disposable gloves was another category that we distributed, and it was an interesting category because gloves are not beauty products. Hairdressers used black gloves when they applied hair color, and nail techs wore latex gloves for pedicure services. Gloves are worn in many professions, especially healthcare, food, and security. I decided 2016 was a great time to get into the glove business. It would later prove to be one of the best decisions.

> 2016 sales were $50 million, and we had 180 employees.

LIFE LESSON TIP: I love going to popular retailers to learn what their best-selling products are. In beauty, these include Lush cosmetics, Bath & Body Works, Sephora, and Kiehl's. I learn about new scents, new formulations, and see what's trending. I also review Amazon's top-100 sellers. The more ideas you get, the more relevant your products will become.

LESSON #79

Nothing Is Forever Except Death and Taxes (and the BUB!)

Thinking back to 2017, little did I realize that I created a conglomerate using TNG as the conduit. Come to think of it, that is the main reason why TNG has been able to succeed over the years regardless of the setbacks experienced. The outlier companies that I created within the conglomerate included: CTS, bebeautiful, The Pavilion, and Beauty Direct. Each of these had a sales manager, and each did about $6 million in sales a year. By 2017, none of these companies would exist.

New Sunshine was our biggest tanning vendor. Trevor decided he wanted out and sold New Sunshine (Trevor didn't even give me a call). Who he sold it to is up for debate, but sources had it that he sold to John Menard, the billionaire who owns Menard's. Others have it that Menard's ex-business partner, Steve Hibert, bought it. The two of them ended up in court, and I would have to write a book on what happened. Suffice to say, it was not pretty, and the new owners went on to buy California Tan and Designer Skin. In 2016, I got a termination letter from New Sunshine. I tried contacting Menard to no avail. It was yet another dagger in the back and forced me out of the indoor tanning business.

Bebeautiful was a victim of Amazon.com and the end of mail-order catalogs. I was OK with closing it down as it was not profitable, and my objective was to sell as much as possible on Amazon.com.

The Pavilion was another story. The glory days of A and A+ salons were coming to an end with the 2007 introduction of salon suites, which became a huge part of the industry. Franchises such as Sola, Phenix, My Salon Suite, and Salon Lofts were opening across America in the most desirable locations. Salon stylist "walk-outs" were always the number-one challenge for salon owners, and before salon suites came along the "walk-outs" would either open a new salon or take over an existing salon. With salon suites, they could just move in and have their own business. Can you think of the last hair salon that opened near you that was not a franchise?

TNG never did business with the owners of salon suites because they rented to hairdressers, nail techs, and spa professionals. They bought their equipment from their contractor. The need for high-end equipment and design services for A and A+ salons came to a crashing end. The Pavilion closed at the perfect time.

Beauty Direct was always one of my favorite divisions because it was my first acquisition and got me into the hair business. As Sally Beauty, Cosmoprof, and Salon Centric grew from 2007 to 2016, many small beauty distributors closed down, as they could not compete. Small beauty distributors had been the sweet spot for Beauty Direct. The business I most wanted to focus on was our own brands, but our own salespeople couldn't sell our brands. I will never forget Martin Park, our all-star Beauty Direct salesperson. He was Korean, and he sold CND and OPI products exclusively to Vietnamese distributors. He lived in New Jersey and would make an annual trip across the United States by car to visit his customers. He was my "in" to the Vietnamese market, but he could never sell ForPro products to his customers. It was further proof that ForPro had to sell direct to TNG and Amazon customers to be successful. I closed Beauty Direct, renamed it TNG Wholesale, and retained two salespeople. Their focus remained on the Vietnamese market for OPI and the few surviving independent distributors.

Even though these four divisions closed down, there was an underlying current sizzling at TNG. TNG brands now accounted for 40 percent of our overall business. In 2017 alone, I added more than a hundred new products. I had no interest in taking on new products as a distributor and only focused on adding new products under our brands. Not only did our customers love the products, we were quickly separating ourselves from the competition. While I lost $24 million in annual business from the four divisions, the opportunity for new growth with our brands was tremendous and exciting.

> **LIFE LESSON TIP:** Fall in love with your life partner but never fall in love with your products. Be willing to discontinue any product at any time for whatever reason. There will always be a new product to take its place.

LESSON #80

What Comes Around, Goes Around: There's Nothing Like Experience to Understand This

While both CND and OPI were busy concentrating on the Vietnamese market, start-ups such as Dazzle Dry and ella + mila were creating buzz and targeting spas through direct sales (smart move on their part not selling to lowly distributors). These brands were upscale, trendy, and vegan. So, what does an entrepreneur do? Launch EMMA Beauty.

EMMA Beauty was the perfect complement to ForPro. ForPro had every nail accessory product, and the final piece of the puzzle would be fulfilled by the EMMA Beauty nail color brand. TNG could now offer salons and spas a complete nail package.

Already having the Raku and Pinnacle nail polish lines behind me, I set out to find a partner to create the products. I headed to Cosmoprof Hong Kong and found the perfect manufacturer. Best of all, they were United States based. They developed the formulation of nail polish and gel polish to my specs so I could compete against CND, OPI, and the upcoming brands. Dazzle Dry and ella + mila didn't have gel polish so that would be a competitive advantage for EMMA.

EMMA polish was 7-Free (no bad chemicals), fast dry, and chip-resistant. I launched new colors every month like Zara did with clothes, to make it a fast fashion brand. For packaging and pricing, I stole a chapter from Essie and I made the bottle square with an ergonomic cap. I priced the polish at $2 compared to $5.25 for OPI and $11 for Dazzle Dry. It was a slam-dunk marketing strategy. I even called the nail polish V.S.N.P. (very special nail polish).

I came up with unique concepts for salons and the EMMA Manicure was just one of many brilliant ideas. I priced the polish low enough for salons to give away a brand-new bottle with each service. The ingenuity of this was that clients would always pick from new bottles instead of gross nearly empty bottles. With the client keeping the bottle, the client could do touch-ups at home instead of coming back to the salon.

EMMA was an instant success. Shortly thereafter, V.S.G.P. (very special gel polish) launched, and I priced it 50 percent below the competition. I added both retail and professional hand and body products including lotions, crèmes, scrubs, and cuticle oils and balms.

I needed a top-notch nail tech and trainer and hired Herman Paez. He was fun, outgoing, and was a great nail tech. He previously worked at CND and OPI, so he had the perfect background. Herman was my product tester, created how-to videos and instruction guides, visited customers, and took care of trade shows.

I also hired a PR company for traditional PR and social media. I went a step further and hired a marketing firm that focused exclusively on influencers. It was a crazy business then (and still is today but in a far different way). I paid influencers based on the number of likes they had, and it was amazing to see how many posts they would receive. If that was not enough, I also put EMMA V.S.N.P. in beauty box sampler programs. All told, I spent more than $25,000 a month on EMMA marketing. It was an investment that paid off to get the brand kickstarted.

> 2018 sales were $54 million, and we still had 180 employees.

LIFE LESSON TIP: It's amazing how products recycle in popularity every generation. I love this tip: Go back fifteen to twenty years and see what products were popular and think about doing a relaunch on one that makes the most sense.

LESSON #81

You Can't Fight City Hall

If there was any year in TNG history that I could freeze and replay repeatedly, 2018 was it. For the first time in company history, retail products became superstars. So much, in fact, I renamed the retail section of thebeautybook "WOW" and placed it first in the catalog. Besides fizzy bath bombs and sets, I added Shower Blasts, Bubble Bath Bombs (holiday scents for all lines too), Buttercup Bath Creamers (they looked just like cupcakes), Shower Jam, and even more aromatherapy oils. We were selling all of these items along with salt lamps and aroma diffusers by the container load. It was amazing.

With bath bombs being so hot, I came up with a concept just for kiddies, Bubbles The Bear Bank. I created a special plastic mold to look like a bear. The top half of Bubbles was the bank and the bottom half stored six bath bombs. It was adorable! It was too bad our retailers didn't think so. Here is another life lesson I will repeat later on: You can't fight city hall.

I am only mentioning nitrile gloves now because little did I know when I launched them that they would become our best-selling product. I sold them in white, blue, indigo, and black. Indigo was the best-selling color on Amazon, but after the pandemic, black would be the superstar color because of TikTok and all the short reels of chefs and cooks wearing black gloves.

With ForPro sales surging and new products coming out almost daily, it was time to rebrand the look of the packaging. Marketing came up with a perfect solution and we then went through the laborious process of updating artwork for all our items. The results were impressive, and I learned why successful companies constantly update their logos and artwork. I'm hopeful the current artwork will be good through 2027 since we have more than a thousand SKUs.

When Dawn Kuhn, my all-time favorite CFO (Disney lover, includer, and the one who told me that "women are always right"), sent over the year-end financials, I almost fell out of my chair. 2018 turned out to be our second-most profitable year in company history.

Here is another life lesson: Never lose sight of your financial information. For me, I check daily sales by department, reps, and retailers. I compare current year versus previous year. Dawn prepares monthly financial statements including: balance sheet, income statement, cash flow statement, employee count, inventory turns, receivable ratio, and freight expense percentage for sales and detailed breakdown for healthcare costs. Better yet, I get the financials within three days.

I also receive a monthly snapshot that shows year-over-year comparisons: sales by division and reps; Amazon sales; brand sales; SKU sales; and factory sales. I also get daily cash balances, which was crucial when we had an active line of credit. You can never have too much information.

> **2018 sales were $52 million and we had 160 employees.**

LIFE LESSON TIP: I always tried to read the mind of the retail buyers that we worked with to launch new products. Terrible idea. Better idea: Share the new product idea before you launch it. Buyers are very good at sharing their thoughts, and it helps to prevent failed launches.

LESSON #82

You Can Make More Money
Doing Less Business

A s I said, 2018 was a year for the record books, and 2019 was not far behind. It was our third-most profitable year, and retail sales of fizzy and aromatherapy products continued to soar. There was one category left for me to get into while the action was hot: candle melts. Scentsy was a direct marketer (direct marketers were big back in the day) of candle melts, and they were the category leader. Their prices were high and although candle melts were sold in most retail stores, I thought there would be a huge market for our customers. So, what does an entrepreneur do? Create Scentworks.

Two of our employees were Scentsy addicts, and they became my product testers. I found a great factory in Ohio to make the candle melts. My product testers told me what Scentsy's bestsellers were. I bought them and shipped them to my factory to duplicate. I created a unique mold for the melts, and then went to my magic website to find the best China factory for candle melt warmers (they did a lot of business with Yankee Candle). I launched thirty-six different melts and twenty-four different melt warmers. It was one of my greatest new product launches. The only problem was that our major retail customer had no interest in them, and I would later find out that our customers who bought fizzy and aromatherapy products didn't love wax melts. Scentworks would become one of my greatest write-offs.

Other than that, 2019 was a really good year for many reasons. One, all our remote distribution centers were now closed. It made no sense to import products from China and other countries and then pay additional shipping costs to get them to our remote locations. That cut overhead without reducing sales. Two, most of our store locations were closed because I only opened them to sell pro hair care products.

Third, my VP of Sales for TNG Wholesale, Vince Fererra, left to go to work for Wella and be in charge of their Vietnamese OPI business. I wished him the best of success and decided to shut down the division. I made the decision earlier in the year to stop selling CND and OPI to Vietnamese distributors because there was no margin and we were always stuck with excess inventory. With Vince gone, there was no reason to keep it going.

Our employee count was down to 120 and we were making more money doing $45 million in sales than when we peaked at $86 million. Life was good. 2019 was also the year I achieved financial freedom: TNG was debt-free. The building was paid for. No line of credit needed. No interest rates to worry about. There is no better feeling for an entrepreneur than achieving financial freedom. I went from $27 million in debt to zero. It was an amazing feat because half our business was now our own brands and that inventory had to be paid for upfront, which plays havoc with cash flow.

The reason I was able to pay off the debt is because I did not take profit distributions at the end of each year. I just paid the taxes and reinvested the rest. I didn't buy a second or third home, private jet, elaborate artwork, wine at auctions, or a yacht. Luckily for me, because the true test of being an entrepreneur was right around the corner in 2020.

> 2019 sales were $45 million and we had 120 employees.

LIFE LESSON TIP: Growth at all costs is a terrible strategy for entrepreneurs unless they have unlimited funding. Managed growth is best. As your business matures, sometimes it's best to focus on the most profitable services/products and shed the least profitable. While this reduces your sales, it increases your profits. Never forget, the reason you are in business is to make money.

PART 6

THE BIG PIVOT THAT MADE ALL THE DIFFERENCE

LESSON #83

Spot Trends First

COVID-19 started on December 19, 2019, in China, and the first cases in the United States appeared on January 30, 2020. During the month of February, as I was doing my daily walk-through at the distribution center, I noticed a lot of orders for three-ply face masks. I also noticed a higher-than-normal volume of orders for gloves and MULTI-CIDE, our hospital-grade disinfectant.

Back then, we were selling a box of fifty-count face masks for $3.49, and our cost before freight and customs was $.75. When I saw the orders, I immediately went to Amazon and found that similar face masks were selling for $9.99 a box. I promptly pulled our inventory off Amazon and our website because I knew something was going on.

The fortuitous thing about the pandemic was that TNG was already manufacturing personal protective equipment (PPE) well before the pandemic arrived. We had the winning lottery ticket. We were making three-ply masks, nitrile gloves, hospital-grade disinfectant (concentrate and ready-to-use), 70 percent and 99 percent isopropyl alcohol, hand soap, and partnered with a factory for gym wipes.

I contacted our factory in China that made our three-ply masks to place a rush order. However, the pandemic was already wreaking havoc in China, and demand for face masks was high. The factory increased our cost per box from $.75 to $11.40. I am not joking. I ordered fifty thousand boxes anyway. We would be out of stock within two weeks based on new demand. I had to airfreight ten thousand boxes.

Airfreight costs in February were still reasonable at $5 a pound. A box of masks weighs eight ounces. Airfreight cost came in at $2.50 a box so my net cost was $13.90. When the masks arrived, I had to increase the price to $29.99, which was well below standard margin (typically take cost multiplied by three for retail pricing). Customers balked, but it didn't matter: I had inventory and none of our competitors did (airfreight costs in March went to $10 a pound and would hit more than $25 per pound in May).

Michigan shut down on March 12, and the United States shut down on March 15. The public did its normal thing and panicked. Suddenly, every retailer was out of toilet paper, paper towels, bottled water, Lysol wipes, Purell hand sanitizer, and nitrile gloves. Gretchen Whitmer, Michigan's governor, mandated all businesses close down except for essential businesses. To qualify as an essential business, you had to sell PPE and essential products. Michigan had to register each business, and our law firm took care of the paperwork. Every TNG employee needed to carry a letter in their car that stated TNG was an essential business in case they were pulled over by the police.

I will never forget driving to the office after March 12. The roads and freeways were empty. It was as if a nuclear blast came and went. It would stay that way until June 1 when Whitmer reopened the state. During this time, all our competitors' stores were shut down, and this would be a boon to TNG.

Late February I decided that COVID-19 was here and going to be a big deal. I contacted all my factories and put them on notice. I ordered four thousand gallons of MULTI-CIDE, bought a full tanker of 99 percent ISP, and ordered multiple containers of nitrile gloves. My Ginger Lily Farm's factory went into hyper-mode producing gallons of hand soap. By mid-March, I learned that we needed additional PPE products including disposable and reusable plastic face masks, infrared thermometers, hand sanitizers, hand sanitizer dispensers, and KN95 masks. So, what does an entrepreneur do? Get everything in stock ASAP!

Dennis was my contact for many of our acrylic containers and dispensers. I've known him for more than thirty years. His father started a plastic fabrication factory on the east side, it was called CF Plastics. Dennis made all our nail polish racks, my patented Nail Taboret (polish rack and tool organizer), retail sign cards, acrylic organizers, and EMMA Beauty Nail Shields. I asked him about reusable face masks, and he referred me to a local factory. I ordered five hundred to start and would eventually order five thousand every week. However, this was just the tip of the iceberg.

LIFE LESSON TIP: Regardless of what industry you are in, there are always things happening in the world around you. Stay alert, and be ready, as an entrepreneur to pivot or capitalize on an emerging market.

LESSON #84

There Is Nothing Like a Crisis to Separate the Winners from the Losers

---

Apple has the largest company valuation in the world. It hit an unprecedented $3 trillion market cap in 2023 (though that valuation has fallen slightly as of this writing). They don't manufacture a single product; they outsource everything in China and India. Foxconn is their main supplier that makes the iPhone. Why doesn't Apple manufacture their products in the United States?

While Tesla has manufacturing plants in the United States, their largest plant is based in Shanghai and is the world's largest factory based on production volume. It has capacity to build 750,000 autos and shipped more than 160,000 to Europe and other Asian countries in 2022. Why doesn't Tesla export cars from their U.S. factories?

Let's take a look at some statistics from WIPO (World Intellectual Property Organization) from 2022.

	PATENTS	TRADEMARKS
CHINA	1.58 M	9.4 M
U.S.	591 K	920 K
JAPAN	289 K	364 K
KOREA	238 K	360 K
VIETNAM	8,500 K	113 K

China leads the world in patents and trademarks. It is no wonder why it is best in manufacturing. Let me give you an example. Dennis from CF Plastics made an acrylic dispenser for me for years. Sadly, Dennis called me to tell me he was retiring at the early age of sixty-one because he could not find workers for his factory. We paid $7.50 for the dispenser. I went to one of my Chinese factories that made other dispensers, and I sent a photo of the item with dimensions. Within one day, I received a RFQ (request for quote) of $2.50. Within three days, the factory had already made a sample and sent it to me via FedEx. Upon receipt, it was identical.

This is what China does best. I am always amazed at the speed and efficiency of Chinese factories and their attention to quality. I have far more Chinese business friends than U.S. business friends because they are always eager to work with me and ensure I am pleased with the result. Chinese children learn English starting at pre-K and are more proficient in reading and writing than many Americans are. They work long hours due to the twelve-hour time difference. They respond to emails within the hour if they aren't sleeping. They have a vast network of partners to assist them with packaging, logistics, and raw material sourcing.

When the pandemic hit, I was amazed at the speed that Chinese factories changed production lines for PPE products. For instance, our factory that made three-ply face masks also made many other disposables for beauty and medical. But with the demand for masks, they were quickly able to convert the other disposable lines to masks. When 3M couldn't make enough N95 masks, Chinese factories transformed almost overnight to make KN95 masks. Chinese factories were flexible enough to handle the demand for PPE products while American factories were not. It took months for Clorox to increase capacity for its wipes and hand sanitizer. 3M never got a handle on N95 masks, and its distributors were constantly out of inventory.

Let's talk about nitrile gloves. One of the first things Trump did as president was to add 25 percent tariffs on hundreds of Chinese products, including nitrile gloves. During the pandemic, the cost of nitrile gloves went from $1.70 a box to more than $12 a box plus 25 percent tariffs, duties, and freight. At the peak, we sold a box of gloves for $39.99. However, here is the thing: It is illegal to make nitrile gloves in the United States. The chemicals used in production are carcinogenic. Chinese factories developed specialized production and ventilation to keep the contaminants contained. Bottom line: U.S. consumers are the ones paying the extra 25 percent tariffs, and the tariffs are still in effect although the cost of a box of gloves has come back to normal levels.

[Sidenote: China's ruling party, the Chinese Communist Party (CCP), and its leader, Xi Jinping, are steering China back to its original communist days. The confrontations facing China and the United States are near an all-time high. However, one thing is for sure: America depends on China for its manufacturing ability. President Biden wants America to step up the pace of its own manufacturing, but there are more than six million unfulfilled jobs with zero prospects of them being filled as generation Z and millennials have no desire to work in factories. Politics and business never mix well together, the outcome is to be determined.]

LIFE LESSON TIP: You are reading my book post-pandemic. Every industry and every business have changed. What was once acceptable pre-pandemic no longer makes sense post-pandemic. Office buildings are empty, work-from-home/hybrid work continues on, employers have more than 9.5 million job openings as of December 2023, and inflation is at 3.2 percent. But that is what makes entrepreneurs ... entrepreneurs: the love of the challenge. The most important tip I can share with you is to learn to adapt quickly in times of crisis. The next few lessons are the most important ones of all.

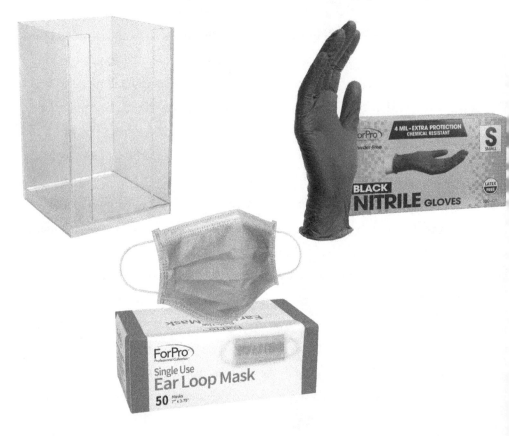

LESSON #85

Anything Goes in a Crisis

Over the past thirty-five years, I have experienced interest rates as high as 20 percent, the .com crash, the housing crash, and everything else in-between. That was child's play compared to dealing with the pandemic. As an entrepreneur, it was my most difficult time being in business, and it happened at a stage of my life that couldn't have been worse. I went from working four-day weeks to working 24/7. I went from never using WhatsApp and WeChat to using it day and night to stay in touch with my Chinese factories.

America shut down, but Americans still had needs that had to be met. People still needed their hair cut and colored. Women still needed manicures and what was better than getting an at-home massage. As a result, hairdressers, manicurists, and massage therapists either set up shop in their home or they traveled to their clients' homes. Some did both. They needed supplies. All our competitors' stores were closed. Only their websites were functional. Being that they were distributors, their inventory levels were low to begin with, and when they went to reorder, their vendors were out of stock. They were not prepared for the pandemic. Suddenly, customers who never ordered from TNG before were ordering. Our regular customers were ordering more often. Our order volume more than doubled in March and would continue that way until reopening in June. However, in March, I had no idea when reopening would be. It might not have been until 2021 or later.

At the same time, essential industries were having difficulties getting PPE supplies. Funeral homes bought all their PPE from funeral home distributors. Within a week, they were all out of stock, and they would stay that way for months. The Michigan Funeral Home Association got in touch with us through a referral in Lansing, and we started selling to funeral homes in Michigan. Word got out quickly, and major national chains started to order from us. The same went for nursing homes, nurse practitioners, EMTs, and doctors.

I started to get phone calls (I had no idea how they got my cell number) from all of the above, each person pleading for PPE. I allocated and re-allocated to meet demand, but it wasn't enough. It got brutal for funeral homes because so many people were dying from COVID, and they did not have gloves or disinfectant for their staff to use while collecting bodies from the hospitals. I will never forget one call I received from a mortician begging me for body bags (that is the one item I did not source).

In the meantime, our orders more than tripled from normal levels. The DC staff had to work overtime to get the orders out daily. Many times, I got carryout dinners for them and had alcohol delivered (bottles of wine and bourbon) so they could go home and relax after working long days.

My China factories were also working overtime to expedite my orders. Many of my U.S. vendors were either closed (nonessential companies) or did not have the ability to convert to making PPE products. I realized that those brands had no value to me or to my customers. With our business already more than 50 percent of our own brands, I had to make the biggest decision of my career. It was my biggest Chance card that I would ever pick up. The question was: Do I discontinue distribution and only focus on manufacturing my own brands? So, what does an entrepreneur do? I picked up the Chance card and it read, "Now is the time to go full-force ahead." And I did.

I first held a meeting with my managers to tell them we were dropping all non-TNG brands effective immediately. That meant all the TISE exclusive hair care brands, CND, OPI, and more than two hundred others would be out and that our focus would only be on our own brands. We had four stores left and I rebranded them "TNG Essential Stores" and assigned a task force to remove all non-TNG brands and restock them with essential products.

The second thing I did was call select vendors to let them know we were done with them. What a great feeling to finally cut them off instead of the other way around.

The third thing I did was abandon The Industry Source name and renamed the company TNG Worldwide. In some regards, this was more difficult than retiring the "Nailco" name. All our customers called us

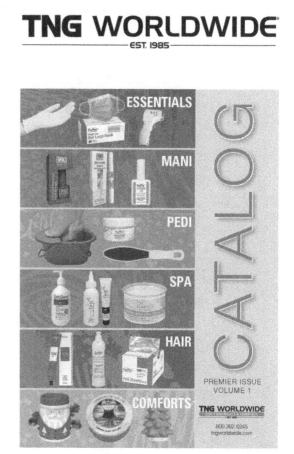

The Industry Source, and now that was to be no more. At least for the website, it was a simple redirection and most customers didn't notice. However, we had to change all the store and building signage, invoices, and so much more. It would also be the end of the biannual catalog. I produced one last catalog in the fall without pricing and, afterward, maintained an electronic online catalog.

The last thing I did was get in touch with a Chicago-based broadcast company that excelled in doing high-capacity Zoom calls. I decided to do a customer invite-only Zoom meeting to let our customers know my new strategy. More than three thousand customers signed up! I displayed pallets of 99 percent ISP, nitrile gloves, EMMA table protectors, and MULTI-CIDE. The meeting lasted more than an hour, and our customers got the message. The distribution center was busier than ever.

I gave up more than $20 million in business in one fell swoop. It was the scariest and riskiest decision I had ever made. Worse, I was sixty-four years old and up to the pandemic, life was good. It was the perfect storm at the worst possible time. It ended up being the crisis that made TNG Worldwide the leader it is today, but the rest of the story gets worse before it gets better.

LIFE LESSON TIP: When life is in turmoil, it's the best time to make the most radical changes because no one cares or is paying attention. Not only that, it's the best time because you are making the changes to make your company financially better. Those that don't often file Chapter 11 or close. It's no wonder that hundreds of thousands of businesses closed due to the pandemic.

LESSON #86

The Internet Lives Forever

Some of my best business friends are Vietnamese. I have gone to Vietnamese nail salons for decades and have understood and admired their culture. When I made the decision to toss out all the nail brands and focus exclusively on EMMA Beauty, I also knew that my focus had to be on the non-Vietnamese nail market. Here's why.

People within the second-generation Vietnamese salon community decided to compete directly with CND and OPI as they thought they were paying too much for nail polish, acrylic liquids, and nail accessories. SNS was the first major company to launch in 1990, followed by LeChat in 1993, Kiara Sky & Cacee in 2005, and DND in 2015. They sold exclusively to Vietnamese distributors. There was little product differentiation between the brands as most of the companies used the same contract manufacturers. There was little innovation. What mostly separated each company was the number of nail polish colors (some exceeded five hundred) and low price point. As more Vietnamese companies got into the private-label business, price points spiraled down. After gels peaked, it wasn't unusual for a

Vietnamese brand to package a gel, nail polish, and powder dip for the same price as one bottle of OPI gel.

One thing that makes America great is competition. The Vietnamese fought hard to win market share and stole business away from both manufacturers and traditional beauty salons by keeping overhead low and prices even lower. However, I do think continual low pricing kills innovation and demand for new talent. Enrollment at beauty schools is at an all-time low for manicurists, and less Vietnamese seem to be immigrating to America to become manicurists. This is one reason you don't see new nail salons opening. It is also the reason you frequently see the same old products in the salon on every visit.

My mission was to grow EMMA Beauty and make it a premium brand at a value price point so that our customers could compete against Vietnamese and other nail salons that kept prices too low. It was a great idea because there was no one left in the industry to tackle the issue. I decided to do an EMMA Beauty invite-only webinar to our nail customers. We had about three hundred customers in attendance. There was a three-minute segment in the webinar where I was very animated and talked about how the Vietnamese destroyed the professional nail industry and killed innovation. I mimicked the way they spoke Vietnamese in nail salons and mentioned there is no other business in America in which employees do not speak English. For more than ten years, I patronized a local Vietnamese salon. When there I used to make the staff laugh if I parroted back to them in my version of their language. Over time, I learned what they were saying. When I asked the owner why they spoke in Vietnamese all the time she told me, "That's what we're used to." I was attempting to be funny during the webinar—and I was just being my energetic self.

As it turned out, someone recorded my webinar and sent it off to a person that represented an organization that worked to fight against anti-Vietnamese sentiments and bigotry. From there it started to hit social media, and by the end of the day, I was on the phone with the representative and apologized. He accepted my apology, and it was over. I doubt there is a single soul on earth who has not had something fly out of their mouth in an animated or humorous—or angry—discussion and realized that they actually inserted their foot in their mouth. I was sincerely sorry—I did not intend to hurt.

Except when it comes to social media and the internet, it is never over. And this is a true life lesson for all entrepreneurs: What goes online never comes down. Even worse, negative social media is very sticky as people love to read about and watch videos on bad news. Good news stuff like donating money for a new building at MSU is as sticky as silicone.

A Vietnamese group at MSU got involved and wanted my name removed from The Pavilion. They went as far as contacting the president. MSU reached out to me, and I told them I was very happy to meet with the group and give them my perspective. They didn't want to meet. No changes were made. In 2022, the same group tried again. The same group failed again. In 2023, we finally came to terms.

As always, I learned my lesson the hard way. My hope is that if by reading this book, you learn my life lessons you will not make these mistakes yourself.

LIFE LESSON TIP: Understand that all Zoom and Teams meetings are being recorded by someone. If you are doing a virtual meeting with customers or employees, make sure your content is straightforward. When possible, have your attorney review it first. Watch being too off-the-cuff. Remember that humor that might work in person does not always translate well. Better yet, consider if you even need to do a virtual meeting. After my experience, I have never done another one.

LESSON #87

Sometimes You Have to Be Lucky to Risk Everything

The month of May was total hell. We were at the peak of the crisis, and we had no idea how much taller the peak was going to be. I was exhausted, and BUB was not happy with me. The pandemic stole me from her, but my passion for my customers was overwhelming. I reassured her that everything was going to be fine, but for now, I had to focus. Thank God for that being my number-two strength. Even though we were a tiny company compared to Clorox, 3M, and P&G, the impact we made with so many healthcare professionals was immense.

I will never forget many things but here is one that was indicative of the times: Hospitals ran out of rooms and ERs were overflowing. One hospital group decided to transform an expo hall to a medical facility. The contractor needed masks to get the job done, and there weren't any available from their traditional distributors. They learned about TNG and we supplied them with masks so they could get the facility built. Those were the kind of stories that kept me going.

Even with all my factories working 24/7, the issue became supply chain logistics. TNG was not the only company that wanted expedited goods out of China. Typical shipments that took thirty to forty days were taking sixty to seventy days or longer. Trains and truckers couldn't keep up with demand. It was the most frustrating thing ever to happen: The goods were ready, but they could not be shipped or moved once they hit the United States. We were in desperate need of more masks and nitrile gloves.

I read about how companies were chartering private planes to move their own cargo. FedEx was our partner, and I knew they had a fleet that went from China to the United States. I inquired with our agent. He told me, "Larry, yes, I can arrange for a plane [it held seven full containers]. However, I have to tell you the rate of the plane before the pandemic was $300,000, now it is $1.1 million, and I only have availability for the next seventy-two hours. After that, the price will be higher, and I cannot even guarantee you a plane at the higher cost."

Wait . . . $1,100,000 just for a plane? There were thirty-eight thousand boxes of nitrile gloves in each container. My glove factory was out of capacity but still managed to produce three containers for the plane. My mask factory was able to produce four containers, 160,000 boxes. Total plane contents were 274,000 boxes. With added costs, it came to $5 a box for airfreight, far cheaper than $15 a box. The investment was well over $4 million.

As you recall in 2019, TNG was debt-free for the first time. It was my firm objective to stay debt-free the rest of my life. Less than a year later, here I was contemplating sinking $4 million into PPE products for which I had no idea how much longer the demand was going to stay strong. It was the second-biggest decision I had to make as an entrepreneur. So, what does an entrepreneur do? Pick up the Chance card. And it read, "De Plane, De Plane!"

To fund the plane and its contents without going into debt, I had to liquidate my 401(k) plan and pay 25 percent capital gains taxes. The net amount was $2.2 million, my life savings. Here I was, in my mid-sixties fucking years old, risking my life savings on PPE. I brought Dawn into my office and told her my plan. She asked me if I was crazy. I told her, "Absolutely, all entrepreneurs are crazy." I went online to my Fidelity account, processed the transaction, and the "submit" button appeared. We both looked at each other. I took one deep breath and pressed the fucking button. The check arrived in two days. It was the biggest check I had ever seen. Dawn snatched it from my hands and deposited it into our Comerica checking account. I called FedEx.

The plane landed in Ohio in the middle of May. I had photos taken of the plane and the goods being unloaded. The trucks showed up a couple of days later. It was a joyous occasion. But only two weeks later, the lockdown was lifted and people went back to work. While demand for PPE was still good, it died down, and we were left holding thousands of boxes of masks (sold all the gloves). TNG still owes me the money I loaned it, and we are still debt-free. To this day, I still can't believe I chartered De Plane.

LIFE LESSON TIP: Yes, all entrepreneurs are crazy, and the successful ones are also lucky. I strongly believe in luck being a factor in many aspects of one's life. At the poker table, there are days I can't lose a hand, and there are days I can't win a hand. When I play chess (no luck involved here), there are days I win four in a row, and there are days I lose six in a row. Some experts say it is karma. I agree. Karma each day is different, and I also think that entrepreneurs have more good days than bad days, because we are inherently optimistic. And it never hurts to be lucky too.

LESSON #88

If You Are a Turtle, You Never Want to Be on Your Back

Unlike any world war, unlike 9/11, unlike the Great Depression, and unlike any other previous event, nothing changed the world like COVID-19. Books have already been written on this subject; I'm only going to tell you my part of the story as it relates to being an entrepreneur.

Lockdown scared people. COVID was an unknown. Unlike the usual seasonal afflictions, one could actually die from it. COVID was like an alien spaceship landing on earth and the "Invasion of the Body Snatchers" coming to life. People became zombies. Restaurants were closed down except for carryout. You had to wear a mask everywhere you went, even nitrile gloves were a thing. Howard Stern was broadcasting that he washed his fruit in a baking soda solution to get rid of any chance the fruit was contaminated with COVID (he was petrified of it). People started washing UPS, FedEx, and Amazon boxes before they opened them.

When lockdown was announced in Michigan, we had a team meeting with all the employees. We needed warehouse workers to process the huge influx of orders. We said that if you were uncomfortable working with a mask, you could stay home (without pay) and come back when you wanted to. Some left. Office employees were nonessential, but we needed them to do typical tasks. Right away, we allowed two to three days a week in the office; employees were allowed to choose. Most chose to come in on Monday and Wednesday; the other days they worked from home. Little did anyone know then that this would cause a permanent shift in employee mentality as they got used to working at home. As of December 2023, offices are still half-empty, and it is estimated that there will be more than 330 million square feet of empty office space by 2030.

Salons in Michigan were allowed to reopen June 15. Salons were already struggling before the pandemic with the onslaught of booth rental suites as I mentioned earlier in the book. Although the government came up with a PPP program, many salons did not know how to submit for it or thought they weren't eligible. Many salons never reopened. This further destroyed the possibility of a resurgence in young people wanting to become salon professionals. The professional beauty industry never recovered. It will be interesting when the baby boomers who opened A salons in the 1980s and 1990s retire, what will be left? Consumers will have no choice but to go to a franchise or salon suite.

Restaurants were another group that we targeted because they needed PPE and bought from food distributors. Restaurants were not allowed to reopen with indoor seating in Michigan until February 1, 2021, and consequently, many closed permanently even with PPP funding. Even reopening at 50 percent capacity, restaurants struggled to stay open and make money. The new world order was cursed.

One huge consequence of the lockdown was the surge in online spending. Americans were bored at home and binged on Netflix until there was nothing left to watch. They spent the government's stimulus money on furniture, home décor, home improvement projects, food delivery, in-home fitness equipment, workout and leisure clothes, and essentials. Companies such as Wayfair, Williams-Sonoma, Lululemon, RH, Peloton, Zoom Video, and Amazon all benefited. Their sales rocketed to unprecedented levels, and many thought that was going to be the new norm. Demand was so high for these products; factories couldn't keep up, and retailers were caught short of inventory. They vowed that wouldn't happen in 2021 and that is the topic of the next chapter.

For TNG, Amazon was a blessing in disguise. Sales of Ginger Lily Farms products soared as everyone was taking showers at home and traveling to Airbnb's. ForPro products skyrocketed as consumers did more beauty treatments at home. Most importantly, we had inventory because we were not a lowly distributor, and I anticipated in advance that this would happen. Although 2020 was the most brutal year in profitability for TNG, it was also the year that transformed the company. This was partly due to the loyalty of 120 Amazonians and one Amazonian expert, Daniel, who rejoined the company at the perfect time.

While most companies remained shuttered, I was still working the innovation machine. I launched more than fifty new products including NHON implements (made in Vietnam and best quality), ecoTint eyelash tint, and Ginger Lily Farms ZeroDerm. ZeroDerm was a personal care line that contained zero harmful ingredients, was fragrance-free and dermatologist-tested. It quickly became one of our best-selling brands.

The biggest oxymoron in 2020 was that I never worked harder in my life and TNG never lost so much money. I told you loyal reader that 2018 and 2019 were the perfect years for the company. How, just one year later, had so much changed? Between De Plane, airfreight costs, duties, overtime, and other extraneous costs, TNG lost more than $1.6 million.

> 2020 sales were $37 million and we had 120 employees pre-February and ended with 55 employees.

LIFE LESSON TIP: We love watching action movies like Indiana Jones, Mission Impossible, James Bond, and others where the main character is on their back but ends up killing his enemy. As an entrepreneur, you will be on your back at the most inopportune times, and you have to figure out a way to turn over. Pandemic lessons taught me that you can come out ahead if you never stop trying.

LESSON #89

The Government Can Mess Up the Best Plans of Any Entrepreneur

Every priority at TNG changed because of COVID. Once I made the pivot to make TNG a manufacturer, we no longer had to deal with education, trade shows, catalog production, travel schedules, meetings, or marketing projects. Gone were all those employees involved in those functions. I also made the decision to outsource our website to a Magento third-party partner and laid off the web team. By the end of the year, we were down to forty-four employees. It was the most amazing transition I ever witnessed, and while 2021 signaled the bottom for TNG, it was the year I told my employees at the annual meeting that my goal for 2022 was to exceed $1 million in sales per employee. Outsourcing was my new best friend while our mission of 100 percent customer success stayed intact.

The first vaccine to combat COVID was approved by the FDA in December 2020 and was available by the end of the first quarter. By March 19, more than 100 million Americans were vaccinated. However, it did not take long for vaccine shots to become a political target and that jumpstarted the divisive political culture in the United

States. For better or for worse, it was vaccines that opened the economy back up and allowed Americans to travel again.

It was also the beginning of the end of the PPE sales boon. Companies that got into the PPE category wished they never heard of the word. Competitors in my industry including Sally Beauty, Salon Centric, and others took huge write-offs. Even manufacturers including Clorox, 3M, and others took huge write-offs because the factories they built or expanded suddenly had no orders. It was like the faucet turned off overnight. Believe me, we had our share of write-offs too, but it was well worth the cost because TNG became a PPE category leader when other companies exited the business.

On March 11, President Biden signed the $1.9 billion American Rescue Plan. This was on top of the stimulus payments the Trump administration gave most families in 2020. Let's not forget extended unemployment benefits, PPP for businesses, tuition loans stalled indefinitely, and employers desperate for employees. This perfect storm created the biggest supply chain issue in the history of America, and as of May 2023, core inflation was still over 6 percent. Let me explain to you loyal reader how this affects an entrepreneur.

Pre-pandemic (or should I say "during normal times" as we will never live in normal times at least until 2030), I would place an order with a factory in China for a full container. The factory took thirty days for production and then loaded the container on a freight vessel. The vessel would port in Vancouver and then rail to Detroit and then be trucked to our distribution center. Travel time was thirty to forty-five days. The delivered cost of the container was $6,000–$7,000.

However, the stimulus meant not only were Americans not working full-time jobs, they were spending big time. Demand soared. Retailers who were sold out in 2020 were not going to be sold out in 2021 so they doubled and tripled their orders for seasonal and home goods. The supply chain was not ready to accommodate the order surge. It takes months for a shipping firm to add capacity. The busiest port in America is Long Beach/Los Angeles, and it has capacity constraints. Once the container is off-loaded at the port, it must go on a railroad or truck. Both railroads and truckers have capacity constraints. Suddenly, there were containers stacked in China waiting to get on a ship. Once they got on a ship and the ship reached port, the ship had to wait up to three weeks to be off-loaded. The container would then sit for days or weeks at a time trying to get on a rail or a truck.

Every industry was affected. What took thirty to forty-five days to receive now took sixty to ninety days (in some instances, 120 days). Seasonal merchandise arrived after the season. Vital parts suppliers were out of stock. Builders had to stop building homes because they couldn't get toilets, faucets, flooring, and other basic items. Outdoor furniture arrived in the fall. Companies like Peloton couldn't get inventory and customers had to wait ninety days or more to get their bikes. Even worse, retailers ordered heavy on the goods they sold in 2020, but in 2021, consumers no longer wanted fleece pants and home goods. They wanted to travel and go to concerts.

Our container costs went from $6,000 to $10,000 to $15,000 to $20,000 and as high as $30,000 in 2021 and into early 2022. Not only this, factories in America and China were raising costs for the first time since the 1970s. It was a double-whammy. Let me give you an example. One of our best-selling items is a hot towel warmer. There are 870 pieces per container. When the container cost was $6,000, our freight cost per unit was $6.90. When the container cost hit $25,000, our freight cost per unit soared to $28.75. We had no choice but to increase the cost of the warmer. This story was replayed every time we received a container. Every manufacturer experienced the same scenario. That is why inflation soared in 2021 and 2022. Only when interest rates were 20 percent in 1979–1980 have I ever experienced inflation like this. But unlike back then, demand stayed strong even with the higher prices.

Most of our competitors either chose not to pay the inflated container costs or decided the risk was not worth it. They stopped ordering or reduced their quantities. Either way, they were out of stock most of the time and we were in stock. We gained market share and enhanced brand awareness. While 2020 and 2021 were years I never want to relive, they set the stage for 2022 and beyond.

> 2021 sales were $29M and we had forty-four employees.

LIFE LESSON TIP: Big government is anti-business. They would rather hand out money and raise taxes and tariffs than let the free enterprise system work. If and when the government gets involved with your company, you have no choice but to play by their rules. But know that most likely all businesses in the same industry are affected. For instance, when the government enacted 25 percent tariffs on many of our items, we had no choice but to pay them. But we did have the choice to capitalize or expense them.

LESSON #90

Anyone Can Succeed Short Term, It's Long Term That Counts

Amazon did more than $514 billion in sales in 2022, second only to Walmart ($572 billion). That is unfucking believable especially when you go back to Jeff Bezos's original premise of being the ultimate bookstore and nearly going broke during the .com crash.

Just about every strategic decision Bezos laid out came to fruition. Amazon really is the "Everything Store" and has managed to be the leader in thousands of product categories. TNG categories include personal care products, pro beauty, and mass beauty.

Amazon's success can be attributed to several significant innovations, with Amazon Prime being number one. Shippers such as TNG use FedEx or UPS, and depending on the customer's location, delivery can range from one to five business days. With Amazon Prime, delivery is same day to two days. Salons, spas, and other beauty customers were used to buying from several distributors because each distributor offered unique brands. However, that meant they had to place several orders and wait for the orders to arrive sporadically. With

Amazon Prime, they could order everything and receive the order quickly with only one invoice.

Another game-changer was that Amazon did not require its customers to have a cosmetology license (with the exception of a few brands). Salon and spa distributors always required their customers to be licensed and most still do. The Amazon platform allows everyone to buy beauty products with or without a license. That too helped to contribute to the demise of the pro beauty industry because you no longer had to be a pro to buy pro beauty products.

As you read earlier, TNG was among the first pro beauty companies to sell on Amazon. This is one reason why today TNG has more bestsellers and Amazon Choice products than any other beauty manufacturer. The pandemic drew more beauty customers to Amazon, and they stayed with Amazon when the pandemic was over. This helped to create a boon for TNG. Daniel capitalized on it.

There are three ways to sell on Amazon: VC and FBA and SC, as mentioned in Lesson #67. TNG used VC exclusively. Daniel quickly discovered that we were losing a ton of business not doing FBA. He went to work.

By the end of 2022, our FBA sales exceeded VC sales. TNG's total Amazon business more than doubled. FBA was the secret sauce that was missing from the Amazon sales machine (secret sauce is also the key to any burger!). Before you start screaming at me loyal reader for not moving ahead with FBA much sooner, let me go back a bit. As you know, our website launched in 1995. I always had a VP in charge of web sales, and I always pressed the VP to launch FBA. But growth was so robust, it was never a priority. When the next VP came in, I would mention FBA and the same result would take place. When Daniel took over, there was no VP in place because the pandemic eliminated that position. For Daniel, it was priority #1.

Some of our bestsellers include: hot towel warmers, massage sheets, pedi liners, nail files, tongue depressors, every category of Ginger Lily Farms, foil sheets, cotton rounds, esthetic wipes, and paraffin. However, there is nothing more spectacular than having the best-selling nitrile gloves on Amazon. All of the pain and tribulations from dealing with the pandemic were worth it, for this reason alone.

Still another reason for TNG's success on Amazon is that I understood what customers wanted better than our competitors did. I also notice trends, weaknesses, and opportunities. That is what an entrepreneur does. Let me give you an example. We have the best-selling foil sheets and sell them in a 500-count box. I noticed that an off-brand launched a five-inch foil sheet in a 100-count box, and it quickly gained traction. So, what does an entrepreneur do? Launch a five-inch foil sheet in a 100-count box. It is now one of our bestsellers and sells more than three times that of the off-brand.

Let me give you another example. Ginger Lily Farms has the best-selling gallons of personal care products. When I looked at the competition for consumer sizes, I noticed that many of them also sold household cleaning products such as dish soap, laundry detergent, and pet products. So, I further diversified Ginger Lily into those categories. We now have the number-one-selling dish soap gallon and have launched laundry soap, garbage disposal cleaner, and ice machine cleaner.

Product innovation is vital for success. Each year I launch at least fifty new products or variations. It keeps the brands fresh and allows the opportunity to capture trends at a moment's notice.

The Amazing Amazon Machine helped propel TNG's sales to over $40 million, and I realized my goal of $1 million in sales per employee. Daniel always says, "Let's Fucking Go!" Based on the way 2023 started out, we have only scratched the surface of the sales opportunity we have with Amazon. Just as exciting, the 800-pound beast is waking up.

> 2022 sales were $40 million, and we had forty employees.

LIFE LESSON TIP: Take a stroll through your favorite supermarket, mine is Kroger. Notice the brands in each aisle. Chips: Lays. Cereal: Kellogg's, Post, General Mills. Condiments: Heinz, French's, Hellman's. Laundry: Tide. Soup: Campbell's, Progresso. Point is, these brands have been around more than fifty years and are still dominant. The same is true with brands in any industry. Long-term thinking is critical for success the moment you start your business.

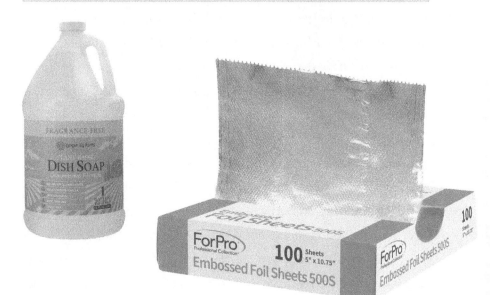

LESSON #91

Never Stop

Walmart operates more than ten thousand stores and clubs in twenty countries and has 2.1 million employees. Doug McMillon is the CEO of Walmart, and one of his biggest challenges has always been trying to balance his store and online business. In 2019, he launched Walmart +, his second major attempt to compete with Amazon. The following year, he launched Walmart Fulfillment Services (WFS) to compete directly with Amazon FBA.

I was always curious about Walmart's online business and how TNG could capitalize on it. When Doug bought Jet.com in 2016 to compete with Amazon, I thought it could be the beginning of an opportunity to engage with them. So, what does an entrepreneur do? Email Doug and ask his advice for doing business with Walmart.

Doug responded almost immediately to me and copied Marc Lore who was the CEO of Jet.com. (Marc was the guy that started diapers.com which Bezos bought to get Marc on his team, another great story.) Marc also responded back to me almost instantaneously and copied the direct report below him. Bottom line: TNG launched more than a hundred products on walmart.com in 2017. But walmart.

com was nothing like Amazon. It was a disaster. We stopped shipping to Walmart in 2021 because sales were disappointing.

Walmart executives will tell you they are at least five to ten years behind Amazon when it comes to technology and distribution. Knowing Doug, I think it is far less. The 800-pound gorilla is alive and kicking, and Walmart is likely the only retailer that can compete against Amazon. On the most recent earnings call, I heard Doug talk about e-commerce business, Walmart +, WFS, and his projected growth rates. Unlike 2016, Doug was feisty and determined. Shortly after the call, I emailed his direct report for e-commerce and again received an almost instantaneous response.

TNG went live on WFS in April with our top-twenty SKUs. This could be another game-changer.

My original sales goal for TNG was always $100 million. We got close at $86 million, but close is only good in tiddlywinks and hand grenades. As an entrepreneur, you are always setting sales goals, but sometimes, they are not as important as other priorities. For me, priority number one has always been profitability and cash flow. However, we are no longer a lowly distributor but a successful manu-facturer. I have restricted selling our brands to other retailers because Amazon does such a great job. Walmart is the second merchant for TNG brands, and I am confident we can get to $100 million in sales with the top-two retailers in the world. Only the future knows for sure. Either way, 2023 turned out to be a record-setting year for TNG in sales growth (44%) and profitability (most profitable year in business).

At sixty-eight years old, everyone always asks me when I am going to retire. I always give them the same answer, "Never. I'm doing exactly what Warren Buffett is doing; working until the end." When his biography came out in 2009, *The Snowball: Warren Buffett and The*

Business of Life, I immediately bought it. It was enormous at more than eight hundred pages, but it was well worth the read and I recommend all entrepreneurs read it. Everything about Buffett is long term, and he is one of the most brilliant businessmen of all time. I took as many key points as possible from the book and still use them today. As of this writing, he is ninety-two years old and still eating See's candies and drinking Coca-Cola (two of his best investments), while managing his portfolio at Berkshire Hathaway. The valuation of his company is $653 billion. Now that my loyal readers is the most amazing statistic of my book. I want to be just like him.

> 2023 sales were $55 million, and we had thirty-seven employees including myself and the BUB.

LIFE LESSON TIP: Never stop and, even better, never quit. Countless times I see people quitting at the gym before they finish their class or they give up on a yoga pose or plank. The hardest workouts are the ones that you want to quit but you keep going. That's what makes us stronger. Entrepreneurs that have this mindset will win more often.

PART 7

THE INTANGIBLES: WHAT THEY DON'T TEACH YOU IN COLLEGE

T hank you loyal reader for making it this far into the book. The fact that you made it here means that you really are in the entrepreneurial spirit and perhaps have learned a thing or two along the way. And if you want to keep learning, the last part of my book is the best part because I get to write about all the intangibles of being an entrepreneur. We all have different mindsets, values, traditions, beliefs, and upbringings. What is constant among entrepreneurs is the spirit of life. We are passionate about what we do on and off the playing field. We have the ability to motivate people, bring smiles to others, and to make the world a better place. The next few chapters will dive into what are the most important intangibles to me that make a difference.

LESSON #92

Giving Back

Rabbi Dannel Schwartz was a senior rabbi at another temple and got "kicked out." So, what does an entrepreneurial rabbi do? Start a new congregation. He started Shir Shalom in 1988 with thirty founding families. We were one of them. Dannel approached me at the worst possible time in 1991. He called me and said "Larry, it's Dannel. I was wondering if I could come by Nailco to see your building and have a cup of coffee?"

I could only give a little money to charities here and there back then because I had no money to give. I suspected Dannel's reason for coming but made the appointment anyway. Sure enough, his vision was to build a new temple in West Bloomfield and he wanted me to be a part of it and make a generous donation. He was a schmoozer, number one, and a rabbi, number two, and won me over. I pledged $25,000 and got my father to do $25,000 as well. The donation was good enough to have the library named "Gaynor Library." It was the first time my name was on a building. BTW, the new temple opened in 1995 one mile away from the office building. Dannel had the brilliant idea for the founding members to walk from the office building to the new temple to celebrate the opening.

At this juncture, I decided it was time to get season tickets to MSU football games. I loved going to the games as a student, but I had to work weekends and could not go to the games after I graduated. Now that I didn't work weekends and the kids were at the age they enjoyed football, I thought it was a great way to get them excited about MSU and going to college.

Little did I know that seats were based on donor level. I wasn't a donor, and my seats were in the end zone. I also didn't know that seat selection was based on how many years you had season tickets. I was years behind my peers.

Fast-forward ten years; I was ready to sign up as a donor at the $5,000 level. On top of the ticket prices, the $5,000 annual donation got me tickets around the twenty-yard line. I then moved up to the $10,000 level and got to the thirty-yard line. Fast-forward another ten years, around 2010, and I was finally at the top level of $25,000. For this, I got the "green padded seats" and was at the forty-yard line, nine rows from the field. The game perspective was so much better! Then the following year they upgraded the highest level to $50,000 and I bought in. I was now on the forty-five-yard line, seven rows from the field. It was then that Dorn, part of the MSU Athletic donor team, approached me about the North End Zone project.

Now for the side story. One of my friends asked me to buy him season tickets because I was at the highest donor level. I told him sure thing. One benefit of being at the highest donor level was getting stadium parking passes. I received two each year, one for me and one for him. In 2019, Dorn told me I could only get one stadium pass and the other pass would be a few blocks away. I told him after all the money I donated, I wanted two stadium passes. He told me NO! I told him to fuck off, and I canceled my season tickets.

Just as the North End Zone opened, I got a call from Sanjay Gupta, then the dean of the Broad School of Business. He wanted to see me at my building and have a cup of coffee. Yeah, right. I said to him, "Sure thing, Sanjay." Sanjay showed up with his assistant and a couple of others from the university. Sanjay said, "Larry, I have the most exciting opportunity to share with you, and there is no one else that I could think of that would be more of a perfect fit." Yeah, right. He then went into an elaborate presentation of the new building, The Pavilion, which would be built right next to the main business building, Eppley Center. On the lower level of the two-story building, he pointed out the Entrepreneurial Lab that would focus on entrepreneurial programs for underclass and graduate students. I immediately thought that he and Dannel were friends. They were both amazing schmoozers.

The grand opening of The Pavilion and the Entrepreneurial Lab was very special. Unfortunately, Sanjay would be terminated in 2022 and MSU would have five presidents in five years. As of this writing, both the current business dean and president are "interim."

I wanted a charity that would appeal to women since most of our employees and customers were women. I found the perfect charity, the St. Vincent and Sarah Fisher Center in Farmington Hills, Michigan. The center was run by Catholic nuns that took in foster kids and raised them until they were able to be on their own. We donated $50,000 a year until they closed down over a scandal. I then went from one charity to another, but none resonated until one day the Farmington Hills police came to our building and asked for me. I came to the lobby and the officer said, "You are being arrested on behalf of the ACS. I'm to take you to the Holiday Inn where you have to fundraise at least a thousand dollars to get out." Back then, it was called "lock-up," and I had the choice to go with him or politely decline. So, what does an entrepreneur do? Ride shotgun with the cop. I ended up raising more than $10,000, which was a record, and the ACS was my new best friend.

ACS launched STRIDES in Detroit, and I was asked to be a presenting sponsor. I signed up. STRIDES focused on breast cancer awareness and research. It turned out to be another perfect charity. Over the next twenty years, we donated more than $2 million to ACS and were a lead sponsor for STRIDES. In 2023, I decided to end our partnership and move forward with Gleaners, one of the biggest food banks in Detroit. Food insecurity is a prevalent issue in Detroit and we are very happy to support Gleaners' mission of achieving a hunger-free community in southeast Michigan. The first gift was for $50,000.

One very important thing Gallup® taught me was the three Cs: external customers, internal customers; and charity. Our pledge for our external customer has always been 100 percent customer success. In giving back, it all started with the Nailco Gold frequent buyer program that was continually updated over the years. We gave back well over $5 million in rewards to our customers.

My wife and I love to give back to others, our community, and our employees—and I think this is very important. To start with, sponsoring charities has been so positive—employees love getting involved. They delight in participating in food and clothes bank collections. We sponsor volunteer days in which talent can work at a charity of their choice for a day. At STRIDES, they brought their families and friends for the walk. Two, you always get back more than you give. Sometimes, the results are instant. Let me give you an example. I hand out bonus checks twice a year with the biggest check at the end of the year. One employee later that day always comes to my office with a bottle of Stag's Leap cabernet and a very nice thank you card. Finally, you don't have to donate, you *get* to donate. I am always amazed at how our employees rally to collect funds by tapping their friends and family. For some, it is a competition. Overall, it really helps to create a team environment.

LIFE LESSON TIP: Giving back to charities is often the last thing on an entrepreneur's mind, especially at start-up. But it is amazing how much you can give back without donating a penny. Both customers and employees love companies that give back and adding logos of companies that you give back to adds intangible credence to your business.

LESSON #93

Make Exercise a Daily Routine for the Best Overall Health

We all know that all the money in the world won't buy you happiness. Alas, it also won't buy your health. I have said it once, and I will say it again: Health is based on three equal parts: genes, luck, and how you take care of yourself. How you take care of yourself is the only thing that you have control over.

One of my yoga instructors, Ceasar Barajas, once said about life, "You are fortunate to have a group of loved ones around you when you take your first breath. You are even more fortunate to have a group of loved ones around you when you take your last breath. What you do between your first and last breath is all up to you."

When I graduated from MSU in 1977, I was six feet four inches and weighed 180 pounds. Fast-forward to 2023; I am still the same height and weight. I am not on a single prescription drug, and I only drink alcohol on days that end in "y." HA!

Some people might refer to me as: OCD; regimented; addicted to life; black and white. They might be right. After all, I can tell you what I will be doing at any time of the day for the next year. I plan medical appointments and vacations a year in advance. They say that no two entrepreneurs are alike, but most likely if you are one, you share some of the same traits as me. Regardless of the amount of wealth, success, and happiness achieved, everything boils down to health and wellness. Let me share my thoughts with you as to how I have lived my life. Perhaps I can inspire you, especially if you are still in your twenties and thirties.

My Twenties

They say that life is wasted on the young. They are right! If I knew what I know now when I was in my twenties, OMG! What was more fun than coming home from work on Friday, getting ready for a night on the town, staying out until two in the morning, then going to the twenty-four-hour diner for breakfast, crashing at 3:30 in the morning and getting up at six to get ready for work? Nothing. The twenties was all about being invincible: unlimited energy and stamina; eat what you want at any time; nothing ever hurt. I joined Franklin Racquet Club in my late twenties and got addicted to aerobics.

LIFE LESSON TIP: Stay out of the sun as much as possible and use SPF 50 sunscreen (I love SuperGoop best!). I wish I knew about sunscreen and skin cancer in my twenties. Don't get me wrong, there is no better feeling than baking in the sun, but you don't want to be an expert on Mohs surgery like I am.

My Thirties

I had kids in my thirties, and I have to say this was my worst decade. Not only did I have to deal with three kids and commuting every other weekend, but I was also working six days a week. Exercise became more important, and I took a yoga class for the first time. It was life-changing, and I highly recommend it. Not only do you stretch your muscles and focus on breathing, it is an amazingly hard workout. Aerobics started to get a bad rap, and I switched to step aerobics. I worked out three times a week including weightlifting. The BUB and I enjoyed dancing on weekends until early morning, and instead of breakfast, we stopped for sliders and fries. Yum!

LIFE LESSON TIP: Sleep is one of life's most important functions for the body and brain. I also get some of my best ideas while sleeping. I love 8-8.5 hours of sleep per night.

My Forties

Is this the beginning of the typical mid-life crisis? Not for me. It was the beginning of many things, however. Annual physicals. No more fast food (I have not had a hot dog, burger, or donut in more than twenty-five years but don't ask me about pizza or French fries). Martini Fridays. Red wine. Running. I switched from Franklin to The Sports Club. I still loved step aerobics and yoga but also played tennis, racquetball, and was introduced to spinning.

Daniel joined The Sports Club, and one day he said to me, "Dad, have you ever thought about running?" I replied, "Not really but I'll give it a try." Mind you, I was in great shape and was now working out five days a week. We went one mile and turned around running at a nine-minute pace. I was out of breath at the end of the run and felt muscles I didn't know existed. We ran for a few times and then Daniel said to me one day after we ran the first mile, "Are you ready to turn the corner instead of going back?" That meant going four miles. I said, "Sure thing." I remember slowing down on the last mile thinking I wasn't going to make it. Daniel was well ahead of me, and I barely finished. The next few runs were better. Then Daniel mentioned the Turkey Trot, and I thought it was a great idea. My first 10K and first timed event! Daniel handily beat me, but I vowed I would beat him the following year. And I did. More importantly, I went on to run more than fifteen half-marathons and did the Turkey Trot each year until I stopped running.

LIFE LESSON TIP: Make exercise enjoyable. I joined gyms that had full-service locker rooms with steam, sauna, and jacuzzi. The after-exercise reward is the best and definitely worth the time.

My Fifties

I have to say this is the best decade of life. Kids are on their own. Vacations are more plentiful. Not too young and not too old. And not working crazy hours.

I ran my first and only marathon in Chicago in 3:42 and finished in the top 15 percent. There is nothing better than running to release endorphins. However, there is nothing harder on the body either. Turning fifty meant it was time for my first colonoscopy. Colon cancer is the fourth most common type of cancer and is the most preventable. Just get a colonoscopy (some doctors are starting to recommend age forty-five). Basal cell carcinoma is the most prevalent form of skin cancer and nearly four million Americans are diagnosed with it each year. I learned more about this than I wanted after going to the dermatologist and being diagnosed with it. He told me it was from sun exposure as a teenager and early twenties. For better or worse, my dermatologist became my new best friend as I have had five Mohs surgeries and countless encounters with his liquid nitrogen canister (–320°F).

I increased my exercise to seven days a week and came up with a brilliant schedule. Daily core work and:

Sunday: Nine-mile run, ten-minute meditation

Monday: Yoga forty-five minutes (I highly recommend the Aaptiv app for yoga, meditation, core, treadmill, and outdoor walking) and core for fifteen minutes

Tuesday: Free weights thirty minutes, four-mile run, ten-minute meditation

Wednesday: Free weights thirty minutes, six-mile run, ten-minute meditation

Thursday: Yoga forty-five minutes and core for fifteen minutes

Friday: Free weights thirty minutes, six-mile run, ten-minute meditation

Saturday: Yoga forty-five minutes and core for fifteen minutes

This is a good time to mention diet. I eat healthy Monday through Thursday (addicted to wild salmon and love Arctic char). Friday and Saturday are splurge days. On Sundays, I make an awesome brunch for BUB, and I clean out the fridge to make an awesome dinner.

LIFE LESSON TIP: If you see something on your body that doesn't look right, see a dermatologist right away.

My Sixties

This is the decade that you say to yourself, "I'm fucking old now, but at least I made it this far." Yadda-yadda-yadda, I love when people tell me that the sixties are the new forties. In one aspect, they are right. Life expectancy in 1900 was only forty-six. It hit sixty-six years in 1950. It peaked before the pandemic close to eighty (women have higher life expectancies by a couple of years). They say it will zoom to 115 by 2100, and I believe it.

Personally, not much changed for me compared to my fifties except for one little incident. I was running with my friend, Jeff Risius, and we always did six miles. After 5.8 miles, we sprinted to the end. In one brief instant, my right hip didn't feel good. I shrugged it off and thought I pulled a muscle. I thought it would go away, but it didn't. BUB told me to see a doctor. I held off as long as possible, and I started walking funny. Running started to hurt more so I succumbed and went to see an orthopedic surgeon. Yep, 100 percent arthritis in my right hip. It was the end of my running days and I was so disappointed. I had hip replacement surgery in 2019, which was easy-peasy.

I replaced running with spinning and never looked back. It does suck however that I have to go through the x-ray scanner at the airport.

I also added an afternoon exercise session alternating with walking, cycling, and swimming for a total time of thirty minutes. I joined Equinox so I could enjoy these activities during the winter and love their Equinox+ app that includes SoulCycle.

LIFE LESSON TIP: Download your exercise schedule every Sunday. Post-pandemic, I am hooked on using the Aaptiv and Equinox+ apps. I download and schedule all my classes on Sunday for the week, and I know what to look forward to.

LESSON #94

Throw Out the Remote Control and Find Hobbies That You Can Get Addicted To

We have all heard the expression, "All work and no play makes Jack a dull boy." You don't have to worry about that with me. I love fun and games. As you know, competition is my number-one strength so when I do play, it is always to win. And I always say, "When I don't win, I'm learning."

For me, fun starts with music. Being a baby boomer, I grew up on rock'n'roll and loved Frampton, Zeppelin, Elton John, The Doors, Aerosmith, and Springsteen especially in college. BUB loved music, too, although softer rock like Fleetwood Mac, Diana Ross, and Madonna, and she knew the words to every song (I can hear a song a hundred times and still not know the lyrics). We listened to vinyl, cassettes, and CDs.

Sirius XM's launch in 2002 had a huge impact on the way we listened to music. I loved it. When Radio Margaritaville debuted on Sirius in 2005, it forever changed my music world. I listen to it daily in the car, when I work out, when I relax with a glass of wine with BUB, and I love the concert replays. Jimmy Buffett is all about summertime, sand, beach, flip-flops, boats, drinks, and having fun. It is the perfect music for me.

After music, I have to say reading books is right up there. Both BUB and I read the same authors and adore reading. When we take a one-week vacation, we read three books. I love anything John Grisham, Steven King, James Patterson, Patricia Cornwell, Lee Child, and David Baldacci to name a few.

Fun on vacation for me now is waking up (very important thing to do!), exercise, breakfast, beach, swim, happy hour, dinner, and bed. Don't get me wrong, I thoroughly enjoy traveling to exotic international countries too. BUB and I have been to Israel, Portugal, Greece, Italy, London, Hong Kong, Croatia, Switzerland, Lima, Machu Picchu, and New Zealand. However, there is nothing like a week on the beach in Mexico (love Puerto Vallarta best).

I love cooking. BUB and I have become gourmet cooks, and it's not unusual for us to spend hours each weekend preparing the menu, grocery shopping, and cooking. BUB is the best sous chef (although she can be irritating when she cleans utensils I am still using, HA!) and the queen of Bounty paper towels (I prefer kitchen towels). I can write a cookbook on our favorite recipes and might do that next. I have perfected smash burgers (chicken/turkey mix), smoked ribs, tuna tartare, Caesar salad, homemade pizza (I love my Ooni pizza oven), frittatas, and blueberry pancakes.

I am obsessed with games. I learned how to play poker in high school. My brother Bob and I went to St. Louis in 2005 to watch MSU lose in their first game of the Final Four. We had an afternoon to kill, and Bob suggested we go to a casino. The casino had Texas Hold'em and Bob proposed we play. After an hour of playing, I was addicted. I played at least one weekend day at a Detroit casino up until the pandemic. We taught the kids how to play poker. Recently I taught my oldest grandson Carter how to play. I think he has competition in his top-five too; he loves to win and hates to lose.

BUB and I were crazy about Scrabble, Perquacky, and War. Now we are addicted to Candy Crush! This came out in 2012, and I still play it daily. I am past level 11,000, and BUB just passed level 13,000.

When *The Queen's Gambit* was released in 2020, I was fascinated. I learned to play chess in college but rarely played afterward. The series was so good, I decided I had to get back into chess. So, what does an entrepreneur do? Sign up for chess.com. It opened up an entire new world for me. I have taken over six hundred lessons on chess.com, do the daily puzzle, and spend at least fifteen minutes daily doing puzzles. I even have a chess coach, Alex Banzea, who is an International Master and resides in Romania. He teaches me for one hour weekly and I just cracked 1200 in rapid, which is good enough to be in the ninetieth percentile on chess.com. I am not alone in being addicted to chess. At the end of 2022, chess.com had more than seven million subscribers. At the end of February 2023, the number grew to more than twelve million.

I have been going to Mexico for nearly twenty years, and I thought it would be cool to learn Spanish. So I went online and found Duolingo. That was more than three years ago and I am totally hooked. I learn Spanish thirty minutes daily and have been in the Diamond league (that is their top league) forever.

Needless to say, watching TV and movies is not my thing. I do love a good series now and then. My favorites are *Succession, Curb Your Enthusiasm, Yellowstone, Stranger Things,* and *Shtisel.* I rarely watch sports anymore as all the Detroit teams suck, and the Spartans continue to disappoint at the highest level.

As an entrepreneur, taking time out for fun and games is crucial for your overall success and well-being. I cannot imagine a world without it.

LIFE LESSON TIP: Entrepreneurs need time for themselves each and every day. Hobbies are the best way to use that time, and when possible, use that time for yourself.

LESSON #95

Celebrate Success!

O nce upon a time, BUB and I were addicted to golf and even joined a country club. This was about the same time Daniel was finishing his stint at the Ross College of Business. My friend Howard and his wife joined too and we would play nine holes on a Friday afternoon and have dinner afterward. We all know the best part of golf is the nineteenth hole, and Howard always ordered a gin martini. I hated gin so I would opt for Grey Goose. The bartender made them extra good because he pretty much filled up the shaker and gave it to us with an ice-cold martini glass and a side of blue cheese olives (yum!). I called it the endless martini, and it was the best way to cap off a long week.

When Daniel joined the company after Ross, we took him to the country club for dinner on Fridays and we started with a Grey Goose martini. We always toasted to health and life. It became a tradition, and to this day, we still celebrate Martini Friday.

Man has to eat, but tech companies got it all wrong when they thought offering employees free food would make them more loyal to the company. The key is not giving away free food but making the food for them. Summertime barbeques at TNG started when we moved to Farmington Hills, and I thought it would be a great idea to have a company lunch in the parking lot. The tradition still lives on. The all-time favorite barbeque is Chick-A-Doodle-Doo because of the secret marinade that makes the best-tasting chicken. As a loyal reader, I am going to share my recipe, and you will want to make extra!

5 pounds of chicken breast filets, pounded

1.5 ounces of Good Season Italian Dressing

1 ounce, Lawry's seasoning salt

3 ounces, red wine

5 ounces of lemon juice

.75 ounces of black pepper

Whisk all ingredients together and then add 1.5 cups canola oil. Put the chicken breasts in a one-gallon Ziploc bag, add marinade and marinate overnight. For best results, cook chicken on a hot charcoal grill, three to four minutes each side. YUM!

There is no better way to celebrate than a good old-fashioned barbeque lunch in the parking lot. Or is there?

Damn right, there is. I already told you about our annual meeting celebrations. Now let me tell you about our 30/60 Celebration. TNG turned thirty, and I turned sixty. So, what does an entrepreneur do? Charter a plane to NYC for the weekend. At the time, we had 145 employees and we just about filled a 737 jet. I booked rooms at the Marriot Times Square Marquis and hired a tour company to handle all the details. We had four charter buses.

The first night we walked to Grand Central Station and had dinner at Michael Jordan's steakhouse. The next morning, we had private tours of 9/11 Ground Zero, Wall Street, Chinatown (had lunch there too), and the Financial District. We had an amazing Italian dinner at Carmine's and then saw *Kinky Boots*. Sunday morning, we toured Central Park and had a private ferry take us to see the Statue of Liberty while enjoying a decadent brunch. It was the most amazing celebration ever and worth every bit of the $500,000 it cost.

Two years later, I chartered another plane and we flew to Cleveland. I held the annual meeting at the Rock and Roll Hall of Fame. It was so cool.

Beginning in 2014, I turned the annual meetings into an overnight extravaganza. At noon, we would close business early to enjoy a gourmet-catered lunch. Then we would board buses and head out for a fun-filled afternoon of activities. We would go to an upscale mall and each employee would have up to a thousand to spend in two hours. Other activities included Broadway plays, touring Meadowbrook Estate, Dave & Buster's, Detroit Zoo's festival of lights, and Greenfield Village. I also held the meeting at cool places like movie theaters, live music theaters, the MGM Grand, and Greektown Casino.

Yet another way of celebrating was BUB's and my idea of the Summer and Winter survival kits. We would go to Costco and select the best items we knew everyone would enjoy. The summer kit always had guacamole and chips, ready-to-drink margaritas, movie passes, a cookbook, lunch gift cards, Sander's Sea Salt caramels, red and white wine, prime filets (everyone loved those), shrimp cocktail, and so much more. The winter kit always featured something warm and cozy in addition to all the great food items (we did a whole ham instead of the filets).

Post-pandemic, everything changed, but we still had to celebrate! Now we do the summer and annual meetings on Saturday morning at TNG starting with a catered breakfast (Cracker Barrel does an amazing job). The meeting lasts about an hour and then we take a chartered bus to Costco. Now everyone gets to make their own survival kit and the employees are totally spoiled with the thousand to spend in one hour. Afterward, we have a steakhouse lunch at a fine restaurant before heading back. It is the perfect day.

LIFE LESSON TIP: Cracking open a Corona and grilling up a hot dog is a great way to celebrate. Going to Ocean Prime and ordering the seafood platter is another great way. Point is, you can celebrate on any budget.

LESSON #96

Awards and Media Mention Might Be
Good for the Ego, But Don't Depend
on Them to Help Grow Your Business

There is one goal I set forth for myself that I failed to achieve: getting on the cover of *Forbes* or *BusinessWeek*. I got close with *Forbes* during the height of the pandemic, but it didn't pan out (I did have a featured story in *Entrepreneur* in 2001 and made the cover of *dBusiness* in 2009).

If you visit me in my office, you will walk down a fifteen-foot hallway. Both sides are filled with framed articles that I appeared in since I started the company. Most of the articles are from years ago when there were trade journals and people still read the newspaper. I thought it was cool to be in the *Detroit News*, *Crain's Business Detroit*, *Entrepreneur* magazine, and various trade journals. As an entrepreneur, being featured in the media helped to confirm your success with peers, customers, and vendors. Or did it?

If there was an award to win, I was all in. I can't tell you how many times TNG won an "Employer of the Year" award, whether it was sponsored by the *Detroit Free Press*, *Crain's*, or *FOX2*. The Detroit Chamber of Commerce held a Future 50 contest each year and TNG won it nearly every time. *Crain's* once held a contest for the 50 Fittest CEOs, and I won both years it was held. *FOX2* did a "101 Brightest & Best Companies" competition for a few years, and we were always included. As an entrepreneur, winning awards helped to confirm your success with peers, customers, and vendors. Or did it?

Looking back, the answer to both questions is "no." Someone once told me that newspapers don't sell by writing about good news; they only sell when they write about bad news. The more horrific the news is, the better the sales. What could be more boring than reading about a company that won an award? What could be more exciting than reading about a company going out of business or embezzling money from employees?

Fast-forward to today, as an entrepreneur: you have to be very careful when dealing with social and traditional media. You can look no further than reading the story about Olaplex. They used social media in the best way and they went public in September 2021 at $21 a share, the highest amount ever for a professional hair care company. Then social media railed against them and as of December 2023, their stock was $2.35 a share.

I have been writing my blog, larrygaynor.com, for more than fifteen years. For me, that is one of the best ways to get your message out to your loyal followers. Podcasts are very popular and have taken over blogs and are yet another great way to reach out to your followers on your terms. Most importantly, however, is to communicate to your employees often and always keep them informed on good and bad news at the company. Nobody likes bad surprises.

LIFE LESSON TIP: If you have a story to tell, the media will find you. If you have an award worth winning, your employees and/or mentors will let you know about it. The best award is having customers buy your products.

LESSON #97

Management 101, 201, 301, 401, 5000000000000001

T he best B schools brag about teaching management, but none of them succeed. Why? Look at who is teaching the classes. You could take all the management classes in the world and still fail miserably managing others. Why? Like being an entrepreneur, management is a talent too.

Entrepreneurs do not make great managers. Truthfully, the last thing we want to do is manage people, but it is one of those tasks that you have to do as your company grows. At one point, I had eight people on my leadership team, and I had eight people on my sales team that reported directly to me.

Let me give you a glimpse of my management style over the years, both pre-Gallup® and post-Gallup®. Pre-Gallup®, it didn't matter who the employee was, I was going to get in my two cents if there was an issue. Employees who made gross mistakes (anything that pissed off a customer was a gross mistake), I just shouted at and asked how they could have made that mistake. It did not matter the location or how many people were around. Then I would go to HR and want that person fired immediately. And in case you forgot, the HR Director was BUB.

I don't have enough fingers and toes to tell you how many times BUB told me I couldn't yell at employees in an open environment. So, I changed it to a closed environment and had the employees come to my office. That didn't work either. Mind you, this was in the early growth stages of the company, so we didn't have a lot of department managers. What worked was this: I had to meet with an employee with a member of the HR team to review the gross mistake and to confirm it would never happen again. The employee would get a write-up and that would go in a file. Three write-ups were required to terminate unless it was a felonious charge like stealing or embezzling. Three write-ups, you ask? Yep. Women are always right.

Every management book tells you that you must do annual employee reviews. I always wondered who dreaded the annual review more—the employer or the employee. It was customary to give an annual raise after the annual review, and the amount of the raise was dependent on the results of the review. Employees who got great reviews were happy because they got great raises. On the flip side, employees who got lousy reviews didn't get a raise and weren't happy. But at least they could not be fired.

Post-Gallup® managing got better. Gallup® had a review program called the "Four Keys," and it was very elaborate. Gallup® recommended quarterly reviews and to focus on employee goals that could be reached quarterly and annually. We did that for a couple of years, and once the employee reached their goals, we moved back to doing an annual review.

I decided not to get personally involved with employee relations and let HR do its thing unless I thought it was a really big issue. Even then, HR would overrule me, and it got to the point it was best

I wasn't involved at all, except when HR came into my office and closed my door.

The good news is that we have always had the best employees so dealing with the few deadbeats was a rare occurrence. In fact, I always compare our HR department to the Maytag repair department: just waiting for something to do although the government and insurance companies keep them busy.

Fast-forward post-pandemic loyal reader, to the best management style of all: hire the best people and let them do what they do best. Only step in when they ask for your assistance. Annual reviews? Upon request only. I cannot remember the last time I did an annual review. Then again, the last time we hired a new employee was in 2019. Hire the best managers too and let them take care of HR issues with the HR department. Only get involved if one of your direct reports has to be terminated.

LIFE LESSON TIP: Post-pandemic, HR is trickier than ever. Document, document, and document. As mentioned earlier in the book, hire the best HR attorney, and when in doubt, call. Prepare an employee handbook and keep it updated. And if possible, hire the best damn HR manager. Even if part-time, the peace of mind is worth it.

LESSON #98

Develop the Best Core Team

Every company, every sports team, and every president has a core team.

If you go to investor relations for any public company, one tab is Corporate Governance. Here you see who is the CEO, CFO, COO, CIO, yadda, yadda, yadda. That is their core team.

The starters on any sports team are the core team.

The POTUS core team is handpicked and made up of his top advisors.

Successful companies, sport teams, and presidents all have one thing in common: They have the best core team.

I did not know how lucky I was until the pandemic hit. So many people quit their jobs or were fired. Many were afraid to come to work. Government handouts were aplenty. In 2021, it was all about the Great Resignation. Suddenly, employees who were not happy at work decided to quit. Millions of jobs went unfilled. "Help wanted" signs were hanging in windows, dancing in the wind on street poles, and even appearing on electronic billboards.

As I mentioned in the previous lesson, the last employee we hired was in 2019. Since the pandemic began, not one employee has left.

The average tenure per employee is over eighteen years. These are incredible statistics, and you would never read about these in *The Harvard Business Review* or *Sloan Management Review*. The bottom line is that all my thirty-seven employees now make up the core team. It is no longer a specific group of employees like pre-pandemic.

Here is the most amazing statistic of all in regard to having all your employees being part of your core team: 100 percent of everything done right. 100 percent customer success? Got it. Ship Amazon orders complete and on time? Got it. Computer issue? Got it. Prep, set up, and tear down company lunch? Got it. Don't bother Larry because he is writing a book? Got it.

They say ChatGPT is going to be the greatest revolution of all time in technology because, in part, it can answer any question in less than a second. I have to say having the best core team is as good if not better than ChatGPT. Why? No matter what the issue is, the team solves it immediately and without my assistance. That is how tuned in the team is. And let me tell you my loyal reader, ChatGPT will never replace the human experience. Just as nail techs, hairdressers, and massage therapists are allowed to touch people (and people enjoy it), there is nothing better than watching the team enjoy a company lunch and the camaraderie that goes along with it.

The core team likes to be referred to as the TNG family. I disagree. Forty to fifty percent of first-time marriages fail and that is between two people who loved each other. And 60–67 percent of second-time marriages fail. And when was the last family event that went well for you? There is always drama and someone getting on your nerves. The poor baby boomers thought they were free and clear when their kids left home; now they have to take care of their mother and/or father. Sorry, but families have too many issues.

Teams win or lose. I like to refer to our core team as the best winning team. Winning teams make more money, share more high-fives, are the happiest, and, most importantly, shrug off mistakes. No one makes less than $25/hour after bonus. The pay gap between the lowest paid employee and myself is six times. I distribute at least 25 percent of the company profits each year. However, money is not the motivator that keeps employees loyal to a company. In fact, it ranks fourth.

According to the Institute of Chartered Accountants in England and Wales, the top-five motivators are as follows:

1. Provide meaningful and challenging work

2. Improve employees' lives

3. Recognition

4. Compensation

5. Culture

The core team is so important to BUB and me that we put them in our will. But who wants to die before giving away money? We have decided to give more money away while we are alive so everyone can enjoy life just a little bit better now. Let me give you an example. You already know about the ten-year and twenty-year anniversary trips employees receive. BUB and I decided to do something special for our employees who have been with us thirty years (we have five through 2023): At the last annual meeting during lunch, we made an announcement and brought up each employee one at a time. I then brought out a cashier's check for $30,000 and BUB gave it to the employee. The shock and tears in the dining room were immense. The appreciation from each employee was priceless. Moreover, since we gifted them the money, it was 100 percent tax-free. This my loyal reader is one of the benefits of being a successful entrepreneur. What are you waiting for?

LIFE LESSON TIP: Starting out, the core team was the BUB and me. When you start out, make sure the first hire is someone that you would hire forever. That is the most important hire you will ever make. If you are an established entrepreneur, then realize who your core team is and develop them to the best of your ability.

LESSON #99

Why a Gallup®-Trained Organization Is Best-in-Class

I firmly believe that TNG's continuous success, especially post-pandemic, is because we are a Gallup®-trained organization. Gallup® is a company lifestyle that transcends daily in all our activities. Employees love knowing their top-five strengths, and I love the stories they have shared with me when they have told their families and friends what their strengths are—and seen they align with what those closest to them think as well.

The core team is invaluable to TNG and I asked them if they wanted to write something for my book. I thought it was the perfect thank you for their dedication, loyalty, and support. I think one of life's greatest rewards being an entrepreneur is seeing how you have changed the lives of so many people, especially all the employees that have worked for you. I am thrilled to be able to share their thoughts with you.

I knew immediately after I accepted the accounting manager position it was going to be a good fit. I didn't know, however, at that time that

I would later become the controller and then the CFO. Larry and Teresa supported me, believed in me, and I am thankful for both of them.

You understand why there is such longevity here. Yes, there are great perks, bonuses, trips, shopping sprees, lunches, etc., but it is more than that: We all want TNG to be successful and to be part of its success. I love the team atmosphere that we have.

TNG's success is contributed to Larry's vision: He isn't afraid to take risks; he is passionate about the business; and is very hands-on in every aspect.

DAWN KUHN, CFO

Hired 6/30/2003

Includer® | Learner® | Relator® | Self-Assurance® | Focus®

Someone once called me a creature of habit. This comment came in regard to my long-term employment at TNG, and at the time, I'd been employed for ten years. Now I'm pushing past thirty years at TNG! It was easy to stay at TNG…. It was exciting! Trade shows, new distribution centers, travel, learning, growth, company culture, amazing parties, and the talent and owners were great.

Call me a creature of habit or lifer, but my basic life and esteem needs were met, and my career came with variety and experiences I would never have found in positions at ten different companies.

If I had to explain my longevity and experience, I would have to describe TNG first. TNG Worldwide—a dynamic Gallup®-trained company in a continual state of change to maintain relevance in the beauty market. Anyone spending thirty-plus years here at TNG has the exposure and experience that compares to working at a hundred different companies.

Thank you, Larry and Teresa, for all your support and generosity over thirty years, you are the best!

JESSE RICHARDSON, LOGISTICS SHIPPING MANAGER
Hired 10/12/1992

Responsibility® | Analytical® | Restorative™ | Arranger® | Relator®

Twenty-five years ago, I was hired to sell hair brands for a brand-new division that was formed. The sales team worked directly with Larry and within the year we were taking the business from all of our competitors. Larry always had new plans to form partnerships with our customers. We had numerous hair shows, business seminars, high-end dinners, hair competitions, Gallup® training for salon owners, and more. During these years, we gained brands, lost brands, and we always bounced back better than before. As a company we always work hard but play hard as well.

I have had some of my most exciting moments at company events. Overnight trips to top hotels, shopping trips, big parties, amazing dinners to name a few. My favorite thing we ever did was go to New York City as a company on a charter flight. This was a celebration for Larry's thirtieth year in business and his sixtieth birthday. The 30/60 was two magical days. Larry had the bus pull over. A few minutes later, we see Larry running across the street dodging cars to jump back on the bus with ten boxes of pizza. He was so excited to get us New York pizza as a "snack." At TNG Worldwide, our favorite thing to do is eat! Our best lunches are with Larry at the BBQ.

JODI BROADDUS, SENIOR SALES CONSULTANT
Hired 12/15/1997

Relator® | Achiever® | Focus® | Learner® | Responsibility®

When I began at TNG, the company was young and so was I. I was eager to learn and take on new challenges but I had no idea about the journey that was in store for me. I quickly learned that a sense of urgency permeated every aspect of the company's operations. The only norm was change. I remember Larry always saying: "Just because we did it that way yesterday doesn't mean that we are doing it that way today." Time and speed were a necessity in every aspect of our daily work. Trust was also a key component. The team had to work together seamlessly, and our sense of competition was never against each other but against anyone trying to take market share away from us.

Over the years, I witnessed the company's growth firsthand as it expanded its operations and took on new challenges. We went through highs and lows, celebrating success and working to overcome obstacles. Larry and Teresa fostered an environment of giving. Whether that was the team giving their all, or Larry and Teresa giving their all to us. Going the extra mile for customers, learning to understand the importance of supporting our community and each other is the fabric of the organization.

Reflecting on this passage I look back on all of the lessons learned, disciplines developed, and memories made. I am eternally grateful for the opportunity to be part of such a dynamic organization and deeply value what I get to do every day. I look forward to seeing how TNG will continue to thrive in the years to come.

MAUREEN MANN, SENIOR SALES CONSULTANT
Hired 01/09/1995
Maximizer® | Strategic® | Achiever® | Ideation® | Learner®

"I love you, man" was something I said in a video the first year that I started working at TNG. That was 1997 and, wow, I never knew how true those words would be today!

Young and clueless about the beauty industry, I accepted a position in sales with the Hairco division in March of 1997. Never did I imagine truly loving my career or the company I work for as much as I do. Furthermore, never did I imagine how much it would play a role in molding me. The opportunities I have had over the years with TNG are incredible; the experiences are second to nothing I have experienced elsewhere ever and relationships will last a lifetime.

Larry, or LG as I like to call him, is like no other individual I have ever met, and certainly is not like any other entrepreneur that I know. You would swear the man has a crystal ball with the accurate predictions he makes. He is highly intelligent, fiercely resourceful, and just a tad competitive. The combination has made him the fierce leader he is and TNG Worldwide the most exciting company to work for.

I cannot write about my experience with the company and not mention the complete selflessness LG and Teresa have when it comes to the team or the community. The giving is never ending, and done with complete joy. If their personal motto isn't "it's better to give than to receive," then it should be, because they have exercised this mentality since the day I started working for them and bleed joy doing so.

ROBIN KING, SENIOR SALES CONSULTANT
Hired 5/14/1997
Responsibility® | Individualization® | Achiever® | Arranger® | Harmony®

When I started with TNG Worldwide, it was just before Larry decided he wanted to move toward manufacturing. I was a consultant at the time so there were many benefits I was not eligible for, but it also meant I didn't have to attend any of the annual meetings (something I now know I missed out on). It was a turning point in the company as Larry wanted to start developing the ForPro brand rather than just selling other third-party products.

On the Monday after an annual meeting, I came into a more subdued office environment as many were concerned about the future of the company. I was worried as well because only a couple months earlier the Snowden affair had occurred with the federal government, and all contracted network administrators were effectively put on hold (as I had been hired to support U.S. Army TACOM in Warren, Michigan). However, over the next couple of years, ForPro became a successful brand along with other TNG brands. I was later hired as a full-time employee, and it has been amazing to see how maneuverable the company has been in responding to world events and market changes. Since the beauty industry changes as fashions change, only a company willing to adapt can survive, and Larry has continuously adapted to ensure TNG Worldwide's success.

CHRIS ISBERG, SENIOR INFRASTRUCTURE ENGINEER

Hired 11/4/2013

Achiever® | Learner® | Focus® | Responsibility® | Intellection®

After coming to TNG nearly twenty-four years ago, I can honestly say that I couldn't have been more fortunate in my career. I've witnessed an evolution in business that I don't think I would have seen close-up anywhere else. TNG, with Larry at the helm, has steered the business by dodging every obstacle and reinventing itself when it needed to stay on top. And with each success or failure, TNG grew or learned.

As a graphic designer, I was able to be part of many transitions when it came to marketing and product packaging development. Whether it was the many catalogs and publications, launches of new divisions, or the creation of new, innovative products, I have always had an opportunity to learn new skills and appreciate the opportunities. Given that, why would I want to be anywhere else?

I'm glad to see the evolution of TNG from a distributor to a manufacturer where control has firmly been placed in the company's hands. The core team that exists now are some of the most loyal, talented, and motivated people that I've come to know. We as a team are lucky to be a part of a still growing and thriving company with a leader who is an entrepreneur to the core. Lastly and just as important, the caring and generosity that Larry and Teresa show their employees is bar none.

SHELLY SCHROEDER, CREATIVE DIRECTOR

Hired 8/9/1999

Maximizer® | Deliberative® | Responsibility® | Relator® | Belief®

When you work somewhere for almost twenty years there are many experiences you'll encounter. Most good, and a few maybe not, especially when you're in the HR field. One of many things I've learned over the years is to treat others the way you want to be treated. This mindset fosters a positive environment with happy and dedicated talent. I know that through Gallup® training, engaged employees give you at least 20 percent more effort than those not engaged where they work. We are all engaged at TNG!

All companies go through difficult chapters, and TNG certainly isn't excluded. But there is one common denominator through it all. Larry and Teresa show a high respect for their employees. They genuinely care about their people's careers with TNG. Extra special is they are vested in their employees' personal lives as well. I recall times when they learned a family member was in need (i.e., non-working appliances). As our motto "Makin' It Happen," that family member ended up with a new appliance. Why? They care about the "whole" employee and not just a piece.

CHERYL GAMBRELL, HR DIRECTOR
Hired 10/6/2003

Relator® | Responsibility® | Achiever® | Strategic® | Developer®

I started picking orders in the warehouse and moved into inventory control. I helped implement WMS systems and had a lot of contact with the IT department. I spent thirteen years in the warehouse before having the opportunity to assist with the implementation of SAP. I moved to the IT department as support for the warehouses for SAP and the WMS systems. I quickly was put in charge of the POS system for our stores. As people left the department, I took on more and more responsibilities. Currently I oversee all things IT and web. I have had a lot of opportunities to learn and grow with the company.

JULIE SZOSTAK, DIRECTOR OF TECHNOLOGY SOLUTIONS
Hired 1/2/1996

Deliberative® | Adaptability® | Achiever® | Significance® | Individualization®

From taping boxes to playing hide and seek in the warehouse to learning how to drive a hi-lo forklift, TNG has been part of my earliest memories. It wasn't until my senior year of high school that I had the epiphany I wanted to be part of the company full time. Joining

TNG, the summer of 2002 was the second-best career decision I've ever made, second only to the decision to come back after a twelve-year sabbatical.

Having had the opportunity to witness the growth and evolution of TNG over the years has been fascinating. The vision and foresight needed to remain relevant for decades as a small business by taking the right Chance cards and knowing when to pivot is a masterclass in entrepreneurship.

I have to admit, when my dad first pitched the idea of writing a book, I was a bit skeptical. I mean, between chess, Español, Candy Crush, traveling, cooking, exercising three times a day, and oh yeah, running the business, how could he possibly have time to write a book? Of course, we all know what a successful entrepreneur with over a hundred life lessons does. He writes a book! And with Focus as strength number two, he did it at a pace that would impress the likes of Stephen King.

I truly believe everything happens for a reason. It can be no coincidence that I was able to rejoin TNG at the perfect time to help continue the company's transition to its next phase as a consumer brand powerhouse. I couldn't be happier to be part of this chapter in TNG's history. And I look forward to helping write many more chapters on our way to $100 million and beyond. LFG!

DAN GAYNOR, AMAZON BRAND SPECIALIST

Hired 8/1/2021

Maximizer® | Command® | Arranger® | Competition® | Self-Assurance®

I always told Larry to write a book, and I'm glad that he finally did because I've always enjoyed his blogs. They are always an interesting take on the beauty industry, spas, politics, and life.

I came to work for Larry during the hotel and spa crash in 2008, and even before I worked for him, he offered to pay my way to a national spa conference and represent TNG as I took two months off between jobs to be with my ailing mother. Larry appreciates and endorses that family comes first, and for this I will be forever grateful.

My background was from a world of opening world-class spas, and this was a new venture for me in sales. I remember the first time I met Larry at headquarters during a training session. He was very intimidating, and I'm not easily intimidated. He reminded me of Howard Stern with his big personality and quick-thinking mind. I was able to raise my children in East Hampton, New York, as a single mother of two girls.

What strikes me about Larry is his true entrepreneurial spirit. I wish I didn't have the fear I had to start my own business over the years as I always worked for other people. Watching Larry, constantly reinventing himself and his business, it has been an amazing journey and learning experience.

The company is an honorable one that always donates to charities and incites the employees to donate each year. This giving spirit comes from Larry, who, with his beautiful and loving wife Teresa, plans amazing and inspirational trips and team buildings for the entire company. Each of these trips ranged from epicurean adventures to a visit to the Rock and Roll Hall of Fame to an amazing trip to NYC (where I learned more about NYC than by living two hours away for many years). So many memories have left lasting impressions on all of his employees.

The one thing that will always stand out to me about Larry is going through all the ups and downs in the industry and what he's observed of major brands. He is loyal to you if you are in touch with him and show him you're trying, even when your heart gets broken or you lose your morale and income, he'll stand by your side. I will never forget the time he paid for my vet bill when my dog almost died after she was attacked by another dog. The owner of the other dog would not pay, and Larry called the vet and he gave his American Express card number. Who does that? Larry!

As he says, life is one-third genes, one-third how you take care of yourself, and one-third luck. I feel lucky I met this entrepreneurial spirit.

CHERYL HARTSOUGH, SENIOR SALES CONSULTANT
Hired 11/17/2008
Strategic® | Relator® | Achiever® | Focus® | Positivity®

I am a nail technician by trade, I worked for over fifteen years in this profession. During that time, I ordered my supplies from Nailco, went to trade shows that Nailco offered, and did some side work for them. I heard how awesome this company was so when I had an opportunity to apply for a position, I jumped at it. I was hired into the material handling department as an inventory control clerk/quality control.

I tested all nail products for quality before receiving them into inventory. After about a year, I was voted by my peers to be a team leader, and a few years later I became an assistant manager for the logistics department. I was honored with awards for Rebel of the Quarter four different years; I still have one of the TVs that was given.

I have had unlimited opportunities to learn and grow with this company. I experienced trips to New York City and Cleveland along with several local travel destinations. Larry makes lunch for the whole company monthly May–September; he is an awesome cook. Most recently, I was asked to be his sous chef, again more learning.

TNG has pivoted a lot during my employment. I am proud to be part of the core team and can honestly say I love my job and enjoy coming to work. Larry and Teresa have given me so many opportunities to grow professionally and personally.

CRYSTAL MEYER, LOGISTICS MANAGER

Hired 12/18/2006

Includer® | Restorative™ | Achiever® | Learner® | Focus®

In January of 1992, I answered a want-ad of a beauty supplier looking for general warehouse help. I drove to the employment center, filled out my application, and waited on a call. Two days later I interviewed with the warehouse manager, Dave Folsom. He informed me that Nailco was a professional beauty distributor and family business owned by Larry and Teresa Gaynor with big plans on growing the business.

The interview went well. Two days later, I received a job offer from another company to be an auto apprentice tech. I accepted the offer since it was in my wheelhouse. As fate or luck would have it, I also received a call from Nailco with a job offer. Now it was decision time for me. Do I work with cars that are my passion or do I take a risk on beauty products? Learning a new business that I had little knowledge of and working in a team environment was appealing and ultimately won out. I was off to be a warehouse worker at Nailco.

My first job was to pick orders for the new division of Nailco, CTS. They had just completed the expansion of the warehouse, and the shelves and packing area were almost completed. I was asked if I would handle "put way" California Tan. Since I worked in retail for years, I took this project and ran with it. My first interaction with Larry and Teresa was on completion of the project. They gave me a glowing review for how well the shelves were stocked and how well I handled the task assigned. That compliment stuck with me. It was at that moment I knew working here was going to be different from other jobs I had.

I remember six months into my tenure the tanning business was starting to grow very quickly, and Dave telling us stories of Larry's vision of building a professional beauty one-stop shop. This is when I knew I wanted to be part of building the TNG future. Being part of a great team, all working on the same goal was the perfect fit for me. I had found a home and ultimately a career.

I grew up at TNG. As the business evolved, I did as well. I've been lucky to have a leader that taught me the importance of continuous improvement. My TNG experiences shaped who I am today, and I have a career I am proud of.

DAN MACE, TNG FACILITIES MANAGER

Hired 1/30/1992

Maximizer® | Developer® | Includer® | Harmony® | Consistency®

So happy that you wrote your business life into a book. You have incredible insight, perspective, and wisdom. You really are a visionary when business is involved. It really is amazing seeing where we started and where we are today. The story will continue ... I know this.

I would like to thank everyone that has ever worked at TNG. No matter the reason why they left, everyone has contributed to TNG's success, past and present. We are a stronger company because of them or in spite of them.

I especially want to acknowledge our amazing core team that we have today. Most of the team has been with us for a long time and have kept TNG going. Without the core team, we would not be the TNG that we are today.

LG has the vision and the core team has been able to process that vision and make it happen. Thank you, thank you for all you do. You are 100 percent appreciated! The ride continues....

TERESA GAYNOR, VICE-PRESIDENT

Started with Larry 7/1/1985

Relator® | Responsibility® | Maximizer® | Consistency® | Individualization®

LIFE LESSON TIP: What are you waiting for? The intangibles are why entrepreneurs are entrepreneurs.

LESSON #100

There Is No Time Like the Present
to Be an Entrepreneur

N
ow for some final thoughts.

Your product or service that you launch should be as much a reflection of you on the court as it is off the court. What does this mean? Some of my favorite brands are: Costco, Starbucks, Rhone, Dolce & Gabbana (they make the best jeans and t-shirts), Kroger, Tod's, Porsche, Equinox, Amazon, and Four Seasons Resorts. These are my favorite brands because they deliver the same level of service that we deliver to our customers.

Now if you ask me which of the above brands I could not live without, my answer would be Amazon. Amazon is like pizza. Can you think of a better overall food than pizza? Have you tried Amazon pharmacy? It is the best and so much better than dealing with CVS or Walgreens. I went to my favorite author's websites to get hints for publishing this book. Stephen King had the most informative website, and he suggested two books, which were linked to Amazon. I bought the books at night and they were waiting on my front porch in the morning.

Amazon is also a great place to search for a product that you want to launch. Instantly, you can see if the product is already available. Remember, the best product ideas have been refined several times. Guy Fieri launched his new chicken franchise, Chicken Guy, modeled after Chick-fil-A. Guy certainly did not invent the fried chicken sandwich but his spin offering twenty-two different sauces is unique.

Caesar Barajas, who I mentioned earlier, has another favorite saying, "Chickens don't fly, soaring eagles do." Entrepreneurs are soaring eagles because they are not afraid to risk everything. Don't be a chicken when it comes to making the most important decisions.

Another final thought is that the best entrepreneurs always prepare a business plan. Just think about getting married. Most brides-to-be hire a wedding planner to take care of all the details: venue, menu, invitations, attire, entertainment, honeymoon, guest list, budget, photography, rehearsal dinner, wedding party, and so much more. And we are talking about a one-day event. The more precise your business plan, the better the chances for success.

Texas Hold'em poker is a fascinating and thrilling game because players can go "all in" on any hand. As an entrepreneur, you have to make the decision to go "all in" or gradually when you start your business. To mitigate risk, it is best to start gradually—don't quit your day job. However, at one point you will need to pick up the Chance card that tells you "it's time to go all in." That is when you decide once and for all if you are a soaring eagle or a chicken.

Be careful of credit card debt; it is a terrible way to finance a new business. As I mentioned in the book, avoid partners at all costs unless the partner is your significant other. If you truly have an innovative product or service, establish a relationship with a local bank. If you own a home, a home equity loan is a viable alternative. Be careful of cashing out your 401(k); you will have to pay a penalty and ordinary income.

Last but not least, the most successful entrepreneurs have a "BUB" that understands their mindset and work ethic. If you have to work 24/7, then so be it. But no one can stand in your way while you do it. Having a "BUB" also gives you another perspective when you need it. Never forget that you are the CEO and president and responsible for making the tough decisions. Only a "BUB" has your best interests at heart.

My journey started in 1985, but it has really just started. Be sure to follow my antics on my blog, larrygaynor.com. If you want to connect with me or need an entrepreneurial coach, you will find everything you need on my website. Thank you for investing your time to read my book and best of success to you.

Namaste,

LARRY GAYNOR

7/1/1985

Competition® | Focus® | Ideation® | Maximizer® | Strategic®

BONUS LESSON #101

Take a Chance!

WHAT ARE YOU WAITING FOR?
LET'S FUCKING GO!

CONTACT PAGE

Whether you are an aspiring or experienced entrepreneur, you need a coach. Why use a specialty or assistant coach when you can hire a head coach that can give you real life coaching utilizing more than fifty years' experience being an entrepreneur?

Larry is a successful entrepreneur running TNG Worldwide and he introduces more than fifty new products a year. Larry has experienced working with everything from start-ups to mega-corporations including L'Oréal, Unilever, Amazon, and Ulta. Along his path, Larry has had to make critical decisions (what he likes to refer to as "Chance Cards" in his book). Those decisions are what makes or breaks small companies. The more informed you are about making those decisions, the better decisions you will make. That is Larry's number one reason for being an entrepreneur's personal coach: To help entrepreneurs make better decisions.

Larry offers executive coaching on a multitude of categories from leadership to the inner workings of Amazon. Larry also offers a vast array of marketing services including logo development, Amazon A+ pages, and sourcing new products.

For more information, please visit larrygaynor.com.

ACKNOWLEDGMENTS

Nobody writes a book thinking that no one will read it or buy it. While I knew the subject matter of my book was fascinating, I wanted to make sure it was entertaining and captivating, that the reader would actually finish the book. To assist me in my goal, I enrolled ghost-readers to read chapters as they were completed.

Most promising was that when I took a break from sending new chapters, they would often email me, "Where are the new chapters?" That suggested that they were engaged and loved the content. I would like to acknowledge the BUB, Maureen Mann, Robin King, Dawn Kuhn, Michael Gaynor (he worked at TNG during college), and Daniel Gaynor (he currently works for TNG) for their dedication to see the project through.

I would especially like to thank Maureen for her super editing skills which made the transcript so much more readable and was enjoyed by the publishers I interviewed.

And a final thank you to Shelly Schroeder for her expert marketing wisdom.